# KELLY
# BLACK, WHITE & GOLD
# HOLMES

MY AUTOBIOGRAPHY

# KELLY
# BLACK, WHITE & GOLD
# HOLMES

MY AUTOBIOGRAPHY

WITH FANNY BLAKE

TED SMART

This edition produced for The Book People Ltd,
Hall Wood Avenue, Haydock, St. Helens, WA11 9UL

First published in Great Britain in 2005 by
Virgin Books Ltd
Thames Wharf Studios
Rainville Road
London
W6 9HA



A catalogue record for this book is available from the British Library.

ISBN 1 85227 284 8

Typeset by Phoenix Photosetting
Printed and bound in Great Britain by CPD Wales

# CONTENTS


| | | |
|---|---|---|
| 1 | Early Days | 5 |
| 2 | Childhood Dreams | 17 |
| 3 | Working Girl | 29 |
| 4 | First Step on The Ladder | 41 |
| 5 | At the Wheel | 51 |
| 6 | In Training | 61 |
| 7 | In the Line of Duty | 69 |
| 8 | Who's Boss? | 83 |
| 9 | Back on Track | 93 |
| 10 | Medals or Money? | 99 |
| 11 | Decision Time | 109 |
| 12 | Medal Hopes | 117 |
| 13 | Breaking the British Record | 131 |
| 14 | Injury Time | 141 |
| 15 | Olympic Fever | 153 |
| 16 | Cursed | 165 |
| 17 | On Home Turf | 173 |
| 18 | Reaching Rock Bottom | 183 |
| 19 | Now or Never | 199 |
| 20 | Going for Gold | 213 |
| 21 | What Next? | 227 |
| | Statistics | 237 |
| | Awards | 242 |
| | Index | 243 |

## Thanks

Writing this book has been an amazing experience. I have spent hours re-visiting periods in my life – it has been humbling, sometimes difficult, but mostly fun. My memories seem so clear and at times situations feel like they were just yesterday but I am aware that these are my memories of how things were and others may remember events differently. Without the experiences I have been through, I would not be the woman I am today.

I want to thank everyone who has been part of my journey however big or small. Without those of you who have given me your compassion, honesty and support, I might not have achieved my dreams.

To my family, friends and all those who have been a significant part of my life, a special thank you – you mean the world to me. You all know exactly who you are.

My thanks also go to Virgin Books who have given me the chance to write my story and to Fanny Blake for all the laughs, late night stress and chocolates!

## My Training Diary
## 1 January 2004

*I have dreamed forever to be the best at what I do. Some dreams come true, but my biggest ones are still out there and I really want them to become reality. I have really gone through a lot to realise my dreams. I have the passion, dedication, willpower and heart to achieve my ultimate goals. I have put my life and soul into this, given up my life to pursue what I know is my destiny. I just pray that for once I can be given the lift to get through this year with no struggles, no injuries and a lighted spirit of guidance.*

*I hope 2004 can bring me more happiness, success, purpose than ever before.*

# 9 MARCH 2005

The limousine swept towards the gates of Buckingham Palace. If only the people waiting outside could have seen through the blacked-out windows. Inside, my mum, dad, granddad and I were fighting for space with two TV crews who were covering the event for the BBC and *London Tonight*. I was on my way to the royal investiture where I would receive my Damehood from the Queen. I had to pinch myself just to make sure this was really happening.

My day had begun early. I had woken at 6.30 a.m., having had a disturbed night thanks to the snores of my mum, who was sharing my hotel room. She had been up early too, excited about the day ahead and already worrying about the time. I had told her I was going to breakfast and sneaked off to the gym instead. I felt much better when I got back an hour later in time for Patricia, my hairdresser, who had arrived to put my hair up. She had already sewn in the coppery red extensions the night before to give the length to create a spiky style that would stand in place of a hat. My Jasper Conran suit in cream silk crepe hung there, cool and sophisticated, with the matching Jimmy Choos waiting on the carpet below. I had gazed at them with a big smile on my face – this was a million miles away from my more familiar tracksuit and trainers. On the side table were laid the diamonds brought to me the night before by James from Boodles – exquisitely simple teardrop earrings, a necklace with two matching teardrops and a ring.

My mum had gone for the whole shebang as well – an all-matching outfit, hat, shoes and bag in a pastel green with navy trim. Together we really looked the part and ready for my big day. My dad and granddad had arrived at the hotel in the limousine that had driven them from home in Hildenborough, Kent. They were spruced up in their top hats and tails hired specially for the occasion. The TV crews joined us and together we made our way to the Palace, very proud and excited.

We dropped off the TV crews near the gates and drove in through the majestic archway into the courtyard where the limo purred to a standstill. We emerged to walk past the guards, along the red carpet and up the stairs. My family were shown to the ballroom where the investiture ceremony was to take place, while I was directed to a room where I waited with the five men and one other woman who had come to be given their knighthoods or to be invested as Companions of the Bath: General Sir Kevin O'Donoghue; Professor Sir Clive Granger; Sir Alan Jones; Professor Basil Markesinis; Air Vice-Marshal Andrew Collier; and Naomi Eisenstadt. I felt nervous, anxious that I might trip in my Jimmy Choo heels and break my neck before I got as far as being made a Dame Commander. We introduced ourselves and chatted until the Lord Comptroller came in to tell us the protocol. When he explained how the men would kneel on a velvet stool to be knighted with a sword, I couldn't help piping up, 'Can't I kneel on the stool too when it's my turn?'

'Ladies don't normally receive their Damehood that way, Dame Kelly.' I think he was slightly taken aback.

'I really want to. Imagine what the Queen would say!' We all laughed at the thought.

'You can have a go now if you like,' he said.

So I did. 'Now I'm ready,' I announced. He just smiled.

The time came for us to walk to the front of the ballroom, where an orchestra high on a balcony at the other end was quietly playing.

As we walked down the corridor I joked with the officer, 'I really want to kneel, I'm going to do it.'

'I dare you then,' he said, smiling again.

'OK. I will.'

I was only winding him up but his face was a picture. He was obviously thinking, Oh my God. She's going to do it.

I spotted my family on the other side of the ballroom. They were beaming with pride. I felt really choked because I knew how proud they were of me, so I gave them a little wave. The atmosphere was hushed as we waited for the Queen to make her entrance escorted by the Lord Chamberlain and attended by two Gurkha Orderly Officers. The guards stood sharply to attention as the royal party made their way onto the dais. We remained standing as the orchestra played the National Anthem. I had tears in my eyes as it brought back the moment when, only six months earlier, I had stood on the rostrum at the Olympic Games to receive my gold medals, first for the 800 metres and then for the 1500 metres.

When the Lord Chamberlain called out my name, I walked forwards and turned to face the Queen. I had visions of hundreds of people watching me trip, arms and legs akimbo, but, thank God, it didn't happen. As I approached the dais, I couldn't stop smiling. I curtseyed; then Her Majesty placed my insignia, a gorgeous medal on a smoky pink sash and a big silver star, on the special hooks that had been put on my suit by an usher. She said that she was delighted to be giving me the award and asked me about the hamstring injury that had prevented me from entering the European Indoor Cup the previous weekend. I replied that it was much better and thanked her, remembering to address her as 'Ma'am' as in jam, not 'Marm' as in farm – something I had been taught when I had first joined the British Army back in 1988. I stepped back from the dais, feeling honoured and proud; curtseyed again and, still smiling broadly, walked along the red carpet out of the ballroom. I had a short interview with the Press Association, before joining the rest of the recipients at the back of the hall to watch the rest of the proceedings.

After the ceremony was over I met up with my family and we all stood around chatting. When I went down into the Ladies, I was amused that lots of the other Honours' recipients who were there unexpectedly asked me for my autograph, which I gladly gave. I still couldn't get used to the fact that, after the Olympics, my face was recognised wherever I went and everyone seemed to know my name. Before going for a celebratory drink in my hotel and then driving home to Hildenborough, I was called outside by the palace PR officer for TV interviews. My family stood in the freezing cold waiting so that we could have our photos taken, along with all the other recipients and their families. We all smiled with real happiness and I showed off my award with pride.

For me, this was a fantastic reward for all my years of hard work. I had come such a long way since the days when I used to run round the fields outside Tonbridge, training as a junior athlete, sharing the same hopes and dreams as so many other young runners. So much had happened to me since then. I had spent almost ten years in the Army, working my way up to be a physical training instructor. I spent more years as a professional athlete, fighting injury, refusing to give in until I had achieved my dream of winning an Olympic gold. It had been a long, hard struggle with moments from which I thought I'd never recover, but I had made it in the end. To be made a Dame was the ultimate accolade.

That night, back in my mum's house in Hildenborough, I changed out of my glad rags, took down my hair and put on a tracksuit and my sister Penny's huge fluffy slippers. As I came down the stairs, my mother burst out laughing. 'If only they could see you now!'

She was right. But I didn't care what I looked like. I was at home where I really belonged, round the corner from the council estate where my story began, where, as a child, those dreams were born that meant so much to me that I would give everything I had until they came true.

# 1. EARLY DAYS

My mother was seventeen when I was born, on 19 April 1970 in Pembury Hospital in Kent. The fact that she had me at all must mean something, given the odds she faced. She was involved with a Jamaican guy, something that in the 1970s was not the done thing – at least certainly not by girls in the whiter than white county of Kent. I was an accident that no one wanted to happen.

When Mum broke the news to her family, who lived in the village of Hildenborough, that she was pregnant, they were horrified and, instead of support, they gave her an ultimatum: have the baby adopted or leave home. In those days, mixed-race relationships were still looked on with disapproval by many of my grandparents' generation. Their daughter was young to become a mother – she had only just left school. They must have been unhappy about the idea of having an illegitimate baby in their home at all, never mind a black one. So my mum left home, moving to London to live with her Jamaican boyfriend, my biological father. But their relationship together didn't work out and it hit the rocks before I was one year old. I have no memory of him at all from those days. As far as I'm aware, he showed little interest in me or in what happened to us. He might as well not have existed at all.

Young and single, my mother found herself with a mixed-race baby and no means of keeping us both. She had nowhere to live. Her only choice was to have me admitted to St George's Children's Home, so that she could go back to her parents until she got herself sorted out. St George's was a large old white Victorian house, just outside Tonbridge and opposite the Unigate Dairy; Mum got a job in the laboratory there, testing milk samples, so that she could be near me. Because she lived and worked so close, she could visit as often as possible. She remembers putting me to bed there. I'd cry so much that she couldn't get off the bed to leave me. I have no memories of my stay there, just a photo of me standing, hanging on to a cot in a room full of other cots, and another picture of all the children in care there.

My mother's recollections of that period in her life are hazy. And I can understand why. Who would want to remember such difficult times? She must have wondered what was going to happen to us both. If she wanted me enough to defy her parents in the first place, then she must have been desperate to look after me herself. She can't have been earning much money and without the prospect of any more, our future together must have looked bleak. Living with her parents can't have been easy, knowing what they felt about me, especially when I was staying only a short distance up the road. I can only imagine how torn she must have felt. Then, after perhaps as many as eighteen months, we were properly reunited again. Mum had found a dingy bedsit to rent in New Cross, a rundown area of south-east London. We had somewhere to live together and she was determined to make a go of it.

My earliest memory is of us together in that bedsit. My mum has poker-straight, long, dark-brown hair that she can sit on. The room is small and dark. I'm on the floor playing with toys when there's a knock on the door. In comes the lady from downstairs, furious about the noise I'm making. She and my mother have a massive shouting match and she slams out again. Mum remembers me as a 'sweet, delicate, little thing' but also that, when I was tiny, I was constantly crying – the source of irritation to our downstairs neighbour. She admits she had no clue how to look after a toddler (at that age, why would she have?) and, without a family to turn to for help, she was finding it impossible to cope. Not long after that the landlord wanted to renovate the building, so we were forced to move on.

Thirty-two years later, Mum told me that the pressure on her from her family to have me adopted was so great that she eventually gave in. St George's had found a couple who wanted me. I don't blame her. She was in such a difficult position and she had tried to do her very best by me. In the same circumstances, I expect I'd have done what she did. But then, when the woman from the Social Services came to take me away, Mum started crying. She couldn't go through with it. So I was saved yet again. This time, she took me with her to live in a mother-and-baby home until a council flat was found for us in Forest Hill. But it wasn't long before things got difficult again. Mum had found a job with De Beers in London, where she graded and cut diamonds. Although she liked the job, the commuting was difficult. Juggling it with looking after me was impossible so I was sent back to St George's when I was about four years old. At least Mum knew I was being looked after properly while I was there.

I remember very little of my stay, but I know that Mum spent as much time as she could with me. One day, not long after I'd last seen her, I was called to the TV room where everyone was sitting on the floor watching Bruce Forsyth's *Generation Game*. 'Kelly. Your Mum's on. Come quick.' I shot downstairs and stood in the doorway to watch my mum and her father, my Granddad Percy, battling against another couple to get a place in the final. Nobody had told me they were going to be on. Or if they had, I'd forgotten. I was riveted. They never made it to the conveyor-belt challenge but my mum left with a Russian clock radio and Granddad won a tankard. 'Didn't they do well?' My mother was on TV. She must be famous. It was a weird feeling being so proud of her when at the same time I missed her and would much rather she was with me.

Other than that, I remember my bed was always covered with cuddly toys, including my favourites, Brian the Snail and Zebedee from *The Magic Roundabout*. My only other memory from those days was being dressed in a yellow bodysuit, with a red plastic 'shell' on my back, an orange scarf knotted around my neck and a pair of antennae on my head. I was Brian the Snail and excitedly taking part in the annual Tonbridge Carnival.

But the unsettled start to my life changed when Mum got together with Mick Norris, an old schoolfriend of hers and the man who was later to become my dad, my support and my biggest fan. To this day he still is. At weekends, she would take me out of St George's to stay with either her sister Sonia (my aunt and godmother) and my uncle Steven whom I loved going to see and spending time with, or with

Mick's sister, my aunt Sheila, who was married and lived nearby. Young, with dark hair, Sheila loved everything sporty. We'd go out into the street where she taught me how to ride a bike. Once Mick's dad made me a pair of stilts and it was Sheila who taught me to walk on them. When I got the same purple scooter as a present from both Mum and Mick and Nan and Granddad Norris, one of them was sold so that I could have some roller skates. Again, it was Sheila who came out to help me master them without breaking an arm or a leg. Mick had helped Mum move house from the mother-and-baby unit to Forest Hill and gradually he just became part of our lives.

I first remember him being around when we occasionally stayed in Hildenborough with Aud and Geoff, his mum and dad, who are my other beloved nan and granddad. Mick was a painter and decorator who worked in partnership with his dad. A slim, quiet guy with wide long sideburns that were fashionable back then, he was laid back to the point of sleeping: something that's always been a family joke. I can picture him in his cowboy boots and a succession of loud, patterned cowboy shirts singing 'Viva España' at the top of his voice. Ever since he'd been there on holiday, he had had a love affair with Spain. But he also loved my mum, and I came as part of the package. We just accepted one another as we were, beginning life as a family in Forest Hill before moving to a top-floor flat on the Longmead Estate in Tonbridge, where I went to the Infants School.

It wasn't long before we moved to Riding Park, at first four doors away from Nan and Granddad Norris, then we moved to a slightly bigger house just next door to them – number 62, where I grew up. It was a three-bedroom, redbrick, semi-detached house with a deep-red front door with white beading and a window above that boasted a white '62'. Inside it was comfortable, although there wasn't much money for luxuries. I eventually had my room done up in my favourite colours, red and white, right down to the light switch and the door. The wallpaper was white with little red flowers, the bedspread was red and white, and there was a red carpet and red curtains. I always had a few toys on the bed, especially my favourite Smurfs and, later on, when I started running, I hung up all the pendants and the medals I won from the English Schools Championships. I was proudest of all of my trophies on the shelves.

My other nan and granddad, Elsie and Percy Norman, lived in the blink-and-you-miss-it village of Hildenborough for over fifty years. My nan stayed at home to look after their five children, Daphne,

Rodney, Celia, Mum and Sonia, while Granddad Percy was a travelling blacksmith. He had a white van that he used to take his equipment to stables all around the area. I remember Mum taking me to see him at work, the warmth of the fire from the dusty black coals, the deafening sound as he hammered the glowing horseshoe into shape on the anvil, the acrid smell of burning hoof. Although they had fallen out when I was born, Mum and her parents had patched things up so that Nan and Granddad Norman had slowly come to accept me. She remained especially close to her dad who grew to love me too. He was short and bald, and he wore a flat cap, corduroy trousers and the sleeves of his soft, old shirts rolled up. He sometimes wore sleeveless, Fair Isle V-necked jumpers too. When he was reading the newspaper, I'd crawl under the table, come up between his knees and try to swing from his braces. Other times, I loved flicking them. I remember him singing songs with me and teaching me silly rhymes:

*Down in the jungle*
*Got a bellyache*
*Can't find a lavatory*
*Poop*
*Too late.*

On 10 April 1977, when I was nearly seven, Mum and Mick got married in St John's Church in Hildenborough. It was their wedding that gave me the first inkling that something about our family set-up wasn't quite normal. Someone at school pointed out that it was weird to be your own mother's bridesmaid. Of course, everyone else's parents were already married. I could see that. So what did that make Mick's relationship to me? But I was so excited about being a bridesmaid with two of my cousins (although less excited about the frilly blue mob cap that went with my blue dress and the little bag I had to carry) that I put the thought to the back of my mind. Nearly all the photos of the day show me behaving badly, either lifting up my skirt to the camera, smudging my face with chocolate cake or making faces.

The first time I really questioned Mick's relationship to me was when my brother Kevin was born in June 1977. He was white. Until that moment, being a mixed-race child had never been an issue for me. I don't remember anyone having made a comment about my colour, not to my face at least. I don't think it had ever occurred to me that I was different from anyone else until my friends at school pointed out that children are normally the same colour as their dad – children can be so brutally honest.

'Why aren't you the same colour as your dad?' they asked.

'I don't know,' I replied, unconcerned, and went on playing. But I carried the question around in my head for a few days, brooding on it. As soon as I had a chance, I asked Mum why I was a different colour to Kevin and my dad. She practically choked when she heard the question but I suppose she must have known that I'd ask one day. She handled it well by being honest and to the point. I'd had a different dad when I was born but he had left Mum when I was a baby. That was it. Conversation over.

But it wasn't over for me. I suddenly resented the fact that my mum was with this guy, Mick, who wasn't my dad and who was stealing her attention away from me. It wasn't that I wanted to see my biological father or that I felt any curiosity about him, but I felt cross that Kevin had his dad there and I didn't. I couldn't help feeling it would be fairer if Kevin didn't either. Then, in 1980, my second brother, Stuart, was born. My feeling of unfairness that the boys both had their father on the scene intensified, although it was less of an immediate issue because, by then, I adored Kevin and went on to feel the same about Stuart. However, my relationship with Mick began to go downhill simply because I knew he wasn't my 'real' dad. I turned into a stroppy teenager, screaming and shouting at him whenever I disagreed with him. Rather than chasing me up the stairs to my bedroom, trying to slap my legs when I'd refused to do the washing up or had given him some backchat, he put up with it all. He took me on as if I was his own. I respect him so much for that and for all that he has done for me.

I doted on Kevin and Stuart. I loved them to bits and wanted to do everything for them. I dressed them, changed their nappies, washed them and played with them. They were like living dolls to me. As they grew up, Kevin always wanted to copy whatever I did, with Stuart following close in his shadow. I remember teaching Kevin to ride a bike, just as Auntie Sheila had taught me. The difference was that I decided he didn't need stabilisers. I just put him straight on the bike and gave him a good shove down the hill. Down he went, screaming his head off, until he crashed in a heap at the bottom. Fortunately he was so young and flexible there were no bones broken, just a graze or two. The other thing they both remember to this day was when I was babysitting them and pretended to be dead on the landing. I was a great babysitter! As they desperately tried to wake me up, they were getting more and more upset. The only time I moved was when Stuart ran down the stairs to try to telephone the police or an ambulance. As I heard him dialling, I let out a great groan. Both the boys rushed back to me and helped me to my feet as I pretended shakily to come round. Why I did it, I don't know. But I'm ashamed to say both episodes have left scars on their mind forever, although we laugh about them now.

Number 62 Riding Park was a good family home. It was in a small estate of similar neat redbrick houses on the fringes of Hildenborough, edged around by fields. All the houses had small front gardens with a low wall that separated them from the pavement. At the back were long gardens. Ours had a climbing frame and a swing while next door Granddad Norris spent ages in the greenhouse or in his vegetable plot at the end of his lovingly kept garden. I'd watch him digging up potatoes, or picking tomatoes and runner beans, or I'd sit in the kitchen with Nan Norris, shelling peas.

Dogs were an important part of our family. My dad had an Alsatian called Champ. He'd lie on the landing outside Mum and Dad's room and whenever I came out of mine, he'd growl long and fiercely. I was absolutely terrified and would run down the stairs or shout to Mick to come and move him. Eventually I got so fed up with him being so aggressive that I decided to fight him back. I thought that my dad would rescue me if Champ turned really vicious. But after a good wrestle, we got used to one another – although he'd still rumble away whenever I passed him. We always had a dog in the family. After Champ came Gemma and after Gemma there was Charlie, a white Heinz (57 different varieties) dog who looked just like a polar bear with a couple of black patches and a thick white woolly coat. He was so gorgeous. As a result, I've always loved dogs. I also had a cat called Candy, but I was allergic to her so practically ignored her.

Christmas was always special. Mum would pin Chinese lanterns to the ceiling and hang shiny paper chains from corner to corner across the room. She loved decorating the tree. Then in the night, Santa would sneak into our rooms, leaving a pillowcase full of useful things like colouring pads and pencils, small toys, *Mr Men* books, Smurfs, tangerines, nuts and chocolate coins. On Christmas morning we weren't allowed downstairs until Mum had had a cup of tea and her breakfast in bed, the dog had been taken out and we'd had a wash. Only then could we go into the front room where our presents were waiting, piled up on the chairs by the tree. The agony of anticipation was prolonged for as long as possible.

The year I remember breaking the rules was when I'd saved up to buy Mum and Dad a tumble dryer. Every Friday I was paid £12 a week for my paper round. For months before Christmas, I'd give £10 of my weekly earnings to my nan and granddad. Every Saturday, they'd take it down to Curry's and put it towards the payment for a tumble dryer. Mum and Dad didn't have one and I was determined to get it for them. When Christmas Day finally arrived, I volunteered to make Mum's cup of tea. I crept out of the back door and hopped over the wall to Aud and Geoff's where the tumble dryer had been delivered. I could hear my mother shouting, 'Where's my tea?' as my nan and I struggled unsteadily with the dryer in the wheelbarrow. We managed to get it into our front room where I tied a big ribbon around it. I dashed back upstairs with the tea as if nothing had happened, although I was bursting for them to go downstairs. Eventually the time came. The look of shock and amazement on their faces was worth all the planning and secrecy. They were so pleased.

Mum loved parties. There were always lots of family get-togethers going on. We regularly went round to my Aunt Celia's and Uncle Mick's house for parties, where all the family including my cousins always turned up. We'd play games for hours eating up all the brilliant food she would put out. It would always make me laugh because Celia, Daphne, and Sonia would always get drunk and my uncle George and Steven always had to stay sober to drive them home when they were in a state. I remember helping Mum with the boys' birthdays when we'd all go to the bowling alley or the village hall. Even now she'll always buy balloons and put up banners round the house on every birthday. At Easter, she has a huge Easter basket with all the mini eggs she can find. I'm not embarrassed to admit that I still get my stocking at the end of my bed whenever I'm at home for Christmas.

Mum was also quite house proud and everything was always tidy. She was strict about meals so we had to eat everything up, including the vegetables. I hated all of them. I'd forever be trying to hide them under my napkin but she would always spot them and make me force them down. Often she would wheel the tea trolley from the kitchen to the lounge at teatime and it would be groaning with stuffed jacket potatoes, sandwiches and cakes. Not all her food was so tempting, though – I drowned most of it in tomato sauce. Once she made roast lamb for Sunday lunch – the first and last time as far as I was concerned. The smell was bad enough but the taste of it was disgusting. Soon after I ate it, I ran upstairs and was sick. I hated it so much that I've never eaten it since. After meals we had to take it in turn to wash up and dry – of course, I always moaned!

The other thing that Mum drummed into me from an early age was that I had to be very polite to everyone. I still am to this day – well, most of the time! On Sunday evenings, she always did the ironing as she tried to persuade me to get my uniform and books ready for school the next day. One family ritual that I particularly remember happened every night. 'Bath, Biscuit, Bed,' Mum would shout, interrupting whatever we were doing. We had to stop and go upstairs to get ready for bed. Bath was bearable. Biscuit was brilliant – I could make those crumbs last for ages. And bed? I wasn't having any of it and would delay it for as long as I could.

I played with my Tiny Tears (the doll that eats, cries and wees) and my red-and-white stripy buggy when I was really young but then I turned into more of a tomboy. If I wanted to, I could get to my toys that had been stored in the loft by climbing onto the landing banisters, putting my legs over the open airing cupboard door and hauling myself up there, but I much preferred playing outside. There was a small gang of us that hung out in the street together: Simon Wickson came with his mother to stay with his nan and granddad (Roy and Marg Spender), who lived at number 58. Blond and cheeky, he was also my first kiss. We were six years old and we used to go to the trees at the bottom of Riding Park and pretend we were kissing like they did in the movies – no tongues of course! There was also Ian Russell, who was younger than us and lived at number 68, and the Porters, Julie, Steve and Tessa, who went to Hildenborough Primary School with me. I have stayed good friends with Tessa over the years although there was one moment when, because she had gone to an all-girls secondary school and become too gobby for my liking, I punched her off a wall into a garden to teach her a lesson. I'm pleased to say she's not gobby at all now really.

The Porters and I would spend hours playing Doctors and Nurses in their house when we weren't outside. Once we found a porn video hidden behind the TV unit. We pulled the curtains and watched it in secret, listening in case one of the Porter parents came in. We fell about with laughter, looking at the weird things the men and women were doing to each other, but as soon as we heard the noise of the key in the lock, we switched the TV off and hid the video back where we'd found it. As we hung around outside in Riding Park, we thought we were incredibly cool, although of course we weren't at all. We'd pass the time playing hopscotch, football, skipping games, tag, Knock-down Ginger (knocking on doors and legging it before we were caught) or British Bulldog. I was just an ordinary 'roughie toughie' young girl.

Being fiercely protective of my friends and brothers often got me into trouble. I can remember chasing Ian Russell for some reason and scrapping with him big time on the concrete outside his house with the other kids standing round cheering us on. I was punching him and I loved it! Another time, I raced after a boy I'd been fighting with, who slammed his front door in my face just as I was reaching out to grab him. My hand went straight through the glass panel. Fortunately my cuts weren't as serious as the damage to the door.

Best of all was going down Riding Lane to the Brook. When we reached our early teens, we were allowed to play in the woods down there for hours at a time. We'd drag out the broken logs and twigs from the stream that flows through it to make rafts. We'd paddle down the water pretending to be explorers, hunting people down. We'd leap across the stream and float any old containers we could. We thought it was brilliant.

One of the best presents I was ever given was a brightly coloured plastic wigwam adorned with pictures of an Apache reservation and an Indian chief with his tomahawk. We put it up in my grandparents' front garden so we could play Indians. Forget the cowboys; we weren't interested in them, just in circling the tent hollering at one another. The squaw's blue and yellow dress, which came with a plastic headdress with long brown plaits and a brilliant blue feather, made me feel just like the real thing. Later on, Kevin and I graduated to the orange family tent that we used for holidays when Mick would drive us down to Cornwall and Somerset. It was massive, complete with a living/cooking space at the front with two bedrooms behind, one main and a smaller one off to the side. I used to love sleeping in it. I'd always take Kevin with me but he'd get scared of the noises and the dark and would run indoors. I'd stay out there on my own, weeing in a little bucket and pouring it out of the back so I didn't have to follow him in and break the spell of being outside camping.

Although my racing achievements so far were limited to winning the egg-and-spoon and the sack races in my primary school sports day, I loved trying any new activity going. At primary school, I was prefect and games captain for my house, Riding House. I was good at all the games so everyone always wanted to be on my team. Because I had the pick of the best we nearly always won. The only activity I tried that was an out-and-out failure was riding. Although encouraged by Mum, I didn't take to it at all. Apart from the expense, I didn't like the fact the horse was doing all the work, not me. I joined the majorettes but didn't stick at it for long. I learned all the techniques and liked all the twirling and throwing but when I saw our uniform – that was it. Instead of the lovely bright colours I'd seen other teams wearing, we were given dowdy brown and cream. I was out of there immediately. I loved gymnastics too, but not for long. I managed the trampolining and floor work but wasn't too good on the beams. Ballet lasted for about three days – just long enough to discover I was an elephant. But best of all was Budokan, a form of martial arts that is something like a cross between karate and judo. Kevin came too, although he was only three or four. I can still see him in his blue jogging suit with his cap, peak turned up, doing all the punches. I enjoyed martial arts and seeing how they could help me defend myself, so Kevin, Stuart (when he was old enough) and I went along to judo classes in the Angel Leisure Centre in Tonbridge as well.

I belonged to the Brownies and then the Girl Guides, going after as many badges as I could. The thing I liked most about being a Guide was the camping, making fires and living outdoors. Putting up the tents, sleeping squashed together in our sleeping bags on the bumpy ground, cooking marshmallows on the campfire and singing songs was my idea of heaven. I remember I took my first secret puff of a cigarette behind one of the tents. One of the other Guides had given it to me and told me that they were going to have a smoke. I followed them, thinking I would give it a try, but I practically choked to death. It was disgusting. I absolutely hated it. I've never had another one.

I loved all the challenges we were set, especially crossing the 'swamp' on a tightrope. Loads of girls fell in but I'd hang on for dear life, determined not to. I hate water. One of my abiding childhood fears was drowning. I'd have nightmares about falling into water as I dropped off to sleep. First of all I'd see those fuzzy stars and then I'd be falling from a cliff or a rock into the water below. It terrified me.

The other recurring dream I had was of being abandoned somewhere by my mother. I used to scream my head off. It probably related back to the times I had been left at St George's. I was certainly always very possessive of Mum and never wanted to share her with anyone. I always liked it whenever she left me to stay at my aunt's or at my nan and granddad's, although sometimes, like any child, I was frightened that she wouldn't come back – even though she always did. When I think about how I behaved in my twenties, I can sympathise with her wanting to get out and enjoy herself. Who doesn't? As a child, though, I found it hard to cope with because I didn't understand.

Looking back, I can see I was quite independent from an early age. I always wanted to forge my own path and whatever I did, I had to do it properly, or at least do it the best I possibly could. Mum is independent too, hating anyone to think she's weak, so perhaps I got it from her. However, she thinks that I may subconsciously have felt that things were expected of me because I was such a novelty in the village, and that I reacted to that. Whatever the reason, I always wanted to give 100 per cent to everything I liked doing. What I enjoyed was achieving things for myself. If I was quite good at something, I knew I could make myself better. If there was something I couldn't do, I'd just switch off. However, while I was at Hildenborough Primary School, I suppose I let life take its course. It wasn't until I went to secondary school that the dreams and ambitions that dominated my adult life began to take shape.

# 2. CHILDHOOD DREAMS

We all stood shivering at the starting line. It was my first ever cross-country race for my school, Hugh Christie Secondary School in Tonbridge and boy, was I regretting being part of the team now? I was nervous, cold and didn't know what to expect. Despite my reluctance to enter, my PE teacher Debbie Page had gently persuaded me. We were competing at Sussex Road School in Tonbridge and I could see the course ahead of me, lined by mine tape and looping around the school playing fields. The wind was blowing hard. On the start line with me were competitors from other local schools. I didn't recognise any of them but Debbie had told me that the one I had to watch out for was Stacey Washington, a girl who had already established herself as a successful junior runner, whereas I was completely inexperienced.

I was quite tall for a twelve-year-old, very skinny with my big Afro hair sticking out everywhere. Stacey was turned out professionally in her crop top, knickers and spikes while I was in my school games kit of burgundy skirt, white aertex shirt, knee-high socks and plimsolls. To everybody's surprise, including mine, I ran a great race. I was leading the field with only 200 metres to go when Stacey sprinted past me to win. I had challenged the number one junior for our age. It was amazing. Despite the cold, the mud, and the fact that I'd always absolutely hated the idea of running cross-country, the excitement of everyone watching me come second was infectious. That was my first experience of winning – or coming close. The sense of self-achievement was fantastic. Beating a field of runners still gives me the huge buzz that I got that first time.

People often credit inspirational teachers they have had at school, those people who fired them with enthusiasm for a subject in a way that influenced the rest of their life. For me, that person was Debbie Page. She was one of two female PE teachers at Hugh Christie Secondary School. She was tall, imposing, full of energy and great at her job. She cared about what we were doing and wanted to teach us rather than just oversee us. Coming second in that race was one of the turning points in my life because it made her notice my potential and encourage me to keep running.

After the summer track season, it was time for cross-country again, when I competed in the Tonbridge and Sevenoaks County Championships. This time I won easily. Miss Page's excitement for me, her pleasure at my winning, and her view of my potential, translated into her talking to Mum, telling her how good she thought I was. She suggested that I join Tonbridge Athletics Club.

I remember us driving there for the first time; my poor mother's heart must have been sinking at the thought of ferrying me to yet another activity, after the ones I had already tried and given up. However, I was looking forward to going there. I'd had a go at every sport on offer at school, but finding that I was really good at running made me want to do more of it. The club met on Tuesday and Thursday evenings as well as Sunday mornings. I took no notice of Mum's veiled threat, 'Well, you'd better stick at this one.' Little did we know!

Tonbridge Athletics Club is in the grounds of Tonbridge School, just outside the town. Founded in the sixteenth century, the school has been rebuilt twice with most of the main buildings dating back to Victorian days. It's a beautiful place set on a hill in about 150 acres, with sports pitches and a swimming pool, and with an athletics track in the dip below with fantastic views across to Tonbridge and the Kent countryside. Neither Mum nor I knew what to expect as she parked the car and we walked over to look down at the terracotta-coloured track. There were several other kids down there training, their tracksuits and bags scattered on the grass. A man detached himself from the group and came up and introduced himself as Dave Arnold, the coach.

'Are you interested in athletics?'

'Yes,' Mum answered. 'Kelly is.'

'Are you looking for a coach?'

'Yes,' she said, having little idea of what that meant or of what she was starting.

'Good.' He turned to me. 'Why don't you jog round the track while I talk to your mum?'

So, yet another gangly kid full of energy and enthusiasm, eager to go, I set off.

Dave must have been in his fifties then. He was quite short, with a huge head of white hair and bushy grey eyebrows. As an ex-marathon runner, he was still very slim and fit. Later I found out that he had been forced to give up running because of ankle injuries. He worked in the planning department for Nestlé and had taken up running again in 1975 when his daughter Sharon had shown an interest in it. He had rejoined Tonbridge Athletics Club and began coaching, gradually building up a regular group of athletes.

After my run, he told me that he had seen a photograph in the local paper of me challenging Stacey Washington in the cross-country. He knew Stacey, but the fact that he had seen me leading her in the race made him take notice of me. For the next couple of weeks I went back to the club where I got into the routine of running a couple of laps, then doing strides, drills and exercises just to see how it went. After that I was able to join in with Dave's group of runners who were my age. There were about thirty of us altogether, although we were rarely all there at the same time. Some couldn't make it every time; some couldn't handle the demands of the training and didn't stick it out.

Dave has always said that he saw something totally different in me as soon as he met me. You've either got that running ability or you haven't. He liked my stride length, the way that I ran. I'm quite bouncy on my legs, quite light, and I run on my toes, unlike a lot of runners whose whole foot has contact with the ground. He thought that was quite weird but never suggested I should try to change it. Running on your toes can cause a lot of injury problems but it's always been good for me, giving me a big lopey stride and the ability to push forward. Similarly, when he noticed that I had a tendency to over-stride, he reasoned that it would work itself out as I became more capable as a runner. The other thing he liked about me was the fact that I wanted to train. I loved pushing myself towards the targets he set and the feeling of achievement when I met them.

I was very lucky to find Dave. Although he was responsible for coaching a group at the club, he always maintained a one-to-one relationship with his athletes. Sometimes in training groups everyone is given the same training programmes and no one is treated as an individual – their particular strengths and weaknesses are not taken into account. That wasn't how Dave worked. He started giving me proper training programmes that involved hill running, track sessions, fartleks (a combination of timed interval training that varies in speed and intensity to build up pace and endurance) and timed endurance runs. The worst of those, I remember, was the route along the main road from the track to Hildenborough Church – two miles and uphill all the way – and back again. But we found that I could cope with his targets and I was always keen to move on to something more demanding.

After a few weeks, I was ready for the next stage, so he started to give me extra training. If one of us couldn't get to the club, he'd come to Hildenborough and we'd run round Hildenborough recreation ground (the 'Rec') together and do timed fartleks. The 'Rec' was a huge grassy playing field on a slight slope at the end of our road with a climbing frame with a slide and swings. Dave would stand in the centre with his whistle, blowing it every time I had to change pace. When I had finished, he would dash over and put his hand round my neck to feel my pulse and check on my recovery rate. Athletes are often advised to use a heart-rate monitor but he has always stuck to this more direct method. As far as I'm concerned, it was one of his trademarks. Once he saw my potential, he set his sights on my competing in the Junior 1500 metres in the Kent Schools Championships in 1983, the following year. He thought I might be good enough if I kept on training. And that was exactly what I wanted to do.

The mentality of a racer came completely naturally to me. As soon as I started running with Dave, I was focused and ready to race. I didn't have any doubts because, as soon as the athletics season started that May, I began winning in the local athletics meets I entered. By June, I had won the 1500 metres at the Kent Schools Championships and had been chosen to represent Kent Schools in the 1983 English Schools Championships in Plymouth. To run in the

Schools Championships is such a big deal when you're a youngster. I remember being so excited. For me, the scariest part of the weekend was staying with a host family in Plymouth. As soon as we arrived, we were taken to a local school gymnasium where our names were called out one by one and off we went with our families – people we'd never set eyes on before. I was to learn that this is what happened each year in whichever town was hosting the Championships. The families always went to great lengths to make us feel at home. That was very important to us when we were in a strange environment and didn't want it to affect our racing by being stressful.

The great thing about the Championships themselves is that they mimic senior athletics championships so that anyone going further in their competing career has a clear idea of what lies ahead of them. The atmosphere at the track was always fantastic, and Plymouth was no exception. It was a real team environment where all the county athletes supported each other, waving banners, banging on the track sides, screaming and cheering. It was a brilliant buzz and a great social event.

Still sporting my huge Afro hair, I proudly wore the pale-blue Kent vest with the white lion on it and dark-blue knickers. Dave had come to cheer me on but I put him out of my mind as I followed the other runners into the 'pen', a holding area known as the 'call room' in senior championships. I was feeling quite confident, having qualified well in my heat the previous day. Standing there, waiting to have my race number and the size of my spikes checked, I had a chance to look at the other competitors in the race for the first time. It can be a nerve-wracking moment but I was so thrilled to be there that my desire to run overcame any nerves. I watched them, remembering what I knew about how they raced, and went through my race-plan in my head. I didn't think of them as individuals. I was only thinking of myself and how well I wanted to perform. I thought that if I gave 100 per cent, then at least I would always know that I'd tried my best.

Even when I was young, my strongest suit as an athlete was my tactical awareness during a race – where I needed to be at which stage. I've always maintained that a runner can be at the peak of their fitness, but if the race isn't run with their head, they've lost before they've started. You have to run economically. You must be in the right place at the right time. You must know when to make your challenge by being aware when you're at your best or when your rival is wavering.

We walked on to the track and lined up just past the bend, poised for the starter's gun. I was on my own; no one could help me now. My stomach was fluttering with nerves. I could hear the Kent Schools team screaming their support in the background as my name was announced but then the noise of the crowd receded, becoming a distant murmur as I focused on what I had to do. The race went off quite fast and I was towards the back of the pack, keeping the front runners in my sights, making sure I didn't let them get too far ahead. I began to work my way forwards but on the last lap I was still quite far away from the leaders. With 300 metres to go, I could see them going, really going for it. We were coming down the back straight towards the 200-metre mark when I suddenly said to myself, 'You can't lose. Come on.' I just went for it. There was a big gap of 30 or 40 metres between me and the two leaders. One of them was the previous year's champion and the other was the English Schools cross-country champion. I gave it everything I'd got, taking one of them at the 200-metre mark and then the other on the final bend to come storming down the home straight to win. Nobody had expected it. Dave went absolutely mad and ran over to give me a massive hug. My team-mates went wild, cheering and shouting.

Winning that race was a huge thing for me. I learned then that in athletics you are the only person who can let yourself down. Your coach can put in all the work to prepare you but once you're on the track, that's it. There's no one else you can blame if you lose, so you must put in the work beforehand and believe in yourself. Experiencing that first hand is how I learned to be a championship runner. Being rewarded with a gold medal in the English Schools Championship made everything worthwhile. Afterwards I went home to more congratulations. Mum and Dad had decorated the house with flags and hung a large banner above the door. Everyone in the street came to congratulate me, as well as the local newspaper. I was made to feel that I had really achieved something.

Of course, running wasn't the only thing in my life back then, although it was the most important. I had left Hildenborough Primary School and gone to Hugh Christie Secondary School when I was twelve. Quite a modern school just north of Tonbridge, it was built round a big courtyard that was used as a car park by the staff.

The large Assembly hall and gym were in the original buildings but the school had been extended with Portakabins that housed the main reception and the classrooms where we were taught French and Maths. The first person I met was Kerrie Havens. I remember her freckles and her frizzy ginger hair like an Afro. She has remained my best friend to this day. We have one of those friendships that stays the same over the years regardless of the length of time we're apart. Even though I don't get to see her very much these days, I know she's always there at the end of a phone.

On that first day of school, wc found ourselvcs standing beside one another in the starters' assembly and then we went to our first class together. We quickly settled into a little clique with four of the other girls and nothing could split us up. Kim Ruck, Lara Craft and me were the outdoorsy ones: Kim was loud and very good at sports (I always thought she should have joined the Army), whereas Lara was the rebel who always dressed trendily, wearing baggy cardigans with her uniform and only loosely tying her tie. We were all envious of Debbie Brazier's long fair hair and her long legs: she was a massive Duran Duran fan with hundreds of pictures pinned on her bedroom wall. Red-headed Lisa Woodward was the quiet one. I was very protective of the others and would never let anyone get away with being nasty about them. Lara and I were the ones who probably stuck up for our group the most. I remember once fighting with a gobby girl in our class called Kelly, though I do not remember what she'd said. It must have been something bad about one of our gang. I rammed her up against the wall while everyone stood there clapping and cheering. That was the first time I properly realised my own strength. We were broken up by a teacher who sent us to the Headmaster's office for a big telling off and a note home.

School was great fun, but academic life was not for me. I had a problem retaining what I'd read despite having had extra reading lessons at primary school. My writing was an indecipherable spidery scribble and my spelling was unreliable too. I was always being told to try harder, to concentrate, to write more neatly. In classes where I had to sit and concentrate on subjects I couldn't relate to, such as French or History, I'd drift off. The only classes where I achieved any success were PE and Design and Graphics. I loved anything creative and could spend ages on a drawing or collage. As for the other classes, my memories are only of being thrown out of French lessons time and time again for constantly talking and interrupting the teacher. In History we learned about the Titanic, but I can't remember anything else, while in RE we scared ourselves by playing with an ouija board whenever the teacher left the room. But despite my reluctance to learn, I only ever bunked off once. Debbie had done it a few times so I followed her lead and went with her to the swings in the park. I don't know how she persuaded me to go because I was always very conscientious about being good and not getting caught doing anything wrong at school. After an hour or so of swinging aimlessly and scuffing my shoes in the dirt, I felt so guilty that I gave up and went back to class.

My favourite subject was always PE. I played all the usual sports but, although strong on speed, I was weak in the skills department. If I was playing netball or hockey, I'd be centre or centre half and be able to run like hell after the ball, but what I did with it when I got it was rather less reliable. My first love was athletics. I started breaking school records in all distances and in fact those records still stand for all the 800- and 1500-metre races that I ran between my first and fifth year. I tried competing in other events too, largely because my athletics club wanted me to. A good junior athlete is often entered for everything in the hope that the club will earn more club points in the county league tables. But I soon realised I was best at middle-distance running. I wasn't fast enough to run the 100 metres. I jumped so high over the hurdles that the other runners shot past me while I was still in the air. I even tried the high jump but just crashed through it. What I did have was the endurance that you need to run the middle distance. I was naturally better at those distances, particularly the 1500 metres, so I stuck with them and enjoyed it.

I was quite a quiet child, confident only when I was with my close friends or family. If I had a job to do or training, I'd get on and do it. I knew Kerrie and the others went to discos and roller discos but I was so into my athletics that I'd always rather go training. Because I was the only kid in the village to go to Hugh Christie, I had to bike there, as there was no school bus. I was given a girlie pinky-purple bike with a wicker basket in front, so I bombed down to school on that. I'd hammer down Trench Road to the nearest school entrance, three miles away, my fingers frozen to the handlebars in the winter. At the end of the school day, I'd climb back on it and head off to wherever I was meeting Dave to work on the latest programme he'd set for me. I was extraordinarily single-minded.

When I was fourteen, in 1984, one of my lifetime ambitions began to take shape. It was the year of the Los Angeles Olympics, when Steve Ovett and Sebastian Coe would be battling for those middle-distance medals once again. In the 1980 Moscow Olympics, Coe had been favourite to win the men's 800 metres but he ran what he later said was 'the worst race of my life' and came second to Ovett. Six days later, he redeemed himself by winning the gold medal in the 1500 metres. Now they were facing each other again.

In the 1980s, middle-distance running dominated British athletics thanks to the efforts of Coe, Ovett and Steve Cram. They were legendary figures in their sport, breaking records and winning medals. Coe was my hero. He was an aggressive runner who didn't give up and his determination was obvious. I identified with that even then. I remember the grimace on his face as he raced. I've been told that I have a similar expression. I may not be the most fluent runner but, like him, I always have had the guts to go for it.

In 1984, Coe arrived in Los Angeles with the weight of public expectation on his shoulders. He was favourite to win the 800 metres so was devastated to come second to the Brazilian Joachim Cruz. Ovett had gone down with bronchitis but ran heroically to come in eighth. Five days later, Coe had reached the final of the 1500 metres. Would he repeat his success of the previous Olympics? I was bursting to find out. Nothing could have torn me away from that TV screen. Ovett collapsed during the final and had to be stretchered off. The favourite was Steve Cram, who was leading the field as they reached the final turn. But suddenly Coe made his move and sprinted to victory, making the finish line metres ahead of Cram. People have compared that moment with my 800-metres gold win in Athens. His eyes said it all, just as mine would in 2004. He was absolutely elated. The only man to have won two successive Olympic golds for the 1500 metres, as well as carrying off two silvers in the 800 metres. What an inspiration. I wondered what it would feel like to be so good at your sport that you could qualify to perform in the Olympics. Watching the 1984 Games inspired me. Maybe one day I could become an Olympic champion too.

My other sporting inspiration, but for different reasons, was Tessa Sanderson. In 1984, she won an Olympic gold for the javelin. By the time I met her, our family had graduated from camping holidays to the excitements of Butlins holiday camp and it was while we were there in Skegness that she turned up to take some of the fitness competitions. I won all the competitions that I entered and so proudly had my photograph taken with her. But, in fact, what impressed me most was her car. It was plush, streamlined and silver with a javelin painted down its side. I just remember thinking, Oh my God. I'd love to have that. Suddenly our battered, maroon, Nissan family estate car seemed a wreck by comparison.

The other major turning point for me came when I was fourteen. A careers officer came into school to talk to us about life in the armed services: the British Army, the Royal Navy and the Royal Air Force. The Navy didn't appeal to me because it meant ships and that meant water – a lifelong fear of mine – and fewer activities. The RAF was the posh service and demanded more qualifications, so that ruled me out. But the Army, that was something else. It was more rough and tough and go-in-there-and-do-it, which suited me perfectly. After talking about the various career possibilities, the careers officer ran a short video called 'Be the Best'. It showcased all the different army trades and what they did: drivers, clerks, Royal Military Police, intelligence, cooks and so on. But the one trade that really spoke to me was the PTIs or Physical Training Instructors. A sergeant stood shouting at soldiers doing every kind of fitness activity from running and general sports to assault courses and gym work. That's me, I thought. I knew immediately that that was what I wanted to do. At the end of the day, I biked straight home and broke the news to my mum.

'I want to join the Army.'

'What?' She couldn't believe her ears. Nobody in our family had ever had anything to with the armed forces.

'They came to school and showed us a video. I'm going to be a PTI.' The words tumbled out of my mouth as I explained what I'd seen and how I knew I could do it.

From that moment on, I nagged her to take me to the Army Recruitment Office in Tunbridge Wells so that I could get as much information as possible about what Army life would involve. Finally she gave in and we made the first of what were to be our annual treks there. I knew I couldn't join up until I was seventeen and three-quarters, but it didn't stop me going along after every birthday to see if by any chance the age-limit had dropped and to get any new leaflets. I wanted to do things that people down the road would never get the chance to do. I didn't want to stay in Tonbridge, but I was still a homebody and I was reassured to know that, being an army PTI, I would be able to telephone or come home quite easily!

In the meantime, I found the sense of challenge that I was looking for by enrolling in the Duke of Edinburgh's Award Scheme. The scheme is made up of three levels, bronze, silver and gold, each more demanding than the last and designed to challenge youngsters, giving them a sense of achievement and an awareness of the needs of other people. It is open to kids aged from fourteen to seventeen, so my school encouraged some of us to participate. Out of our clique, Kerrie, Lara, Kim and I decided to give it a go, along with a couple of the boys in our class, Steve Clark and Paul Cork. It seemed like a great opportunity to get out of school and make a difference. We were the only ones from our year and school house that took it as an option at CSE level.

'Train, plan and complete an adventurous journey in the countryside' was one of the categories we had to enter for our bronze badge. So in July 1985, we went on a survival course that was combined with the study of Kent village churches. Kerrie's father dumped her, Lara, Kim and me in Shipbourne, Kent. We were laden down with our backpacks, bedrolls and a tent. We'd been given a map and a compass and told to find the local church, and then make our way to the campsite at Stansted. Map-reading was not our strong point. We got hopelessly lost and ended up huddled together under the trees in our long yellow hooded macs in the pouring rain, nibbling our Kendal mint cake, waiting to be rescued. Although we didn't realise it, we weren't far from the camp so our careers teacher, Mr Mort, found us quite easily and led us, bedraggled and relieved, back there. We spent the night under canvas, far too excited to sleep.

The next day we had to find the churches in Trottiscliffe and Mereworth, where Kerrie's mum was to pick us up. This time we managed to map-read ourselves into a field of stampeding cattle. I legged it to a tree, climbed it and hung on for dear life. Kerrie was struggling over the fence with Lara and Kim right behind her – all of us screaming our heads off. Despite these disasters, learning orienteering, map-reading and other skills such as camping without a tent and making fires all stood me in great stead for the Army.

When it came to the category for the silver medal – 'Do something different' – Lara, Kerrie and I were sent to help a landscape gardener. We'd imagined we'd be mowing a lawn and weeding, perhaps doing a bit of strimming. Not at all. The gardener was working on a redesign that involved brickwork, gravel, carefully planned planting and an awful lot of digging. She really made us work. So much so that Lara and Kerrie did a runner, leaving me with all the dog-work because I didn't want to let the lady down. Besides, I was such a perfectionist even then that I couldn't leave the job half done, so I humped and heaved stones, helping to make a rockery, and dug till my hands were blistered.

I would always help someone else if I could. One year, I felt so sorry for the old people in the block of flats opposite our house in Riding Park because thick snow had meant that it was difficult for them to get to the shops. I had got to know some of them when I volunteered to do their shopping for them. Seeing their predicament, I asked my granddad for a spade and spent the day clearing and gritting the path so that they could get in and out more easily. They were watching me out of the windows and rained down 10p pieces and sweets to say thank you.

By then, I was beginning to be interested in supplementing my pocket money, so I did paper rounds for the local newsagent, as well as delivering eggs that a supplier would drop off at our house every week. I'd walk round Hildenborough wheeling them on a trolley. I also started cleaning windows for Roy and Marg (Simon Wickson's grandparents) and for Aud and Geoff for a couple of quid a time. I then convinced Roy to let me clean his car inside and out. I would spend ages on the car, but he gave me a fiver and that was wicked! These were my first steps towards financial independence.

# 3. WORKING GIRL

While I was growing up, I can honestly say that I was completely oblivious to any kind of racism. So much so that I thought I was just a different shade of white. I've since been told that some eyebrows were raised at Mum's predicament in our small village community when she was pregnant with me, but I was never aware of anything. Nobody ever gave me any problems. Apart from when my brothers were born, the only other time I noticed I was different was when I was about eight. Whenever we sang Boney M's 'Brown Girl in the Ring' at school, I was always the one who ended up in the middle of the circle! I just thought I must be the best and loved being the centre of attention as they sang, 'She looks like the sugar in the plum – plum plum.'

The one aspect of my mixed race that I could not ignore was my hair. While I was young, my wild curls were pulled into two bunches that stuck out over my ears. At one stage, I made Mum cut them off. It was a terrible mistake and I hated the result. As I got older, I inevitably became more self-conscious and by fourteen or fifteen, I was starting to worry about it. I didn't know what to do with this natural Afro and neither did my mother. As far as we knew, there weren't any specialist black hairdressers anywhere near

Hildenborough to ask for advice and neither of us had a clue how to tame it. I wanted to grow my hair like my friends at school so, during one summer holiday, Mum took me to a Lewisham hairdresser who gave me a perm. It was brilliant. It made my hair drop down into the long curls that I'd dreamed of. The snag was that they didn't give us any instructions about the aftercare, probably assuming we knew what we were meant to do, but we didn't realise I was meant to go back to have it treated. Without that follow-up treatment, the curls got incredibly brittle and all broke off. I was devastated, especially as my friends came back to school with their new long hair and I was stuck with my short cottonwool hair. I was so embarrassed that I spent the term wishing time away until it grew again. In those days, I wanted to do so many things with my hair but couldn't because I didn't know how. At least when I joined the Army, I knew I'd be able to hide it under a hat.

From the moment I'd made my decision to join up, I couldn't wait to leave school. But I had the small bridge of CSEs to cross before I could. I was told I needed to pass English and Maths for the Army. In the end I took several subjects but my results were unremarkable. I had desperately wanted to do PE but I was one of the only people in the school who did. I couldn't do it on my own so that was that. I was a bit disappointed not to get the highest grade for Design and Graphics, but the worst thing of all was getting an Ungraded for Physics. You'd have thought they might have given me a few points for writing my name at least. I passed the rest and went into the Sixth Form but, by then, my athletics was becoming more and more important to me and besides, I wanted to earn some money for myself so that I didn't have to rely on Mum and Dad at all.

My sights were still firmly set on becoming a PTI. During what was to be my brief period in the Sixth Form, interested pupils were invited on an away-day to the army barracks in Maidstone to see what it was like. I dragged a reluctant Kerrie along with me. After lunch we attempted the assault course. I was in my element, absolutely loving it, but Kerrie didn't share my enthusiasm at all. Just the vision of her stranded half-way over a wall with me trying to push her over is enough to reduce us both to helpless laughter even today. It may not have been the career for her but my mind was entirely made up. As far as I was concerned I was going to have a twenty-two-year career in the Army. I wanted the challenge of something I could do for myself, something I could test myself against and I looked forward to the opportunity of helping other people by training them to achieve their goals. I liked the thought of the discipline. I would do whatever it took to be a PTI. I couldn't wait. I did some work experience with Kim at the Angel Leisure Centre, thinking it would stand me in good stead for my career. All I wanted was to join up, so what was the point of pursuing school any further? I told my parents I was leaving.

Since winning the English Schools Championship in 1983, I had stepped up my training with Dave and had come second in the 1500 metres at the 1984 Junior National Indoor Championships and second in the English Schools Championships, a very tight finish where I was just pipped at the line.

The following year was a bit of a blip. For some reason, I found it increasingly difficult to train and race. My motivation was lacking. It may just have been that I was fifteen and, like most teenagers, had become curious about discos and was spending some time trying to make a bit of money for myself as well. It was also at about this time that I went out with a guy, another runner coached by Dave. We'd hang out together, do some runs and even went to a few discos in Tonbridge, usually with Kerrie and the some of our gang. We got on well but I was too busy to want to keep it going, so after a short time we drifted apart. Whatever else was going on, I never bunked off from any of the training sessions Dave set me. If I missed even one, I knew it would mean that I wouldn't be as good as I could be. I carried on training on the track at the club and going for runs with Dave across all the fields surrounding it. We would even run in the dark, round and round Hildenborough Rec. In the winter, I lined up for those dreaded cross-country races. By competing in them, we were building up my strength and endurance, as well as breaking the monotony of winter training. All I can remember is standing on the start lines, freezing cold, and often finishing the race in tears simply because I hated running in such awful conditions.

I came into the 1986 season without as much confidence as I should have had, but I did manage to qualify for the English Schools Championships in the 1500 metres again, this time held in Portsmouth. Dave came with me, and the night before the race we talked about tactics. Katherine and Jojo Tulloh, who were the twin daughters of Bruce Tulloh, one of Britain's top long-distance runners in the 1960s, were expected to win. Dave and I agreed that my main objective was not to let them get away. When it came to the race, I stuck at the back of the pack, running in eleventh place out of twelve runners. The Tulloh twins were at the front, running as a team, taking it in turns to control the pace. It's hard to explain what happened to me but I just switched off – the weirdest sensation ever – until the 400-metre mark, when I was woken by the bell and the sound of Dave's voice, yelling, 'Kelly. Go.' Suddenly I came to and went for it. I passed the other runners, chasing the twins, pulling them back in the final straight, but it was too late. I nearly overtook Katherine but not Jojo, who crossed the line first. I was pleased I'd made it into third place but I was angry with Dave who insisted I'd given the race away. It wasn't until he showed me the Grandstand recording that I saw he was right. That race was a turning point for me. I decided then and there that I would never ever give up on a race again.

By this time, most of my friends were going out in the evenings, working and spending time with their boyfriends. I was much more single-minded. I went out with a couple of boys but they came a firm second to my athletics. Even the one from Eastbourne who bought me an Easter egg (I think I'd be a chocoholic if I let myself!) and flowers. He was a nice guy and the egg was huge – but I didn't fancy him. I ate the egg though!

I ran my last English Schools Championship in 1987 in Birmingham, winning the Seniors 1500 metres. For the first time, I competed in international races too. Earlier that year, the European Olympic Committee initiated the mini Youth Olympics for young runners in the European Community. I was picked to run with Stacey Washington and Julie Adkins from Tonbridge AC. Mum came over on the ferry to Pappendal, Holland with Dave and Julie Adkins' mum and dad. In the opening ceremony, just as in the adult Olympics, we paraded with our teams around the track, all wearing our uniforms and carrying our flags. We felt so proud to be there. I had been selected for the 800 metres, my first major international race at that distance, and got through the heats to the final. This time I ran with the pack, not getting too far ahead or behind, and then in the home straight I pulled away and gave it a strong finish. I was astonished to win. I stood on the rostrum, with Mum and Dave shouting loudly in the background, turned to the Union Jack as the National Anthem boomed out, and wondered if I would ever stand there again as a senior. I went to two other international meets where I won my races, one of them in Germany where I met several other athletes including heptathlete Denise Lewis and triple-jumpers

Connie Henry and Michelle Griffith, for the first time – all of them competing as juniors.

Dave was dead set on me getting into the European Championships, but when I ran in the qualifying heats in Birmingham, I missed the qualifying time by about a tenth of a second. I was gutted I hadn't made it.

However, I'd been spotted at one of the international meets and, out of the blue, I was invited to apply for an athletics scholarship at Minnesota University. For a moment I was tempted. I 'ummed' and 'aahed'. Did I really want to live so far from home for four years? The idea of being that far away from my family and friends was weird. Besides I wasn't sure how I would cope with the cold state of Minnesota and being in a completely different environment. But still, I was all set to take the exams. Then I realised that their intake would be in September 1988 whereas I could go into the Army six months earlier in March. Decision made. I sometimes wonder how different my life would have been if I'd chosen a different path.

Until I could join up, I made a living from various jobs. My first after I left school was at the local newsagents-cum-sweetshop in Hildenborough. At last I graduated from doing the paper rounds to working behind the counter. I thought that sweetshop was the best place in the world. It was the old-fashioned kind with shelves lined with big jars of sweets: humbugs, sherbet lemons that fizzed in your mouth, strawberry bonbons with their chewy centres surrounded by fruit-flavoured powder, orange aniseed twists, the winter mixture of stripy and plain boiled sweets flavoured with mint, cloves or aniseed. Carol, one of the other shop women, and I ate them all the time when Chris, the boss, wasn't there. Then we made a bet with each other to see who could stop eating sweets for the longest. Carol gave in after a few days but I stuck to it for a year. For a whole year, not one sweet passed my lips. That's when I realised I had the willpower to do anything I wanted to if I set my mind to it.

There was a big window on the right of the door where I'd arrange the displays, especially at Easter when I put all the eggs there so that anyone coming in would be tempted to buy one. I'd pin up the small ads in the little window on the side of the shop and spend ages stocking up and arranging all the chocolate bars. I loved the shop so much that recently, when I was injured and couldn't run, I even considered buying the place and revamping it into a newsagents and coffee shop, but then things took off for me again so my concentration went back to the track.

Soon after I was seventeen and three months, Mum and I went down to the Tunbridge Wells Army Recruitment Centre. By this time she had totally come round to the idea of my joining up. My independent streak, my strong will, my ease with other people and my aptitude for sports all seemed to point towards the Army being a successful choice of career. I completed what they call a Domino test, a multichoice test that covered Maths, English and General Knowledge. The number of points I scored determined which trades I was eligible for. To my disappointment, I got the necessary points but the next intake to become a PTI was full and I had to choose another trade. Among my options were clerk (no way was I going to sit in an office), cook (no way was I going to spend my life in a kitchen) and HGV driver. I chose driving because at least it involved being out and about and I'd end up with an HGV licence, a skill that I thought might be useful one day. My aunt Sheila's husband Paul was a truck driver and I had often been out with him on weekend jobs, so it didn't seem such an unfamiliar profession. I had already saved up to buy a white S-reg Ford Escort ready for when I passed my test. As soon as I did, I ripped off the L-plates and bravely took off on my own to buy a Chinese takeaway so we could celebrate. But once I'd put the bags on the seat and got back in, I turned the ignition and there was just a dull click. I had no idea what was wrong so Mick had to come out and tow me home. So much for my first outing. But at least I had the basic skills that I could build on once I'd joined up. All I had to do was wait until the following March. My plan was that, once I was in the Army, I would do everything I could to get a transfer to train as a PTI.

Before that, I started working at the Princess Christian Hospital for mentally handicapped adults in Hildenborough. Mum worked nights there as an auxiliary nurse but during the day I was a nursing assistant. There were various wards that each dealt with different levels of problems with both men and women. I worked with Nan Connor, who was head of the department, and Deirdre Morgan, an auxiliary nurse, at one of the hospital buildings called the Oasthouse in which the patients were all men aged anything from twenty to seventy years old. One of my jobs was to help them into the shower, wash them, help them out, dry them and dress them. I had to teach them about using toilet paper as well as washing their hands. The

Oasthouse had a very long lounge with two round turrets at either end. The men would all sit on their chairs in there except for Eric who paced up and down with a big smile on his face, holding his ears and making a 'brrrr' noise. At the end was the small office where Nan worked, organising the ward, ordering meals and making sure all hospital appointments were kept. To the left was a large bathroom area that contained toilet cubicles, a shower and a big bath, with a chair-lift and cupboards for all the patients' clothes, which we neatly folded and stacked, carefully labelling them with name tags for each patient.

There were around twenty men, all of different abilities and personalities. Two of the patients particularly touched my heart. One was a smoker who used to get taken down to the newsagents to buy his cigarettes. I spent a lot of time chatting with him and decided I would teach him about money, which he didn't understand at all. We practised and practised until he knew exactly how much he needed for the cigarettes and for the bus fare to the newsagents and back. At last D-day arrived. I took him to the bus stop outside the hospital and waited for the bus with him, then off he went on his own. I had already called the newsagents to warn them he was coming and to ask them to be sure that he was given the right brand of cigarettes and the right change, and that he got on the right bus back. While he was gone, I waited nervously inside the main hospital building where I could see the bus stop. At last the bus came into view and pulled up outside. The doors swished open and out he stepped, proud as punch at having managed the journey all on his own. It was fantastic to have helped him achieve this new level of independence. I never knew whether he was able to keep doing it after I left but at least he had done it once and knew that he could.

Johnny Bray was a lively Down's syndrome guy in his late sixties. Over the time he'd been in the hospital, he had physically deteriorated and, by the time I knew him, he was hunched over in a wheelchair. When he was moved to our ward, I used to take him to Rehab where he'd be strapped onto a bench that was tipped upright to straighten him up. After a couple of hours of standing like this, he was able to walk a few steps. I used to volunteer to go with him whenever I could. I'd spend the time playing games and puzzles with him on the tray that was set up in front of him. Then, when his time was up, the staff would release him and he'd walk towards me with a huge beaming smile on his face. It was so brilliant to see him doing this that I'd have tears rolling down my cheeks. I'd seen photos of him dancing around and it seemed so unfair that although he still seemed full of life, he could do so little. Three weeks after I'd left to join the Army, one of the staff phoned me to tell me that Johnny had died. I was heartbroken. But I've never forgotten him. Helping these men towards little improvements in their lives was one of the most rewarding jobs I've ever had. It was also a demanding job, and it made me appreciate how hard doctors and nurses in general hospitals must work.

While I was working at the Princess Christian Hospital, I had my first major asthma attack. I have always been troubled by various minor allergies and asthma. I had gone with another member of staff and a small group of patients to the Flambards Theme Park in Cornwall. We were staying in an old cottage. I woke very early one morning, hardly able to breathe. The hairy blankets that I was lying under must have been full of dust. I panicked before struggling to my feet. I sat in a chair, hyperventilating, trying not to wake anyone up. My chest tightened as I gasped for air. I hadn't brought my inhaler so had no way of relieving the tension caused by my restricted airway. I was terrified. Somehow I made it through to the morning, whereupon I was immediately taken to the local doctor who put me on a nebuliser and gave me Ventolin and Becotide inhalers to relieve the symptoms.

One day, Deirdre, the other nurse on Oasthouse ward, persuaded me to go to see a Tarot-card reader. I tagged along with her to a house in Tonbridge where a very ordinary-looking woman showed Deirdre into the small living room while I waited in the hall. Eventually Deirdre emerged, saying she didn't believe a word of it and it was my turn. I went in and sat on the opposite side of a table to the woman who was dealing the cards. I didn't feel at all nervous, largely because I wasn't taking it seriously. I'd only gone there for a laugh.

'Someone's been looking for you,' she said earnestly. 'They know you're in their life but you don't know anything about them.'

What rubbish, I thought.

'Somebody is desperately trying to find you.'

Oh, please.

'You don't know who they are but one day you'll find out.'

Yeah, right. I couldn't get out of there fast enough. Deirdre and I laughed all the way back to the hospital as we compared notes and dismissed the whole experience as a load of nonsense.

Only a couple of months later, I was in Sainsbury's with Mum, doing the usual shopping. I went ahead into the next aisle to pick up some baked beans. As I was taking them back, I heard a woman say, 'That's Kelly.' I turned round to see a white woman talking to a mixed-race girl, slightly younger than me, sporting those all-too-familiar bunches that I used to have. I didn't recognise either of them so I couldn't understand how they could know who I was. I dashed back to Mum. When she heard what had happened, we both went back round so I could show her who they were. While I hung back, she went up to the other woman, whom she obviously knew, and chatted to her briefly before we carried on with our shopping. On our way out of the shop I asked her who they were.

She stopped for a moment, then said, 'That's your sister.'

'My sister? But I don't have a sister. What are you talking about?' I couldn't get my mind round this at all. She explained that after she and my biological father had split up, he had gone to live with someone called Linda, the lady in the supermarket. The girl, Lisa, was their daughter and therefore my half-sister.

I was stunned. It was not a nice feeling at all. I had been aware that the girl had looked like me but it hadn't crossed my mind that we might be related. I was intrigued to know more. Suddenly I had another family I didn't know. I had a sister. I also had another father. I had never given this man a thought before, but now that I had had this unexpected reminder that he existed, I was curious to see what he looked like.

After that, I badgered Mum until she agreed to telephone Linda and arranged to take me round to visit them and to meet Derrick, my biological father. To my surprise, they only lived six miles away in Tunbridge Wells! My curiosity was quickly satisfied as soon as I'd seen him. He probably felt as uncomfortable as I did. The whole visit was incredibly awkward. Mum obviously would rather not have been there at all, and admitted later that she was worried that I might switch some of my affection for her to Derrick. That was never going to happen. The tension between Mum, Derrick and Linda was as taut as a piano wire as we sat around the living room making polite conversation. I also found I had a half-brother, a baby boy called Danny. I much preferred playing with him or talking to Lisa than talking with the adults.

The weird thing was that Lisa told me she had known about me and wanted to meet me for ages. So perhaps there had been something in what the Tarot-card reader had predicted after all. What I couldn't get over was the fact that she was only two years younger than I was and I had got to the age of sixteen without ever knowing about her. Derrick got out a photo album and showed me pictures of his huge family. I looked at them but these people didn't feel as if they were part of my life. I wasn't really interested in meeting them. I had my real family at home in Riding Park. They were all I wanted. I suspect we were probably all equally relieved when it was time for Mum and me to leave.

Although I was unaware of it, things were falling apart at home. Mum had met another man, Gary. I have no idea when or how she met him. The first I knew of it was when I was playing pool with some of the other staff at the Princess Christian Christmas party. I looked up across the room and saw her with another guy who I didn't recognise. He was tall, dark and in his thirties. Other members of staff had brought their partners but Mick wasn't there. I couldn't believe my eyes. How could my mother do this in front of so many people we knew but, more importantly, in front of me? What about Mick, who was at home with Kevin and Stuart? I went mad. I stormed out and went round to my friend Hugh's house. He was one of my first boyfriends – tall, slim, with dark hair, very 'Officer and a Gentleman' and lived in Riding Lane, not far from the hospital. The last place I was going that night was home, where I would have to see my mum.

When we heard a car pull up, Hugh looked out and saw that it was Gary with Mum. It wasn't until later that I found out that he and Hugh were cousins. I ran out of the house, yanked Gary out of the car and punched him in the eye. I charged round to get at my mother, but she scrambled across the seats and out the other side, screaming. She ran inside while I sped off home in my car. I grabbed some clothes from my room and drove round to Kerrie's house, where her mum said I could stay for as long as I wanted. For the next nine months or so, I refused to have anything to do with my own mum. I wouldn't see her or speak to her. I felt she had let us all down. I stayed with Kerrie's family for a couple of months, just long enough to tide me over until I embarked on my army training course. I was really badly affected by what was happening at home. My mother was my only real security net and now I felt that all my childhood fears were coming true and she was going to leave me for good. It seemed as if everything was spinning madly out of control;

I wanted to pull it back so everything could be as it was before but I didn't know how. So I decided that if I couldn't control our life together, then I could at least take charge of my own.

As I believed I had lost my mother, I reasoned that I couldn't justify making any assumptions about my biological father based on one meeting, so I thought I'd try to get to know him better. Some time earlier, Mum had told me that she'd lost Linda's telephone number but I didn't believe her. So, first making sure the coast was clear, I snuck home one day to get some more clothes and I searched through the obvious places until I found it. I called Linda and asked if I could come and see them. She was very welcoming and let me go round there as often as I liked. I became very close to both her and Lisa.

Whenever I see Linda, I cry with laughter because she's unintentionally so funny. She's always worried that there's something wrong with her and can exaggerate the most insignificant thing: a cold becomes pneumonia; a stomach ache must be appendicitis. Luckily, she's one of those people who can laugh at herself. Lisa is outgoing and very talkative. She's not at all athletic, as I discovered when I once took her to the gym and nearly killed her as she tried to keep up with me. She's always in touch with the latest look, is very thin and has the big curly ringlets that I always longed for. Once Linda took Lisa, Danny and me up to London to visit Derrick's family. The thing I remember most about that visit was meeting his mother, May. Even at seventeen, I was the spitting image of her. It was weird to find someone who I could see I resembled. I didn't visit them again. I didn't want to get to know them better because they weren't part of my life or my real family, although Lisa gave me a photo of May to remember her by.

Derrick, however, was another matter. Although Linda apparently always told him when I was coming, he'd either be at the pub or on his way there so he was only able to stay for a couple of minutes, trilby on his head, long mac at the ready, barely having time to say hello. He did turn up at the party he organised in a Tunbridge Wells night club, Chez Moi, to celebrate Lisa's sixteenth birthday, my upcoming eighteenth, and my leaving for the Army. But it didn't take long for me to realise that he was not going to be any kind of real father to me. He hadn't been there for me once too often. Even Linda, who'd been with him for nearly twenty years, was annoyed that he hadn't made the effort. She understood my attitude towards him exactly. From that point on, I nicknamed him the Sperm Donor and, once I'd left for the Army, I had no contact with him again. I have never seen him since and have no wish to. Mick has always been everything I could have asked for in a father. I don't need another. At that time in my life, when I believed I had lost my mother for good, he provided me with all the support I needed.

On 17 February 1988, I took my final oath to join the Army and enlisted at the Tunbridge Wells Army Recruitment Office. I was signed up at last.

# 4. FIRST STEP ON THE LADDER

Dressed in my jeans and armed with a bag of clothes and toiletries, I arrived at Guildford Station to find about another thirty teenage girls all in the same state of nervous anticipation. Some, like me, had arrived independently by train and were smiling hesitantly, saying hello and chatting with one another, wondering how we were going to get on. Others were saying emotional goodbyes to whichever family members had driven them up there. I can remember feeling incredibly excited. I'd waited so long for this moment and nothing was going to spoil it. I couldn't wait to meet the other girls so dived straight in. There was such a mixture of people and a few loud characters who seemed confident and fun, so I headed for them and got chatting. It wasn't long before we were all shown on board a coach to be driven to the Women's Royal Army Corps barracks in Guildford. This was to be our home for the next six weeks while we were inducted into the Army and given our basic training.

The barracks were two miles from the town. As we drove in, a guard was on the gate. We were told that the building on the right was the guardroom where we had to sign in and out if we were to leave or return to the camp. In the distance, we could hear the shouting of an instructor taking a platoon for drill on the parade square – a sound of things to come.

We were immediately shown to our living quarters in a large block. The many bedrooms lined a long corridor with large 'ablutions' at the far end where there was a changing area, showers, baths and basins. I was sharing a small room with three other girls. As the sergeant and corporal came in we stood to attention by our beds as ordered, our bum cheeks squeezed tightly together with nervousness. Our metal beds were 'barracked' so the heavy brown blankets were folded to a certain size, box-shaped, and perfectly stacked on the mattress with the sheets. Then the pillowcases and the pillows were on top. Each of us had a small wardrobe and a side unit. Spartan but functional best describes it. I couldn't have cared less. I was looking forward to whatever they were going to throw at us.

On that first day, I was given my rank, Private Holmes, and told to memorise my regimental number – WO804968 – I will never forget it. We were then taken off to the Medical Centre to have a full health check-up before going to the Quartermaster's store, where we were told to stand in line and wait. Eventually it was my turn. The tailor measured me and I was given my green beret and our WRAC cap badges (a lioness rampant inside a laurel wreath topped by a crown). For everyday use, I was given a set of green short-sleeve summer and long-sleeve winter shirts, combats with DPM (camouflage jacket and trousers with disruptive pattern material), lightweights (green trousers), twists (to fold the trousers under), thick green socks, a dark green belt, two pairs of black boots – short DMS (Doc Martens) with shiny toes and worn with puttees (a long piece of khaki material with ties that wraps around the ankles), and 'combat boots high' (long boots). There was also a Bergen backpack for when we went on exercise and green stripy skeleton webbing with attachable green canvas bags to hold various items on combat fitness tests (eight-mile march/walks). The PE kit consisted of a green sports skirt, white aertex shirt and plimsolls. The parade uniform, or 'Number Twos', was a green jacket and skirt, black shoes, flesh-coloured tights (at least, they were flesh-coloured if you were white), another set of shirts but this time in white, belt and a cap with a really shiny peak. Most exciting of all was a gas mask and green overalls with black rubber boots and gloves for protection in the gas chamber. I was also handed billycans, cutlery and a black flask to use on expeditions. We were given two green canvas kit bags, one large and square, and the other long and rectangular just like I'd seen in the movies. The icing on the cake was the dog tags with regimental number and name – just in case we got lost in battle!

So, fully equipped, I went back to my room and joined my roommates as we put everything away. All four of us got on brilliantly. All my clothes from Civvy Street were folded and stashed in the wardrobe and, for the first time, I put on my new lightweights and a shirt so I was turned out identically to everyone else on training. The worst thing was the beret. My first reaction when I saw it was: how the hell am I going to get my hair underneath that? The beret came flat, but the idea was to shape it so that it lay flat on the left side of your head where the cap badge sat, then to fit it to your head down the right-hand side. The way to get it right was to put it in hot, then cold water alternately until it shrank and then, at night-time, to mould it on your head until it became the shape you wanted it to be. Dealing with it that first day was horrendous. I still had my Afro hair that I knew was not going to give in easily to the pressure of a beret. In the end, it became a joint effort. My roommates filled water bottles so that we could damp my hair down and then they contributed litres of hair spray to stick it to my head. The beret was on.

When we went into our first classroom, we had to take off our berets. Immediately my hair sprang out from underneath it, huge and sticking out everywhere. Everyone was laughing, including the NCOs (Non-Commissioned Officers) instructing us. Until I eventually got my hair cut short, I was continually teased about it. I didn't have any trouble fitting it under the peaked caps but the berets were a lasting nightmare.

During the next six weeks of training, everything we needed to know was drummed into us. Inspections were a big part of our basic training life. They could be 'bull nights', kit inspection or bed inspection. It didn't matter which because they all instilled similar degrees of anxiety. For bull nights, we had to 'bull' our parade shoes, polishing them until they shone like glass. We'd all sit in the corridor for ages, spitting on our cloths, then putting on the black polish and rubbing our shoes in small, small circles. After a few rubs, you blew on the shoe and repeated the whole process again and again until you'd got the pair of them as shiny as can be. Then we'd hear the bang of the outside door and knew the sergeant was on her way in to inspect them. If somebody's weren't right, they'd get absolutely bollocked.

The real bane of my life was kit inspection nights when we had to show all our kit properly pressed. Some of the shirts had a double-edged pleats down the back so the panel between them had to be exactly the right width all the way down. The creases in the sleeves had to be razor sharp (I still do them like that to this day) and the trousers had to be perfect. The shirts were a really big issue. To begin with we'd iron away but the creases still came out squint or not sharp enough. Then someone came up with the brilliant idea of using starch. It made the shirts as stiff as a board and horribly uncomfortable to wear but the creases stood out brilliantly.

As we all got to know one another, we discovered each other's forte. Some girls could iron skirts really well, others could iron shirts and some could bull shoes. My forte was bulling the shoes, so I'd shine someone else's in exchange for them ironing my shirts. We could only do that when the NCOs weren't around though, so the moment we heard the noise of the main door outside our corridor, we'd all rush madly around getting our things back before they appeared.

On bed inspection nights, everything in our rooms had to be perfect. All the beds had to be barracked and everything hung up or put away neatly. On one of the first inspections, the sergeants and the corporals started at the bottom of the corridor. They went into the first room. We held our breath. Suddenly loads of crisp packets and chocolate bars came flying through the doorway. One of the recruits had hidden them in her wardrobe and the sergeant was just flinging them out of the room. We couldn't stop laughing. Then we heard one of the girls shout, 'NO!' as all her kit and her bedding were thrown out of the window because they weren't neat enough.

As the NCOs reappeared, we pulled ourselves together, desperately trying not to laugh because we knew we'd get into so much trouble. At the same time we were all panicking that when they came to our room, the same thing would happen. That time our room just managed to pass, but my badly ironed shirts were regularly flung on the floor and once my bed was tipped over because the blankets weren't piled exactly right. When it first happened to me, I hated it, but as the weeks went by, I got used to it.

Although I've never been to university, I imagine that the sense of being in a place with other people your own age who are all just having a laugh is very much the same. When we got into trouble, we took it seriously, but always saw the funny side of it at the same time. We just had to be careful no-one in command saw us.

The one time I got into big trouble was when we were learning drill. Lined up in three lines on the parade ground, we stood at ease with our legs apart and our hands behind our back, facing the sergeant.

'Squad.' As the command was barked at us, our arms were braced down behind our backs.

'Squad. Shun.' We stood to attention, our arms coming to our sides with fingers clasped into our hands and thumbs pointing to the ground.

'Squad will move to the right in threes. Right turn.' We turned to the right exactly together, our boots sounding in step.

'By the right. Quick march.' As we moved off smartly, one of the recruits led with the wrong foot, camel marching. If that ever happened, we found it absolutely hilarious. It was made all the worse by being so nervous in front of the sergeant. This occasion was no exception.

'Squad. Halt.' As we obeyed, we hopelessly concertina-ed into one another, thanks to the one who was out of step. The girl next to me and I were beside ourselves with laughter. I couldn't stop giggling but didn't dare make a noise in front of the sergeant. My shoulders were shaking as I desperately tried to control myself. I could hear the measured sound of marching behind me. It stopped right by my shoulder. 'Private Holmes,' bellowed the sergeant directly down my ear. 'Get off the parade square, now!' Those sergeants had the power that came with rank and were not afraid to use it. To be sent off on your own is the worst thing that can happen to a recruit. We'd all come on the parade square as part of a platoon, a team. She was screaming at me, 'Private Holmes.' I had no choice but to turn and march off. I was completely terrified, thinking I'd had it. My career would be over before it had begun.

I reached the sergeant's office and stood to attention outside it, waiting until she came. The platoon came in a little later, all of them looking over at me with some sympathy. We all knew I was for the high jump. Eventually the sergeant appeared and I followed her in, standing on the other side of her desk while she crucified me, concluding, 'You're on show parade for five days.' I was dismissed. By that time, laughing was the furthest thing from my mind. And being on show parade was a real pain. It meant that every night at 7 p.m., just as everyone else was relaxing back in their rooms or going out to the Naafi, a little social club with a bar, pool tables and music, I had to report to the duty officer in the guardroom at the gate of the camp, wearing my Number Twos. Everything had to be spick and span: bulled shoes, pressed jacket and skirt, straight tie and no fluff on the cap. Other recruits from the other platoons would be waiting there at the same time, waiting and waiting until someone from the guardroom came to inspect us. We could be there for ten minutes or we could be there for an hour. If anything was wrong they'd either give you hell or send you back. Twice I got sent back, once because I'd scuffed my shoes while marching down there and the other time because I had creases in my skirt. After those few days, I was very strict with myself about when I did and didn't laugh.

Part of the course took place in classrooms where we learned about the rank structure and rules and regulations. Unlike the classes I remembered from my school days, I enjoyed these. I wanted to be there and found the information we were given interesting. But, of course, what I enjoyed most about the course were the activities, although I didn't find them all easy. One of the more difficult was weapons training. We began by using SMGs (submachine guns) on the shooting range. The target was a long way away and I found it incredibly difficult to hit, but I knew I had to pass all the different sections of training, including this one, if I wanted to pass out. We normally knelt or lay on the ground, aiming at the distant target and waiting for the order to fire. When we'd completed the set number of rounds, we had to get up and walk to the target to count the number of points scored. I dreaded it.

One day, I was next to another girl who found it as difficult as I did. We were so nervous and our weapons had such a big back kick that we missed almost every time. As we walked down to the targets, I was telling myself, 'Oh my God. We're going to fail.' Then she whispered, 'Look, I've got a pencil. If we're quick, we can use it without anyone seeing.' When we reached the targets we stabbed them with the pencil. By the time we'd finished it looked as if we were the hottest shots in the group (we'd allowed ourselves a few misses for authenticity). The inspecting sergeant was pleased with our success and failed to notice the lead marks round the holes. We were through.

Swimming was the other torture as far as I was concerned. I had never conquered my fear of water to become a strong swimmer. The dreaded day came when we had to pass the swimming section. Eccles, a lanky mixed-race girl in our group, was in front of me. She jumped in the pool and nearly drowned. She couldn't swim at all and had to be dragged out. I was next and kept saying to myself, 'I mustn't fail. I mustn't fail. I'm not going to get kicked out because of this.' I jumped in and started treading water. I just about managed to keep myself afloat. Then we had to swim four lengths of a 25-metre pool. That's a hell of a long way when you're not much of a swimmer. There were two other girls in the pool at the same time. They were much better swimmers and were fantastically good to me. My hips kept sinking and my legs felt like dead weights, pulling me under. I couldn't get them up to kick on the surface. So, whenever the NCO wasn't looking, the girls would grab me underneath my waist and haul me along, spluttering and splashing. How I passed that section, I'll never know. But I did.

There were several PTI direct entries in our intake. I was a bit jealous of them because they were following my dream. I couldn't help thinking how, when I went off to trade training as an HGV driver, they'd be off training as PTIs. As a result, I was tremendously competitive with them so would do everything I could to beat or better them in sports and PT. I didn't just want to prove to them or to the PTI that I was as good as them; I wanted to prove it to myself. They were fit, but so was I, and I gave it everything I'd got, especially in the Basic Fitness Test. That consisted of a half-mile squaded warm-up, then a mile and a half running as fast as we could. I always came in first and even achieved the camp record. I loved being top, especially in the assault courses we had to tackle. Over walls, under netting, through tunnels, climbing cargo nets, running – you name it. I thought it was brilliant.

As far as I was concerned, everything we did was fun. Even doing the gas chamber training. We'd enter the little hut, a few of us at a time, dressed in our NBC (Nuclear, Biological, Chemical) suits. Then the $CO_2$ gas was released. While we were in there we'd have to learn to sip water from the black flask as if we were in a war environment. It was so difficult. I'd be struggling with my gas mask and my lips would be burning as I fumbled for the white powder that we had to dab on any bit of exposed skin. Choking, I'd take a quick sip from the flask and then cover up again. The last exercise we were required to do was to remove the mask and say our number, rank and name before diving out of the chamber. Somehow I managed it but a couple of the girls, however often they practised, couldn't remember their number and had tears running down their cheeks as the gas stung their eyes. The sergeant in charge pushed them out of the hut, yelling that they were pathetic. The agony wasn't over yet. We then had to shout 'Gas, Gas, Gas' and throw ourselves on the floor as if we were in a real wartime situation. That was just one of the various possible emergency scenarios that we practised.

We did get time off to relax, whether it was just going to the Naafi with mates or going out into Guildford. After being in a mixed school it was odd to be in an almost all-female environment but the other girls were great. We were all in the same boat and we helped each other get through it. I particularly hit it off with Harvey, a good laugh and a potential PTI, and Lynne, an energetic and sporty northerner who was also going to be a driver and became my closest friend. There was also 'Penfold', who was nicknamed after the bumbling, bespectacled hamster sidekick of Danger Mouse. Once, just to pass the time, we joined with everyone else in mocking-up a wedding scene. We all took part for a laugh, improvising costumes from whatever we could find. Lynne took down the net curtains to dress like an angel and gave one to Penfold for the bride's veil. I was the vicar, complete with buck teeth, dressed in black and white. I remember a 'mother' crying her eyes out, and a 'baby', complete with nappy and a mock dummy. Everyone gave performances worthy of an Oscar. I loved the spontaneity of the occasion and the fact that everyone got involved and made an effort to play their parts without any rivalry or bad temper. It was this camaraderie that made the Army such a fantastic place to be.

On the fourth weekend we were allowed to go home for a break but I couldn't wait to get back to barracks. There was nothing to do at home with Mick and the boys, except go next door for Sunday lunch with Nan and Granddad. I spent the whole weekend dreaming about the Army or clock-watching. I had become so attached to the new people I had met and to the environment that I was in that I was homesick for it all. I missed those new friendships and the busy, demanding life. That was the longest weekend in the whole six weeks of training.

Of course, I'm aware of the criticisms levelled at the Army for their treatment of recruits, particularly with all the publicity surrounding the sad events at Deepcut Barracks. But during those six weeks, and indeed in all my years in service, I never came across any racism or any bullying. To me, bullying is about picking on one person, abusing them and giving them a hard time. I didn't see or hear of that happening once. A couple of girls in other platoons did try to commit suicide while I was in Guildford but we never knew why. One nearly hanged herself; the other tried to shoot herself on the range. We were all shocked, of course, but because none of my friends knew them, it didn't feel as though they had anything to do with us. We had no choice but to get on with our training. It's true that the pressure on all us recruits was intense. To be able to take everything that's thrown at you during those days of training, you've got to really want to be there and to succeed. If you're not in the right mindset, it's hard to detach yourself from the discipline and to cope with being bawled at. The training is very tough and if someone joins up to escape their home-life, or if they are expecting it to be like a job that provides bed and board, they might well not have the strength to cope.

As far as I'm concerned, the Army is about discipline and respect. The NCOs shouted at us on training to get the best out of us so that, when we got our first posting, we would be the best. I never saw promotion as a way of getting power to wield over others. I knew I'd only get a rank if I'd done my job well. For me, it was a way of improving on what I'd done and a measure of my success. I saw everything I went through as another step on the ladder to a lifelong career.

My greatest embarrassment happened on the day we were all passing out. We had survived the basic training and were nervous but excited to be going to our next camp for trade training. Everyone was dressed in their Number Two's ready for our last parade, waiting for our parents and friends who were coming along to watch. The covered bleachers where the officers would sit had been put out to the front of the parade square. Everyone was hanging out of the windows, trying to spot their parents as the cars came through the gates and were directed left to the car park. Suddenly a car appeared in the middle of the parade square. Someone yelled, 'Who's that driving across the parade square?' I looked out. It was only Mick. I nearly died of shame while everyone else was creased up with laughter. The parade square is absolutely sacrosanct. No one sets foot on it unless on parade or doing the drills. There were car park attendants directing the traffic right around it but Mick had managed to drive straight past them and was making his way slowly and rather uncertainly across the square. The parade sergeant was beside himself, stomping and shouting at him. But Mick took no notice and drove blithely on, slow as you like, pausing occasionally as he tried to find the right way. I couldn't bear to watch any more but I wasn't short of people who, when they weren't laughing, were only too glad to report where he had got to.

After the ceremony I met up with him. He had brought Kevin and Stuart, Kerrie and Lara with him to see me on the big day. It was great. Since everything had gone wrong with Mum, I had become much closer to Mick. I had come to rely on him a lot and found myself able to confide in him. It was the first time that I realised what being a parent means. He had been there for me through thick and thin and never wavered, however difficult it might have been. I know that now, and love him for it.

Mum did turn up, unexpectedly, by train. It was the first time I'd really seen her since I'd walked out at Christmas. By this time, she had moved out from Riding Park, leaving Mick with Kevin and Stuart, and gone to live with Gary. I was disappointed that she hadn't come up with the family and I was shocked that she looked so thin. I felt angry that, after the passing-out parade, she didn't make the effort to come out with us into Guildford on my special day but instead went for the early train back to Hildenborough. I wasn't going to let it completely spoil the day, so undeterred, the rest of us went off into town where I showed them around and we celebrated with a meal. I had proved that I deserved my place in the Army and I was off to the next step – trade training in Leconfield where I would train to be an HGV driver.

When I got back to barracks that night, I couldn't help thinking about Mum and what had happened between us. Deep down I didn't want to fall out with her but since she had left home, she seemed to me to have changed so much. I couldn't understand why she wouldn't want to come and celebrate with me, especially as she hadn't seen me for ages. I didn't really appreciate the extent of the difficulties that she and Mick were going through or the fact that it might have been awkward for them. I just felt as though I had lost her altogether. If I'm honest, the way she behaved set our relationship well and truly back as far as I was concerned. We didn't speak again for some months after.

# 5. AT THE WHEEL

How many people am I going to kill? was the only thought running through my head as I drove through Leconfield behind the wheel of a green four-ton army truck for the first time. As I approached each zebra crossing in the impossibly narrow streets of this quaint old town, double de-clutching to change gear, I was praying no one would suddenly dash out in front of me. It was one of the most nerve-wracking experiences of my life so far. I'd learned to drive in Civvy Street, so learning to handle these monsters was a little easier for me than for some of the other girls. Despite being small, I could haul myself into the cabs of the vehicles, but sometimes I had to use a cushion to give me the extra height I needed when sitting at the wheel.

The inside of the cab was very basic. It had black seats, a huge flat steering wheel and large foot pedals. It was nothing like driving my pride and joy, my white S-reg Ford Escort. Nonetheless, it was fun learning.

I didn't miss athletics at all. I had quite consciously given up the sport to join the Army. This was my career now. Having passed through training at Guildford, I had been sent up to Yorkshire to the Defence School of Transport in Leconfield near Hull for my trade training as an HGV driver. Lynne from the basic training course was also there, so settling into the new environment wasn't so hard.

Leconfield Barracks operated as a functioning army base as well as the driving school so it was much bigger than we were used to. The soldiers and recruits were mainly men and wore a different cap badge from us as they were signing up for the Royal Corps of Transport. Whether it was passing their civilian test, moving on to more advanced driving skills or mastering the different types of transport, from motorbikes to heavy goods vehicles, people came from all over the country to learn to drive there. The barracks had sixteen kilometres of nursery road circuits and five kilometres of cross-country tracks on site. Driving Land Rovers through the thick mud and over the mud banks was a real laugh. We had to practise handling the vehicles in different terrains and situations. The most scary thing was driving up a bank so steep that the only thing I could see out of the window was the sky, while feeling the vehicle was about to tip over backwards. Somehow it always held its ground but I never felt safe whenever we did that exercise.

We had to know the Highway Code back to front and learn the basic mechanics of the vehicles so that, although we might not be able to fix them, we'd know what was wrong with them if they broke down. The mechanical engineers were the ones who came in to sort them out, but the basic maintenance training has stood me in good stead throughout my life. As for washing the vehicles down – we seemed to be doing that all the time.

Parades and kit inspections were still a part of daily life but they didn't happen anything like as often as in basic training, although we did have to march in squad everywhere we went around the huge barracks! We also did a lot more sport. There were so many soldiers at Leconfield that we had plenty of opportunity for all the team sports like rounders, volleyball and basketball in the gym. Tournaments were held for almost everything you could want to play. The other thing I enjoyed was Troops PT: all the team exercises designed to encourage team-building and co-ordination.

Leconsfield was where I got what I regarded then as my first proper wage. I remember lining up outside a vast hangar waiting to be called in to an officer sitting behind a desk. 'Private Holmes.' I stood to attention and marched in to be given that precious pay packet: a small brown envelope with the princely sum of £54.38

after deductions for food, accommodation and tax. I then saluted (during basic training we were told that you must always salute an officer who was wearing his/her cap badge and beret); about turned; and marched back out. That first wage meant so much to me that I've still got my first pay slip.

The one episode during those fourteen weeks of training that really sticks in my mind is a hellish night drive on the Yorkshire Moors. Normally, we travelled in convoy, but this time all the trucks were sent off at different intervals to make their own way to the camp. Another female private and myself were given a map and the co-ordinates of the location where we had to be by 11 p.m. We confidently set off in our truck, but, sure enough, we got completely lost. Eventually we pulled up in a village and I leaped out to ask a policeman directions.

'We're so lost. Can you help us?'

He took a long time, studying our map, turning it this way and that. Eventually he looked at me. 'You're way off the map.'

'Well, do you know how we get back on it?' We were meant to arrive at the base camp at any moment and our time was running out.

He directed us as exactly as he could, given that we didn't have a map that covered where we were. Before long, we were completely lost again, but we gave it lots of welly, trying to get to our destination. Midnight came and went. 1 a.m. 2 a.m. 3 a.m. The rest of the unit would have arrived hours ago and were due to leave for home at around 7.30 a.m. At 4 a.m. we were still driving, surrounded by nothing but moors, moors, moors, with thick grey fog creeping across the ground, swirling around us. By this time, I was behind the wheel again and the two of us were arguing, each of us blaming the other for being such a bad map-reader. One minute we'd be at a recognisable point on the map, the next, we'd gone off the page again.

'Read the goddamn map,' I shouted in frustration. I was beginning to lose sight of the funny side of the adventure.

'I'm doing my best but everything looks the same,' she snapped back. 'I don't think we're even on the map.'

'You're bloody joking. Not again.'

Our bickering disguised the fact that we were both scared stiff that we'd never find the camp at all. If we didn't turn up there to join the rest of the convoy, neither of us had a clue how to get back to the barracks. I was having visions of us driving about for days, never getting off the moor.

We must have gone round and round in circles. There were sheep everywhere, lying on the road – I barely avoided them as they abruptly materialised out of the fog. It was the bleakest place I'd ever been – not a house or farm in sight, no landmarks that we could distinguish. It was only three hours now before the others would be getting up to leave and we still had no idea where we were. Then suddenly, at 6.20 a.m., more by luck than judgement, we arrived at the camp. As we distinguished the outline of the other trucks through the darkness, we cheered loudly. We had made it after all. Having almost given up hope of ever finding them, I cannot describe how relieved we were.

Immediately we saw that everyone else had cammed up (camouflaged) their vehicles with large hessian netting when they'd arrived for the night. We knew that if any of the officers came out and saw that we'd just arrived we would be in big trouble. We quickly cammed up our truck so that it looked as if we'd arrived the night before and climbed in the back to grab a short kip. If we'd stumbled into the accommodation, it would have made it blindingly obvious that we were late. This way, there was just a chance no-one would notice. We were both absolutely knackered after driving and arguing all night. We had just got our heads down when, before we knew it, everyone began coming out, uncamming their vehicles and starting up. After our marathon, where were we going to find the energy to drive all the way back? We emerged blearily from the truck and were immediately spotted by the sergeant.

'What on earth are you doing in the back of the truck?'

'Oh, you know. We got up early so we could sort things out,' we lied. 'Just wanted to make sure everything was OK.'

If anybody suspected what had happened to us, nobody said a word. So, completely shattered, we joined the convoy and drove safely back to barracks. Our reputation as competent map-readers miraculously remained intact although it took us both several nights to catch up on lost sleep.

The great thing about Leconfield was that, unlike basic training, the time after a day's work was always pretty much your own. There were so many of us, we had a pretty wild time with parties in the evening or socialising in the Naafi, where we let our hair down with plenty of drinking and dancing to visiting bands. I've never been a drinker, but without my athletics training to hold me back, I was free to go out and enjoy myself as much as I wanted. Of course, there were plenty of affairs that went on among some of the male and female privates. We weren't hermits. But as far as I was concerned, nothing serious went on with anyone. I did get friendly with someone because of the close environment in training but it was nothing serious. I was to find that during my early twenties, I was quite a jealous person when it came to relationships. I was always worried that things would end before I had given them a chance. I tended to pre-empt anything bad happening – especially when drinking was involved. I didn't like the way drink could change people, making them unpredictable or unpleasant. As I've got older, my attitude to drinking hasn't eased much, so it is what fuels most of my rows in my relationships with other people. My mother leaving home had deeply affected me too. I think that, as a result of her going, I lost my trust in other people generally even when they hadn't done anything to deserve it.

After fourteen weeks, I emerged as a qualified HGV driver and was on the move again. I was posted to 53 Squadron, Marchwood Military Port, Southampton, where service or civilian shipping is loaded and discharged in the support of worldwide military administration, exercises and operations. My job was to pick up and deliver stores either going to or from the port. It was all pretty straightforward – unless I overslept. Usually I cycled or caught the little train from outside the barracks down to the MT (Military Transport) Depot. I should have been down there at 7.30 a.m. but one day I slept through until 9 a.m. Heaven only knows how I got away with it but I managed to sneak down to the MT without being seen, take my vehicle from the side of the building, drive to the Quartermaster's and pick up the stores for delivery. By the time I reached the civilian warehouse, hours late, the manager was going mad, having rung everyone he could think of to find out where his goods were. Fortunately the guys in the Quartermaster's were good friends and kept their promise not to say anything. They knew I'd be for it if I was found out. Thank God it was in the days before mobile phones, so I could get away with the excuse that I'd broken down on the way to the warehouse and had no way of contacting him.

Another time, I wasn't so lucky. I was caught trying to sneak my vehicle away from the MT. I had forgotten what time my pick-up was and had been chatting too much to some friends in the barracks.

Again it was hours after I should have left. I was reported and hauled up in front of the commanding officer. The commanding officer was someone I didn't want to cross. He had the power to give you a bad report at the end of your posting that could destroy any promotion prospects. If the offence was serious enough, he could strip you of your rank (if you had one), put you in jail or give you extra duties. I was given a roasting and four days of extra duties, which meant I had to be on duty in the guard room all night, sleeping in there too. It was bad enough having to do it once or twice a month in the normal course of duty, but to do it for several nights at a time, when all my friends were going to the Naafi or out to clubs without me, was horrible. I was careful not to let it happen again.

I lived in the barrack accommodation that occupied big three/four-storey blocks. Occasional inspection nights or parades occurred but they became much more a thing of the past. I made many great friends there and we had a good time together, often going on a small open boat from our port to Southampton Docks across the water. We'd make our way into the town and go to the clubs. It was the era of acid when the yellow smiley face beamed from everyone's clothes. None of us touched drugs of any kind but the acid music was wild. We'd be there for hours, dancing, throwing our arms about and enjoying ourselves, dancing and singing, 'Aciiiid. Aciiiid. Too strong.' I'd always been very independent so now that I was living away from home I found that I could cope very easily.

At Marchwood, I began to take my first steps towards becoming a PTI. Not once had my ambition wavered. It was just a question of waiting till the right moment. Marchwood was only a small barracks. It did have a gym, but it didn't have a woman PTI. The male PTIs were great but most of them had no idea how to take the women's sports that we wanted to do, such as netball and rounders. Because I was really keen, I went to the gym a lot and got on well with Ray, the staff sergeant there. He was a cool guy, strong and fit, who was an expert in judo. When I got a chance, I explained to him that I really wanted to be a PTI but hadn't been able to get on to the direct intake when I joined. He understood that I needed experience in the gym if I was ever going to be able to transfer to one of the PTI training courses. It was all I had ever wanted to do. I tentatively asked him whether I could take the girls for PT. Every lunchtime I'd go up to the gym with the PTI guys and play basketball, and then, when I was able to, I would arrange games and physical training sessions for the girls. We had a great time and it was such a laugh. I was in my element.

Among the PTI staff was Kriss Akabusi, the 400-metre hurdler with an incredible laugh. He was a huge athletics star at the time, running in civilian races and major international championships. Although he was a PTI warrant officer, I hardly ever saw him. The Army was going through one of its phases where people who excelled in a sport were allowed lots of time off to train and compete. However I did chat to him when I got the chance. He was a great help to me, making some calls to the commanding officer to see if I could take the girls for PT and to find out when the intakes were for the next PTI course at the PT School. Thanks to him and to Ray, I was taking the girls for PT lessons before I knew it, either early in the morning, at lunchtime or after hours. Organising the various fitness classes for them was a way for me to get the right sort of experience and got me into the gym through the back door. Another plus of taking the classes was being given my own room. I was so happy to have that privacy at last. First of all I was given one of the large rooms, which I made cosy by putting all the wardrobes and units around my bed with posters on the wall. Then I got a 'bunk' room that was normally reserved for NCOs – I felt very important.

Eventually I was admitted on to a pre-selection course at the Duchess of Kent Barracks, Aldershot. It was obligatory to go on one of these courses if you were already in the Army and wanted to change trades. If I passed, I would be able to take the PTI training course at the Physical Training School at Aldershot at last. But I didn't pass. They failed me, and I was absolutely gutted. Physically I was very strong and could do everything that was asked of me, but it was my co-ordination and skills that let me down. My hockey, badminton, gymnastics and swimming (of course) weren't good enough. The selection committee also wanted to see confidence in the way the candidates instructed. I couldn't project my voice properly then, shouting from my throat instead of my stomach. It looked too weak to them.

I went back to Marchwood, very unhappy, but my boss at MT and Ray sent me on every skills course they could think of. These were held at the Army School of Physical Training in Bulford, another army camp just north of Salisbury. Badminton, hockey, basketball, judo, swimming – you name it, I did it. I was so determined not to fail the next selection course that I knew I had to be perfect in every one of them. Afterwards, I'd practise everything I'd learned with the guys in the gym. I also took the girls for circuit training or assault courses, arranged league events for various sports and tried to get them as fit as possible.

One day I had phoned Mum to thank her for a ring that she had sent me for my eighteenth birthday present. It had arrived months later while I was in Bulford. It felt strange having hardly been in contact with her for so long. To my astonishment, she told me that she and Gary had got married the day before. I hadn't had the slightest idea that was about to happen so I was horrified. Perhaps I was still hoping that things might return to the way they once were with Mick and the boys, even if I knew deep down that they wouldn't. I couldn't believe she would marry without telling me. Now I see that she must have felt she couldn't win. I was going to go mad whenever she broke the news to me, before or afterwards. My hostile reaction to their affair must have made her nervous of saying anything. She was right to be, I guess. I did not take the news at all well and hung up on her. Relations between us took another step backwards.

It was around this time that the army athletics team got in touch with me. They had heard I'd been an international athlete as a junior so were keen to get me involved again. They have the elite army athletes who compete both internally and against the RAF and the Navy. Naturally they want the best team possible because winning the annual Inter-Services Championships, which is where the Army, Navy and RAF send teams to compete against one another, is regarded as the highest achievement. I was reluctant to become part of it. My athletics days were in the past.

However, Kriss Akabusi encouraged me to go with him to Southampton Athletics Club where he trained. I really didn't want to. I couldn't be bothered to start training again. Kriss wouldn't take no for an answer so eventually I gave in. While we were at the track, he introduced me to Tony Fern, the civilian middle-distance coach for Southampton AC and I agreed to train with him. So it was back to track work, long runs and hill training, but I didn't take it very seriously. The only reason I did it was because the army athletics team were bugging me to join them and I thought I'd better do some training or I'd be completely useless. So, in 1989, I decided to give it a go, and I got into the team. I was selected to run in the Inter-Services Championships at Cosford, in which I won the 1500 metres and came second in the 800 metres. At the beginning of 1990, I was put in the cross-country team and came third in the Army Cross-Country Championship and fourth in the Inter-Services. Lack of specific training meant that I was only good enough to make up the team. I didn't like running cross-country any more than I had when I was a junior but I was encouraged because I was a good runner.

The nice thing about joining the athletics team was that I met loads of new people: Sue Sharp, another PTI and a very good distance runner; Liz Bennett, an officer and 400-metre hurdler, who became the team manager; Dobo, a huge black guy and discus thrower who no-one would mess with if they saw him in the street. In fact he was a lovely guy, always having a laugh, making everyone feel at home on the team and always helping people out if he could. Jackie Gilchrist was a very energetic, outgoing PTI and successful army heptathlete, who was always easy to spot thanks to her distinctive long ginger hair. Originally from Edinburgh, she was six years older than me and cared a great deal about the team. She loved organising and making things happen. Another 400-metre runner was Michelle McBride. Like the rest of us, she had loads of energy and would have a go at every event if it meant the team would get maximum points. Each year, we'd come together to be part of the team. These were the people whose particular friendship and support were to help me later in my career.

At that stage I was hardly training at all. I just wanted to be out in the Naafi or at the Southampton clubs, not training in the cold, the wet and the dark. I remember one army cross-country race at the beginning of the season where I ran abysmally. Afterwards I was showering in the changing rooms and caught sight of myself in the mirror as I came out. I looked so fat. Now I'm a muscley eight and a half stone but then I was nine and a half stone of pure blubber. That was the start of things changing for me. I began to eat a bit more healthily, trying to cut out my favourites – chocolate, sweets, pizza and crisps. I sometimes used to like drinking cider. That went too. As a result, I began to win. But I still didn't have the focused mentality of an athlete. Nor did I want it. I was far too busy having a good time for the first time in my life. I felt free and I was thoroughly enjoying army life.

Finally, another pre-selection course came up towards the end of 1990. This time I really went for it. I could do all the skills and took my certificates along with me to prove it. I'd learned how to project my voice properly so I could bellow instructions with the best of them. I put everything I had into everything I was asked to do and they passed me: I was accepted onto the PTI training course. I was on the way to achieving my dream at last. It was the end of HGV driving at Marchwood and the start of a whole new career in the Army.

# 6. IN TRAINING

In April 1990, I moved to the Duchess of Kent Barracks at Aldershot. It was to be my home for the following nine months as I completed the PTI training course. There were about thirty of us whose target it was to be promoted to Lance Corporal and to become full-time Physical Training Instructors.

Training took place at the Army School of Physical Training, the home of the PT Corps. The course was relentless. For the first of three sections, we had to become coaches, umpires or referees in loads of sports – rounders, netball, basketball, volleyball, badminton, tennis, judo – pretty much everything except rugby and boxing, and, although I hated it, I had to do the swimming because they kept drumming into me that I had to have my Bronze medallion to be a PTI.

The only way to get it was to learn to swim properly, however much the water scared me. I swam and swam, trying to get better. But it involved more than just swimming. We had to complete various exercises, one of which involved making a float out of our lightweights. I remember being in the deep end, fully dressed, and I could feel myself being pulled under by the weight of my clothes. Somehow I had to get my lightweights off, tie a knot in the ends of the legs and then throw them inside out so that they would fill with air and act as a V-shaped float, while all the time treading water. I was beginning to panic as I felt myself going under yet again. Gasping for breath, I threw the lightweights on to the side, grabbed the edge of the pool, and hauled myself out.

'Get back in that pool.' The instructor's order reverberated around the walls.

I hesitated, trying to get my breath.

'Get back in that pool.' He was really yelling now. There was no mistaking the fact that if I didn't, I was going to be in big trouble. I tossed the lightweights back in and I hurled myself back in after them. This time I knew I was going to drown for sure. So, I managed to swim to the side with my lightweights and pull myself out of the pool. That was it. The instructor charged round and chucked my lightweights back in and ordered me back into the pool. This time I didn't even try the task again; I just rescued my lightweights and got out the other side. He gave me a big rollicking. I answered back that I wasn't prepared to die for him, only for my country. He didn't seem to care whether I drowned or not. Eventually he accepted that nothing would get me to do that particular task but he made up for it by making all of us swim backwards and forwards across the pool until I was exhausted. Despite my efforts, I never really got over my fear of water and dislike of swimming, but I persevered, learning to dive for bricks at the bottom of the pool, life-saving and improving my strokes, until I finally got my medallion.

Most of our time was spent in the training school's big old-fashioned gym, complete with ropes, wall-bars, leather-covered vaulting horses and boxes, and with photos of notable PTIs ranked on the wall. The PT Corps was a men's corps with the Corps badge of crossed swords with a crown on top of a black and red patch, and navy beret. As far as they were concerned, they were the best. They didn't want women in the Corps and that was why I was still a Women's Royal Army Corps PTI. Things were set to change a couple of years later.

The first phase of training went into great depth and was hard but I loved every single part of it. Having got through it, we moved on to the second part – drills and command tasks. It was then that I ran up against a problem. For reasons I never was able to fathom, the commanding officer, Captain Durban, seemed to take against me. All it did was make me stronger. Whether it was my personality (then quite 'bubbly' because I loved being on the course), or something to do with my being on the athletics team, we just didn't connect. I have no idea why. What I do know is that a lot of the students didn't get on with her. We felt that since she wasn't a PTI herself, she shouldn't have been in a position to be criticising what we did.

I was initially made aware of her feelings about me when we all had to report to either her or the warrant officer to see how we were getting on. The first time we were called in, she told five of us to buck up our ideas. I was shocked. Perhaps I'd done something wrong on the drill? After that I made sure I didn't put a foot wrong. Later during the course, we had to report again. This time I was one of three who got a warning. None of us could believe it. I had been in the WRAC for a while now and had been referred over from another unit, unlike those who had come straight from Civvy Street. My experience in the Army should have stood me in good stead. All the other trainees agreed that I was completing all the sections as well as, and definitely as good as, them. What was I doing wrong?

Eventually we reached the end of the second section. We had to go upstairs into the offices in the barracks, where we would be told whether we'd passed or failed. As I walked behind the others down a long corridor past the offices, it felt like a long walk to the scaffold. I was certain that the three of us who were listed would get something extra to do. I was called into one of the side offices. I stood to attention in front of the warrant officer sitting behind a desk, which was empty except for the papers she obviously needed at that moment. The captain sat in a chair to my left, looking grimly down at her knees.

'Do you know why you've been called in, Private Holmes?' asked the warrant officer.

'Yes, Ma'am.' Because I was last in line, I thought I must be the first to be told.

'Private Holmes. I regret to tell you that you have failed your course.'

What? I couldn't believe I'd heard right. I stood there with my mouth open, unable to speak. With one short sentence, my dream was shattered.

'Private Holmes. Do you understand what we're saying?'

Something inside me snapped. The most intense rage flooded through me. They couldn't do this. 'How can you possibly fail me?' I couldn't stop myself. 'This is my dream. It's all I've ever wanted.'

By this time I was shouting – not something a private was ever allowed to do to a senior officer. I turned to the commanding officer, screaming at her, 'You've had something against me all this time. Why?'

So far she had said nothing, letting the warrant officer break the news. Then she looked up and spoke for the first time. 'But you can still do your army athletics.'

That was it. I went absolutely crazy. 'Athletics. I don't want to do the bloody athletics. I want to be a PTI. If I can't complete the course, I'd rather leave the Army.'

That made her sit up. She knew that if I left rather than meekly going back to being an HGV driver doing a bit of athletics on the side, there would be an investigation. But I didn't want to be an HGV driver for the rest of my life. I had deliberately used being a driver as a route to becoming a PTI. Being one was all that mattered to me. However, the Army would not be keen on losing a good athlete and would want to know why.

'You don't want to leave the Army. Think about it. Think about it,' they both advised.

'Think about it. I don't need to think about it. You've ruined everything.' Without even waiting to be dismissed, I turned on my heel and walked out, slamming the door behind me. I was aware that I was in breach of all the rules that dictated how to behave in front of an officer, but I was beyond caring. Without waiting to explain to the other trainees, who had heard every word of what had gone on, I went straight downstairs to the personnel office and demanded my P45. I was so devastated to have had my childhood dream shattered by someone who didn't know me, and who hadn't even tried to get to know me, that I felt my behaviour was completely justified.

The person I spoke to refused to give it to me before they'd found out what was happening. They were as shocked as I was. I was the only person to have failed the first part of the course. I was absolutely distraught. As far as I was concerned, the career I had longed for was over.

The next day was the start of a break that divided the second and third parts of the course. I went home to stay with Mick and my brothers in Hildenborough. Whenever I went home on leave I always tried to go round to see Mum, despite disliking her new husband. Sometimes Kevin and Stuart would be staying there and, of course, I always wanted to see them too. One time I had noticed that

Mum was putting on weight, and I asked Stuart if she was pregnant. I wasn't at all pleased when he told me she was. It was hard hearing that from my little brother. But once again, I suppose I had made it difficult for her to tell me herself. She must have known there was no way I was going to be pleased for her. But despite all of our ups and downs, I didn't want to lose touch with her. After all, she was still my mum, however much I'd been hurt by everything that had happened. I still loved her deep down. I just found it difficult to accept the changes in her life because of the way it had affected the rest of us. The visits helped, however, and gradually I found I could turn to her for advice again. She was a huge support when she found out I'd been thrown off the course. She couldn't believe it and told me that we should find out what was going on. However, because everyone was on leave, we had to wait for a week or so.

What was I going to do with my life now? My world had caved in and it was hard to see how I was going to dig myself out. After a few days, I went to the job centre in Tonbridge. I knew I had to get a job of some sort to support myself. They sent me for an interview at a hotel in Tunbridge Wells with a private gym and a leisure complex. At the interview, I told them everything. I explained that although I'd failed the PTI selection course, I'd learned a lot and wanted to carry on working in sport. They offered me the job of managing the entire centre and said I could start in a week's time. I guess I was relieved to have found a way of earning a living but, despite the wonderful facilities on offer, something didn't feel right and it didn't compare to my army goals.

When I got home, there was a message to ring the training school in Aldershot. When I spoke to personnel, I was told I had to get back there at the end of the break. I didn't understand it. I thought my time in the Army was over. Now, I was totally confused.

By the time I arrived, the other girls had gone off to Wales for three weeks of adventure training, the third part of the course. I was told to see the Lieutenant Colonel, another officer at the training school. She asked me to explain what was going on. As I told her, I realised she didn't know that I'd been chucked off the course. She was quietly furious, said she thought I had the potential to make a good instructor, and wanted me to join the others at the adventure-training school. Still confused as to my position, and still fuming about the way I'd been treated, I walked into the dormitory in Llanrwst two days after the others. They were all pleased to see me but just as puzzled as to what was happening. No kind of explanation had filtered down through the ranks. The chief instructor of the adventure training school, Captain Watkins, took me on one side. I had established a bit of a reputation as an athlete and at the PT school so he'd heard I was good, but he had also heard about the drama going on back at Aldershot.

'Look, Private Holmes. I know what's going on,' he said. 'One of the warrant officers at the PT school has told me just to grade you on what you do here so that we can put a case forward for you. We'll grade you on your attitude, on how you apply yourself and on what you achieve. Then we'll either recommend you to be selected or we'll agree with what happened.' It seemed fair enough.

I slotted back in straight away, getting top grading in top rope (rock climbing) and abseiling (just like being in the commandoes), middle grading in canoeing (I never took risks because I was too scared of the water). As a result, the warrant officer wrote me a blinding report and I was formally admitted back on the course. I'll never know why it all happened. All I know is that the Lieutenant Colonel told me they'd sort out the problem and, not long afterwards, Captain Durban left the PT school. I certainly never had to have anything more to do with her or she with me.

On a more positive note, it was in Aldershot that I met Chalkie, a tall, stocky, mixed-race girl with a shaved head and a heart of gold. We met because she lived in Duchess of Kent Barracks, having been posted to 41 Squadron as a driver. She and I hit it off immediately and have remained good friends ever since. Together we got up to some mad escapades. Most of all I remember all the commotion she caused when she was out in her truck. Chalkie was guaranteed to have an accident wherever she was. Normally it didn't involve anyone else. How she passed her test I will never know.

The only long-lasting repercussion of my having failed the second part of the course was that I wasn't awarded my lance-corporal stripe along with everyone else. Although I had proved myself on the physical side of the course, I was still required to demonstrate that I was responsible enough to earn the rank. I was told that I would be constantly tested, but in fact one test was enough. I was asked to set up a display board for an officers' conference. The display was to demonstrate the proposed changes to the PE kit. I went to enormous trouble to make 3-D models of everything, folding bits of coloured card, then pinning them onto a board. I worked late into the nights, drawing on everything I'd learned in my school Design and Graphics classes. I was really pleased with the result and, as it turned out, so were the officers. The officer in charge called me in to say she'd had such good reports of my work that I was being made a lance corporal on the strength of it. She apologised for everything I had been through, but explained they had no choice but to go through the process. By then, I didn't care any more. I had got my qualification, the thing I wanted more than anything.

Mum, Gary and Penny (their baby daughter) came to my passing out day where we had to perform gymnastic and aerobic displays. I was uncomfortable seeing Mum and Gary together and was disappointed that the arrangements we'd talked about for them to bring Lisa hadn't come off. I'd been looking forward to seeing her. If she had come, perhaps she would have been able to help bridge the gap between us. But although I was unhappy about Gary being there, I was really glad Mum had made it. Afterwards all the new lance corporals had to wait to be told where they were going to be posted. I was very apprehensive, hoping I wouldn't be sent to Germany or Northern Ireland. It was with huge relief that I heard I was to be a PTI for York Garrison at Imphal Barracks in Yorkshire. I celebrated big time that evening. I had achieved my first dream. My life seemed to have turned a corner at last.

# 7. IN THE LINE OF DUTY

'It's that bloke Wesley Duncan on the telephone again,' yelled one of the girls who had rooms downstairs by the public phone.

'Tell him I'm training,' I shouted back. 'Tell him I'm busy. Tell him anything but get him to go away. Please.'

I had met Wes after the 1990 Inter Services Athletics meet when he had introduced himself as an athletics coach for Middlesex Ladies' Athletics Club. He had seen me almost lap the other runners to win the 800 metres and invited me down to London to visit the club. He wanted me to consider joining it. I wasn't interested in the slightest and refused the invitation point blank. The idea of becoming involved in civilian athletics didn't appeal to me at all. All that disciplined training at the expense of so much of the rest of my life? No thanks. But whatever I said or however often I refused to speak to him, nothing worked. He kept on bugging me as the months went by until eventually I was so fed up with it that I agreed to take his call.

'Kelly, I want you to come down to the club. You've got to give it a chance,' he begged.

'I'm not interested. Really.'

'You've got so much talent. You must start running again.' On and on he went.

I kept putting him off. 'Why me? I'm a blob. I'm not going to run.' I lost count of the number of times he called me.

When I was posted to York in 1991, Wes tracked me down and, after the 1991 inter-services meet, he began calling me again. An insurance salesman by day, Wes was a talent-spotter for Middlesex Ladies. He had been in the RAF so he regularly went to the inter-services meets to get together with his mates. He has since told me that he noticed me partly because I was the only black female soldier at those meets but, more importantly, because he saw I could run well without having to work too hard at it. Apparently, I was once so busy chatting with friends that the race had to be called up twice. I ended up putting on my spikes at the last minute, after I'd got to the track, delaying the start. Another time he saw me popping a sweet into my mouth just before I was due to race, while everyone else was earnestly warming up. I impressed him as an athlete. He wouldn't let me alone and kept on calling every few weeks. But, as hard as he buzzed around, I still swatted him away. I had just started my first PTI job and I was having far too good a time. It was living up to all my expectations.

Imphal Barracks is just on the outskirts of York, where, at the time, I felt as if I could have stayed forever. Whenever I had time off, I'd go with friends into town, wandering through the Shambles where the upper floors of the higgledy-piggledy houses projected out over its narrow flag-stoned streets, shopping or having tea at Betty's Tea Rooms or Taylors. Surrounded by very high walls, the barracks themselves were beautiful. The addition of modern low-rise blocks to accommodate 2 Signal Regiment didn't spoil the effect of the older, more traditional buildings. Going through the gate, the guard-room was on the left and the barracks, smart with pretty trees planted everywhere, were laid out in front. They were organised round the parade square, which was used for the most part as a car park, with the sergeants' mess, WRAC's accommodation, York Garrison and Military Transport on the right-hand side of it and the majority of 2 Signal Regiment's offices and accommodation on the left.

At twenty years old, I didn't know what to expect from my first post. The face of the Army was changing in the early 1990s. The WRAC was being gradually disbanded and amalgamated into the British Army. Up until then the WRAC had operated as an entirely separate entity with its own officers and trades. All of us were going to be gradually deployed within different units of the Army. The first change that affected us at York was that women were admitted to the Signal Corps. It seemed very strange seeing them in the barracks wearing blue berets when we were used to female military being dressed in green. That wasn't the only difference. They were deployed to their own unit within the Signallers and didn't mix professionally with York Garrison, although we all shared the same accommodation. Needless to say, the guys in the Signals didn't have a clue how to deal with the fact they had women in their regiment. As a result, the women would find themselves in a PT class of men, being asked to do the same exercises without any allowances being made for their physical differences. It was way too tough for them. I was asked to help because I knew how to approach and apply PT training to women.

In fact, what I found was a gym that seemed to be pretty much taken over by 2 Signal Regiment. As far as I could see, the women of York Garrison didn't have nearly enough opportunities to use it. I talked to them, asking them what they wanted out of their physical training sessions. Once they had told me they wanted to do more sports and to do them in a more organised way, I was a woman on a mission. I began by organising all sorts of tournaments between the units – hockey, netball, volleyball and rounders – before we branched out and started challenging civilian clubs in the town. This was great fun for us because through the year I could take the girls out to civilian matches and we could host a return match at the barracks.

At one of the matches I held at the barracks at the beginning of 1993, I met a civvy girl called Emma who was playing for the police. At the end of one match she pointed out to me that I had made everyone, including the civvies, carry the hockey goals up the long fields at the back of the barracks and all the way back to the gym. All the civvies were knackered. Without thinking I'd just ordered them along the same as the soldiers! After that Emma and I got to know each other and went on to become great friends. Because Emma's diabetic, she's not allowed to be a full-time member of the police so has the role of a 'special'. I only have a very few close friends because I tend to be wary of people in general, but Emma became one of them. These are people I would trust with my life.

PT is compulsory for everyone in the Army. Naturally, different instructors have different approaches. Mine was always based on learning the capabilities of the people I trained and trying to improve them. I never thought I should just give a class something to do for the sake of it, or as some sort of punishment. Neither did I ever assume that everyone would be at the same standard of fitness and be able to achieve the same tasks. I planned every session I took so that it had a specific purpose. I set up indoor assault courses and made them into circuit training lessons for variety. None of the women was going to get an easy ride with me but I did try to make the sessions as much fun as possible so they wouldn't realise how hard they were working. I spent ages on the planning and organisation because I wanted everyone to leave longing to come back for more. PT might be compulsory but it wasn't hard to get signed off if you tried. However, I found my classes were always full. That meant a lot to me. Gradually, I started bringing the Signals ladies into our sessions until I was coaching them as well for all the sports where we had tournaments. Luckily they were all allowed to join the same teams for competitions so that made it a lot easier for everyone.

Meanwhile, I also started fitness sessions for the half a dozen or so civilian women who worked in the barracks, among them secretaries, some of the medical staff and wives of the officers. They were mostly middle-aged women who didn't do much to keep fit. Once I started classes for them, they were keen on trying assault courses. To begin with most of them couldn't hold their own body weight, jump over or crawl under things and climb ropes, but they kept on practising in the gym. It gave me huge pleasure seeing these women complete a circuit when two months earlier they wouldn't have got half way round. It was great to see them glowing with achievement.

I organised competitions for them. I did all sorts of activities with them, mainly at lunchtimes, like circuits and weights or badminton, and organised coastal walks to take their mind off the physical exertion. These women were so enthusiastic, applying themselves until they were ready to enter a civilian assault course tournament. I don't remember where they were finally placed, but the important thing was that they really enjoyed it. That's what I loved about my time at York – helping people to achieve things that they didn't dream they were capable of and seeing the pleasure that they derived from doing it. I didn't care what time my day began or ended.

Because of the difficulties I had had in PT school, I was called before Captain Tanya Collier Jackson, who was the WRAC Commanding Officer working for the Garrison. Tall, with blonde hair, she was also sports mad, joining nearly all the teams I organised and also running in the cross-country team. Normally I would have expected to be given a report after my first year, but she felt, after everything that had happened, that I deserved to have one after the first six months. This time she gave me an A1 (excellent, ready for promotion now). Getting that report was fantastic for me. It vindicated everything, proving to me that I could be as good at my job as I had always believed. Now I knew that she believed I was good too. That was a great feeling. I'd got there. I could do this. I was beginning to feel more settled than I had ever felt before, and I knew I could carry on successfully in this role for years. However, my feelings of elation were shortly to be punctured by a three-day expedition into wilds of Cumbria.

There have been three times in my life when I have genuinely believed I was going to die. This was one of them. There I was lying in a green army tent for two, with rain leaking in through the sodden canvas and a wild wind whipping round me, ripping the tent pegs into the air. The temperature had dropped to –5°C. I lay there shivering next to the other NCO sharing the tent, listening to her sob. We were wearing all the clothes we had brought with us, layering them on as we'd been instructed, but they were all soaking wet, as were our sleeping bags. I have never been so cold in my life. We lay awake all night, shivering, talking and crying, encouraging each other to hang on. I was sure that if we went to sleep we'd die. Every so often one of us would have to get up and venture outside into the howling storm to anchor down the tent pegs that were flying everywhere. We knew that the other four expedition tents were somewhere close by, but we couldn't see them in the pitch black or communicate with the others because they were all having the same problems and, anyway, it was impossible to make ourselves heard over the sound of the storm. In and out of the pouring rain. In and out. Every time we lay down again, we felt as if we were going to be lifted up and swept away. The night seemed to go on forever.

When we had started out that morning, the weather hadn't been so bad, although we knew how unpredictable mountain weather could be. There were ten of us in the party: we were all PTIs, Jackie Gilchrist was there as part of a B2 advanced instructor's course, and there was an expedition leader. We had been given the map co-ordinates, and the objective was to find our way to a specific location in the mountains, camp for one night and then return to Ripon Barracks. We'd orienteered our way up and up through the rugged mountainside, making our way towards Lake Tarne. The wind began to get up, whistling across the unprotected landscape. When it whirled Jackie's map away into the distance, that was the last straw.

'That's it. I've had enough of this. I'm not going any further,' she shouted in her broad Scottish accent, having a complete sense-of-humour failure, and sat down angrily on her rucksack.

'Come on, Jackie. We've walked this far, we might as well try to finish the damn expedition.' I tried to persuade her. But she wouldn't budge.

'Let's go. I want to get the tents up before the storm breaks.' The instructor was keen to get on while we could.

Peer pressure got the better of Jackie in the end and she grudgingly agreed to press on with us. All of us desperately wanted to turn back but the instructor would have none of it. As we approached the summit, the weather began to close in. We hadn't yet made it to the spot where we planned to make camp when the heavens opened. Within minutes, everything we were carrying was soaked. As darkness fell, we struggled to put up the tents, battling against the driving rain. The temperature dropped below freezing. We were in the bleakest of landscapes, with nothing we could use for protection. Because it got dark so early we had to get into our tents at about 4 p.m. and stay there, nibbling our remaining dry rations, until 6 a.m. the next morning, when light began to leak through the clouds and we could get off the mountain.

By then we were exhausted, freezing, and wrinkled as if we'd been soaking in a bath all night. In a way, I suppose we had. All the girls emerged from their tents in a terribly emotional state. None of us could quite believe the ordeal was over or that we had survived it. Still shivering with cold, we had to pack everything up and make a move down the mountainside. Even then we had one more exercise to complete. Someone had to be taken down on a stretcher. I was in the worst state of all of us, unable even to feel my feet, so I was the one who was chosen. I was so relieved because they had to wrap me up in foil blankets so, although I wasn't moving, my circulation did begin to get going again and I began to warm up. Even our instructor was shaken by the experience, admitting that it was the worst he'd ever been through. It was absolutely terrifying. Never have I been so glad to get to the end of an exercise. The sight of our truck waiting to be driven back to base was one of the most wonderful things I have ever seen. It was only then that I knew for certain that our ordeal was over and that we were going to survive.

The Army demanded a lot of me but I still managed to find time for a few activities of my own. I had always been interested in martial arts ever since I was a kid. Once I started running as a junior athlete, my coach Dave had advised me not to continue with them in case I injured myself. But now, as I had decided my championship running days were over, I was free to have another go. I had done some judo while I was on my PTI course, getting my yellow, orange and green belts, but once I was in York, I got into it in a big way. One of the reasons I enjoyed it so much was because it was quite different from everything else I did in the Army. It combines skill, strength and self-defence and gets rid of aggression in a controlled manner. Two of the Signals girls and I went to sessions with some of the guys. They took place in one of the Signal Regiment's blocks opposite the guys' accommodation block. There was a small room where the dojo mats were laid out, then, off with the shoes and on with the gi (the judo suit), we stepped onto the mat, bowed and got on with practising our throws and holds.

After a few months we reached a high enough standard to enter a civilian competition, but I had a problem. Competitive judo is organised by weight categories and I was 59kg, just 2kg over the lighter weight category limit of 57kg. I knew that if I didn't get down to it I would have to go into the heavier class with a weight limit of 63kg. That would mean I'd be facing big bruisers who would slaughter me. I had to stay in the lower category if I was going to survive. So on the day of the competition itself, I went running wearing black bin bags under my kit so that I sweated like mad. Then I'd weigh myself; run again; then weigh myself, until I was safely below the weight break. Desperate times need desperate measures, and it did work! Often competitors in a weight category sport do this but I don't recommend it as a safe training method.

All I remember about the competition itself is that I was slammed to the mat in the second round but managed to get up to fight again. Then suddenly I was thrown for what seemed like miles before being pinned to the mat by my opponent. And that was it. Ippon! (Ten points). It wasn't the end of my interest in judo though. I went on to get my blue belt, competing in army and civilian competitions, and eventually winning the Army Judo Championship.

One sport I hadn't tried before was skiing, but I was always up for anything. We were sent on an expedition to Aviemore in Scotland, driving our trucks up there in convoy. My close friends on the trip were Stu, a tall guy who worked as an Akai (assistant PTI) in the gym with me, and Bev (Stu's fiancée), who was in admin. She looked a bit like a ginger-headed Bette Midler and was so funny. None of us had skied before so we knew it would be a scream. It hadn't snowed very much so there was only one piste that was any good and it was always unbelievably crowded. After one of our lessons, we decided to give it a go on our own. We managed to get down to the bottom, mostly on our arses, crying with laughter all the way as we slid over all the icy bits and slowed down where the grass was showing through.

Bev and I decided to have another go, so we climbed aboard the chair-lift. Both of us were dreading having to get off at the top, not to mention the fact that we knew we might break every bone in our bodies on the run down. We both got off, with me moving cagily over to one side, hands on the ground, bum in the air, not daring to stand up, while Bev struggled to get her skis pointing anywhere but downhill. She failed. Suddenly, I heard a yell and looked up to see her flying off down the slope, unable to stop, screaming 'Heeeeeeeelp' as she bounced over the bumps, her hair streaming out behind her. Somehow she managed to stay on her feet as she weaved in and out of the other skiers, knocking people over, crashing through the lines of beginners side-stepping up the slope. 'Watch out. Beep, beep.' Eventually she fell in a heap at the bottom where I found her when I finally managed to get down there myself. We were laughing so much, tears rolling down our cheeks, that we could barely stop when a furious instructor left his group and came over to us. 'You may think you're so good,' he began, 'but there are beginners on this slope. You should respect them and watch where you're going.' What? Neither of us could believe our ears. He thought she was an arrogant professional when in fact she couldn't ski to save her life. It still makes me laugh when I think about it to this day.

I was loving almost everything about my life as a PTI and had completely forgotten about Wes Duncan when I received a letter in the post. It was from him, telling me once more how much I impressed him as an athlete and inviting me to join Middlesex

Ladies again, even though I lived in York. Finally I gave in. By then I'd become a good athlete for the Army, so thought I'd give it a go.

That September, I found myself in Harrow, on the outskirts of London, on a mild sunny day running in a five-kilometre cross-country race wearing the green and white vest of Middlesex Ladies (even though I wasn't a member). The course was hilly and demanding. I hadn't run in a cross-country for years and was very rusty. What on earth was I doing? I didn't even like running cross-country. But Wes was very persuasive.

His wife Anne had picked me up at Wembley Park Station and drove me to their house in Alperton. Wes is a Trinidadian, small and fit-looking, then with his hair shaved on the sides of his head and longer on top. Anne was in her forties too, white, half-Czech, and wore glasses. She was very friendly, always smiling, and whenever I see her now and we talk of my achievements her eyes always well up with tears. We immediately hit it off, getting to know each other as we drove to the race. Wes has always said that ours was a 'meeting of minds'. Certainly we've never looked back. The race went well that day. I was the first Middlesex AC lady home, finishing seventh. Wes was delighted.

Later on, he came to see me run in the Inter-Services Cross-Country Championships at RAF Brize Norton. This time the weather was not so runner-friendly, making it much more the race I loved to hate. I started well, up front with the leading runners, most of them well seasoned in cross-country. It was all going well until we ran into some woods where I hit a muddy patch. Wes was yelling encouragement, 'Come on, Kel.' He had such a loud voice I could always tell where he was.

I slowed down and bawled back at him, 'I can't do it. I don't like this.'

'Come on, Kel. Of course you can. Keep going,' he shouted.

I had no choice. I could either let us both down or I could run on. So, gritting my teeth, I picked up the pace again and somehow finished in the first ten.

We got to know each other better that winter and talked a lot about what we could do about my running. Although my heart really wasn't in it, Wes was right in thinking that for a professional athlete, competing on the civilian circuit is crucial. The standard of racing is inevitably lower in the Army because it's impossible for soldiers to devote themselves 100 per cent to any kind of sports training. The Army comes first. The result is that you don't learn as much because there are not the same opportunities or as many events as those that are offered by the different levels of competition in Civvy Street. The competition inevitably isn't as sharp in the Army, whereas the County Championships, Area Championships and UK/Amateur Athletics Association (AAA)'s Championships take the sport to a completely different level. Wes believed I had the potential to be very successful and he wasn't going to let go.

The episode that made up his mind as to my potential happened on one of the shortest, most miserable days of the year. He had pestered me to come down to race in a cross-country event in Bournemouth – hundreds and hundreds of miles from York. The weather was awful. I borrowed a friend's car and drove south through thick fog, arriving just in time to compete for the club. Wes has always said that the fact I came down in such conditions, especially for a race I didn't particularly want to run, showed him that I had the sort of grit and determination to make a professional athlete. He was so persuasive that I agreed to start training with him, but there was one thing I made clear right from the start. 'The only way you can get me back running is if I only race in the 800 metres. I am never doing 1500. No way.' My reckoning was that the 800 was shorter (two laps as opposed to three and three-quarters) and therefore easier. Little did I know that it's a lot faster and very tough on the civilian circuit.

After that, with my go-ahead, he began to work on my commanding officers, explaining what he saw in me, trying to convince them that they had someone special and to persuade them to release me into running with a civilian club. His belief in me was so strong.

Meanwhile I continued to take my work very seriously, letting it occupy most of my time in York. I didn't have much time to go out. On Saturday nights a big group of us would sometimes go off to clubs to dance and have a good time, but I stayed away from the pub scene. The ways I enjoyed myself tended to be more sedate, maybe shopping or having a meal out. In my block I made friends with a few girls including Lyn and Sue. Loud and from the West Country, Lyn was a great all-rounder but was an especially good hockey player, while Sue, a Welsh girl, was also sports mad and came down to London several times to cheer me on when I'd got back into running. We often preferred to do our own thing in the evenings and would retreat to my room where we'd watch videos, or I would write to Kerrie or plan the next day's classes.

Having said all that, my abiding memory is of my twenty-second birthday when I went out with loads of the guys and girls to celebrate. We started quite early at a pub near the barracks, playing pool and drinking. I had a couple of bottles of Diamond White cider so my head was already spinning when I had a third. At the next pub, I downed one more and was given a 'Blastaway' (a lethal cocktail of Diamond White, Castaway, orange juice and wine). The next thing I knew I was lying, completely wasted, on the floor of the Ladies. Thinking I'd gone home, all my friends had left except for one guy who worked in the gym. By now, we were the last people in the place. I felt completely weird, detached from everything going on around me. It was like being in a dream. All I remember is two bouncers carrying me out and putting me into an ambulance. I can only dimly remember what went on at the hospital, but when we arrived back at the barracks I was in a right state. I walked through the guardroom to the back where I lay on a concrete slab in the cell. No one is allowed to be drunk and disorderly on entering the barracks but those on guard duty couldn't believe that this was the fit PTI they knew who didn't drink. They thought it was hilarious. Eventually I somehow staggered back to my room. I lay there unable to move as it spun dizzyingly round me. I had a meeting scheduled with my commanding officer that morning, but, when I woke, I couldn't make myself get up. By my bed was a note from the General Hospital, so I knew I hadn't imagined it. It said: Drunk. Smells of alcohol. Eyes open to speech only. I ended up staying in bed the whole day.

Needless to say, by the following day, the entire garrison had heard about what had happened. Everybody was taking the mick, knowing that I never really went out and certainly didn't drink much. Whenever I walked past anyone, they'd shout, 'Heyyy, Kelly.' I was the talk of the whole unit. My God, the shame. My commanding officer was away on leave that day, but when she eventually came back, she was quite cool about the whole episode. I was dreading what she would say but she obviously felt I'd suffered enough and let me off with a warning. After that, drinking became an even rarer occurrence for me.

That summer I was in the barracks watching the Barcelona Olympics on TV and day-dreaming. I was keenly following the athletics as always when I realised that I recognised one of the long-distance runners. Lisa York, one of the British athletes racing in the 3000 metres, had been a junior competing at the same race meets as me. I had certainly beaten her several times over shorter distances. I was watching her, riveted, to see how she got on, when it dawned on me. If she could make it to the Olympics, then maybe I could too. Why not? The dream that I'd had as a junior athlete started to take shape again. I couldn't shake it out of my head. I decided to take Wes and my training more seriously.

I had been going down from York on a regular basis to see Wes at weekends. We did a lot of weight training together and speed work on the track. Training became a lot more specific. He introduced me to plyometrics that are great for developing explosive power. I was already very strong but he wanted me to become more like a runner again and work on the areas needed specifically for that.

Wes would set me a training plan for the following week. Then I would write to him letting him know my times and how I was getting on. The trouble was that, every time I got back to York and had to train on my own, I often couldn't be bothered. The only way for me to get the training done was to combine it with some of my lessons. So, if I had a run scheduled, I'd run with the guys at lunchtime, or, if I had to do a circuit, I'd do it with my class. It was much more fun that way and kept me motivated even if it meant I didn't always achieve the exact times or speeds that Wes had set.

Throughout 1992, I competed for Middlesex Ladies in nearly every athletics meeting, with Wes briefing me about the runners before each one, advising me who to watch out for and why. I won the Southern Championships, and the Inter-Services Championships over 400 metres and 800 metres. That was a significant moment in my career. Suddenly I was beginning to make my mark on the athletics circuit. But Wes and I had something far bigger in mind. This was only the first step on the ladder. Our sights were set on 1993 and the World Championships in Stuttgart. Now I had a new goal in view, although it still took second place to my army career.

I went down to race for Middlesex Ladies on the August Bank Holiday that year. I stayed over with Wes and Anne and on the Monday, Wes took me to the Notting Hill Carnival. We parked at Wormwood Scrubs and walked down Ladbroke Grove until we reached the bridge by the tube station. By the time we got there, the party was in full swing. The sun was beating down and we were surrounded by riotous colours and costumes as the floats and dancers made their way through the streets. The insistent rhythms of the music, the strains of Calypso, the steel bands, the cries of the dancers and shouts from the crowds, the smell of street food wafting around us – it was amazing. I tried a Jamaican pattie while Wes stuck to Trinidadian specialities and tucked into a roti. Most of the time, my eyes were popping out of my head and I held on tightly to Wes's hand so we didn't get separated in the crush.

Being at the Carnival was one of the weirdest experiences I've had. Suddenly, there I was hand-in-hand with a black guy surrounded by people from the Caribbean, Africa and elsewhere. It was a complete culture shock. I knew I looked like one of them yet, inside, I felt white. That's how I had been brought up. I wasn't uncomfortable exactly, but I had never been in that sort of environment and I didn't know how to react to it. As we got nearer the sound systems, the beat just took over and I found myself moving to the music without thinking. We stayed there all afternoon until I finally dragged myself away in the early evening in time to catch the train back to barracks, back to the real world again.

As the year came to an end, I was due for my next posting. I was unaware that Wes had been trying his damnedest to influence things by talking to my superiors in the hope of persuading them to send me on a posting further south. However, before I left to go anywhere, I had to be given another report. This time, I was awarded an O1, the highest grade of achievement, and promoted to Corporal. My new posting was to the Army School of Education at Beaconsfield, just west of London and conveniently close to my athletics club and my coach. Had Wes's calls had any effect? We'll never know but I like to think so.

The Army School of Education was a potential officers' unit that was largely attended by university graduates (mostly male) who wanted to become officers without having to make their way through the ranks. There were also a lot of overseas students wanting to join the British Army, as well as soldiers who were to be deployed to different parts of the world and needed to learn a new language. As it was a training unit, it would be a different challenge for me after York, but it was one I was confident that I was more than capable of meeting.

# 8. WHO'S BOSS?

A group of guys – potential officers who were straight out of university – came into the Beaconsfield gym, chatting, chatting, chatting. I told them to be quiet. But some of them carried on chattering, refusing to take much notice of me. I might only be small but that didn't mean I was going to be a pushover. Somehow, I knew I had to impress them and let them know who was the boss. Now that the WRAC was being disbanded, I had decided to dress more like the PT Corps, wearing my lightweights and a PT Corps vest, white with red piping, with the crossed swords but no crown. I made sure everything was really spick and span, with sharp creases in the right places, so that I stood there, looking ready for business. I roared at them (from my stomach not my throat, as I'd been taught) and, finally, I got their attention.

'Right. We're going on a three-mile run, out of the camp, past the assault courses, through the forest and round the Bowl.' The Bowl was like a vast crater surrounded by hills that made a demanding cross-country course not far from the barracks.

No reaction. I could tell that these guys of six feet and over were looking at all five feet three of me and wondering how the hell I was going to be able to instruct them in anything. But that didn't worry me.

'We're going to do this now. Anyone who gets back after me will come into PT at 5.30 a.m. for the next two weeks.'

I could see them all looking at me then exchanging confident glances that said, Ha! That'll be easy.

At this stage they were totally unaware that I was a runner because at this stage, I hadn't had any major successes that had been in the public eye, only in the Army, so I was thinking, This is great! I am really going to show them up here!

I let them all go off, and then shut the gate behind the last one, before starting to run after them. Most of them made the fatal mistake of charging ahead, thinking they'd easily beat me. As none of them knew I was a runner I had a strong psychological advantage. Many of them weren't nearly fit enough to keep up the pace they'd kicked off at. One by one, they were burning out and slowing down. I started catching them, overtaking a few. We reached the Bowl, running up and down the surrounding hills. By this time, most of them were flagging and I picked them off, one after another, until there were only a few left in the distance. I could see them ahead and pushed myself on, all the time repeating to myself, 'Come on. Come on. You've got to get them.' So I ran and ran, catching almost everyone. Then we were back in the forest, nearly back at the assault course, and by now there were only about three guys left ahead of me. At last I was at the gate with only the path back to the gymnasium to go, and one runner in front of me. I pushed myself as hard as I could and just got to the steps before him.

Over the next fifteen minutes, the rest of them staggered in, puffing like mad, looking absolutely dead and thoroughly fed up at the thought of having such an early start the next day.

'Squad. Stand in line.' I ordered.

They stood to attention and this time they didn't say a word.

'Right. Tomorrow, everyone is to be here at 5.30 a.m. And at the same time every morning for the next two weeks. No questions. Dismissed.'

From that day on, I had established myself. I got a lot of respect from everyone who came to PT, simply because that group told the one after them not to mess with me and then the word went round.

It wasn't long afterwards that I was taking the same group for rope climbing. By this time they were listening to my instructions and doing everything I asked of them.

'Line up at the rope.'

They lined up in groups of three or four behind the six ropes.

'Up the rope.'

Some did manage it, using their feet and clumsily hauling themselves up, but others could not manage it at all.

'Look. This is how I want you to do it.'

I stood there with the rope in front of me. Then I went up it using only my arms, hands into the chest, one on top of the other (just as I had been taught in training), keeping my legs together and absolutely straight, not using them at all. Just arms to the top and arms all the way down. The men's jaws dropped. I was strong and one of my strengths has always been being able to support my own bodyweight. I suppose I was showing off a bit, just to prove that I had a right to be in charge of them and that I was a PTI people could look up to.

I had quickly learned never to ask the men to try to do anything I couldn't. Rather than leave them to struggle, my role was to show how to do everything first. I always thought as a PTI you should explain, demonstrate then put into practice, leading by example. I loved demonstrating the assault course, whether it was getting over a six-foot wall on your own, or showing where to put your feet on a rope bridge so as not to fall off. Similarly, when it came to command tasks, I made sure that I gave clear instructions so that when I gave the men a scenario I was sure I could show them the way. I might tell them that they were lost in a rainforest and had a fast flowing stream to cross with only a few rocks to assist them. Equipped with a few planks of wood, a rope and a knife, they had to transport 'ammunition' or an 'injured' soldier from one bank to another.

At the beginning of 1993, when I had arrived at Beaconsfield, I found that the permanent staff were pretty relaxed about taking PT. When I started taking the classes for them, hardly anyone turned up. As far as I could see, nearly everyone was 'on remedial', which meant they had been signed off from PT by the medical centre. As soon as I realised, my immediate reaction was, 'Right. I'm going to change this.' I went straight to the medical centre to get a list of everyone on remedial and the reasons why. My argument was that even if one part of the body was injured, there was no reason why the rest of it couldn't be exercised in some way. I discovered that at least half of them weren't so badly injured that they couldn't go into the swimming pool, so I gave them an ultimatum: either come to the gym for weight training or we'll go on a bus to the High Wycombe pool at 5.30 a.m. So that's what we did. A lot of them chose swimming and I went with them. Luckily I didn't have to swim because I had to act as a life-saver as well as the instructor. Their life was in my hands in that pool. If only they'd known my record with water! I didn't care about having such an early start to my day. It was my job to give them training of some sort. If that was the only way to do it – fine. I loved it. At the same time, the numbers in the PT sessions increased. They were held within working hours, on either side of lunch, mid-morning or afternoon, or after work. Another of my strengths was getting them to enjoy the session. I knew if I could get them to do that, then it became more of a social event that they would look forward to instead of a chore that they were forced to attend.

Jackie Longhorn was Staff Sergeant in charge of the gym. She was tall and energetic and wanted to be a 'sneaky beaky' like her husband, doing undercover intelligence work. Although we weren't in the gym for long together, we got on well. Then, when she left, they put me in charge of the gym and gave me a sergeant's pay, as they couldn't find a direct replacement for her. Giving me a whole unit to look after showed me that the commanding officers recognised I was capable of doing the job on my own and looking after an entire unit. That lasted for at least six months and I was very happy with the arrangement. Then, before my next posting, a guy from the PT Corps took over.

After-hours activities were something else I loved. We had a Gurkha regiment at Beaconsfield who were excellent at volleyball, so we were able to have some great games. I set up volleyball training so we could have tournaments against them and then against civilian teams. I'd spend ages designing really flash notice boards detailing the league tables in all the various sports. The circuit training classes were the other things that were hugely popular. I had full classes in the early mornings, at lunchtimes, afternoons and evenings when I devised a programme that I called Body Blast – a mixture of aerobics, step-aerobics, circuit training and weights. Once it was all set up, the class would start with a warm-up then split into groups and move round the various stations on the blow of my whistle. They would work really hard and I'd join in with them a lot of the time. That's how I got so strong. Everyone seemed to love the sessions. They were always packed and, at the end of the year, I got my second O1 for my work there.

Jason Dulforce was an athlete I'd met on an endurance 'get together' training weekend near Manchester. We had escaped to go to buy some chips when we couldn't wait for dinner. He is a lovely guy, very polite and very handsome, with long eyelashes and long finger nails that I envied. He is also mixed race, having grown up with his black mum and white father in London. He once came with me to an army wedding where lots of people asked questions about our relationship. We just laughed and refused to answer directly, enjoying keeping the others guessing. He started visiting me more in Beaconsfield where I took him to the Naafi. The guys just stared at him. They were used to me keeping my personal life to myself and it was the first time I had brought anyone into the camp. Normally, I used to just go into town with the girls I'd got close to.

I remember sitting there with him when one of the permanent staff came up to us to say hi and to ask if he was my brother because he thought we looked so alike. I burst out laughing. Just because we were both mixed race didn't mean we were related. For days afterwards, the relationship between Jason and me was a constant source of speculation. Were we just good friends? Were we having an affair? Who was he? It was at that point in my life that I vowed that I would never talk about my private life to anyone and that is how it has been ever since. I realised that people assume what they want without bothering to find out whether or not it's anything close to the truth. I am friends with those people whom I trust completely. I have relationships with people I like, people I get to know and maybe fall in love with. But as far as I'm concerned, it's nobody's business but that person's and mine.

I've only ever been really drunk three times in my life. Well, everybody has been once or twice haven't they? The second time was at Beaconsfield when, yet again, I went out with friends to celebrate my twenty-fourth birthday. The town itself is really quaint with several good pubs that were popular with people from the barracks. This time, I distinguished myself by having too much cider and going to sleep at the table not long after we had got there. I was heaved out into the street where everyone was trying to get me back to the barracks. At that moment, the gutter seemed a more attractive place to be and I collapsed in a heap in the road. The next thing I knew I was in a police car with two friends making my excuses. 'She's an athlete. Honestly. She doesn't drink. She's an athlete. It's her birthday.' They drove us back to barracks with me on the point of vomiting in the back seat, and with my friends panicking that I would.

The next day I was summoned to see the commanding officer. As I walked through the admin office, everybody went quiet. Nobody would look at me or acknowledge me. I was told to wait. By this time I knew I was going to be in big trouble. This CO always did everything by the book and I could tell by how serious everyone was that they knew something terrible was about to happen to me. He called me in and I stood to attention, expecting the worst. And I got it. He looked up from the papers on his desk and glared at me.

'Right, Corporal Holmes. We have a complaint from the Beaconsfield Constabulary that, last night, you were sick inside a police vehicle.'

Had I been? I didn't think so. My memories of the whole evening were vague to say the least. Perhaps I had been sick. I couldn't remember.

He went on. 'They have sent us a bill for nearly £250 for cleaning the vehicle.'

I couldn't believe it. Had I really been *that* sick? There was absolutely no way I could pay that out of my wages. I stuttered something to that effect. The CO carried on writing something on a piece of paper in front of him.

'Corporal Holmes. If you don't pay the bill by the end of the week, then I will have to charge you with being drunk and disorderly. I was thinking I would rather you collect the car, bring it to the barracks and clean it thoroughly.' As he went on and on about the seriousness of what I had done and how I'd brought the Army into disrepute, his voice rose until he was shouting.

At last I was dismissed. As soon as I got outside, I sat in the nearest chair with tears welling in my eyes. I had tried so hard to do the right things at this unit because I liked being there so much. One night out and I had stupidly blown it. Where was I going to find the money? If I didn't, the CO had made it clear that there would be more repercussions from the police. The admin staff were asking me what had gone on. They had heard the shouting from outside the closed door. When I tried to explain, all they did was rub it in, pointing out again how much trouble I had got myself into.

About quarter of an hour later, the CO emerged from his room. I looked up and thought I saw a faint smile on his lips as he quickly looked the other way. Suddenly everyone, including him, burst out

*Left* Holding on for dear life in St George's.

*Below* I used to share my sweets. Me with my Granddad Percy.

*Left* My first camping experience with Simon Wickson.

*Left* My mum was young once!

*Below* Kevin, my little shadow.

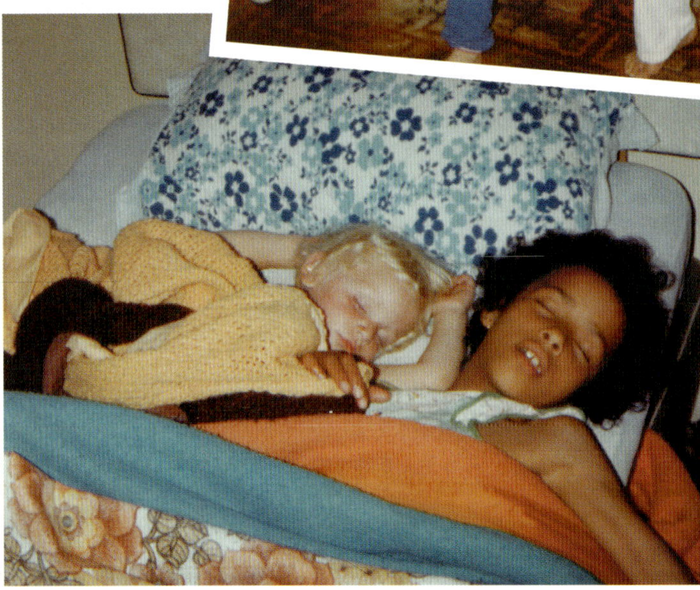

*Left* We always had so much energy.

*Right* Mum says I was a sweet, delicate little thing.

*Below* I loved being the centre of attention.

*Left* My first ever race in 1982 for Hugh Christie Secondary School. I never liked cross-country, but my plimsolls did me proud.

*Below* English Schools Championship, 1983.

*Left* Mum and Dad were so proud.

*Right* Our little gang (Kerrie took the photo).

*Below* We thought we looked so cool. Me with Kev and Stu.

*Right* Is that a wig, Kerrie?

*Below* Running in the army.

*Above* Spick and span in my Number Twos.

*Above* Of course, I liked being in charge.

*Right* I was a good shot – promise.

Above left  *Lost before I started. World Championships, 1995.*
*Courtesy of Getty Images*

*Above right*  You can't always win.
*Courtesy of Getty Images*

*Right*  Dave helped me for years and here he is dedicating his time to me and more youngsters again.

*Above* In the battle zone. *Courtesy of Empics*

*Below* No pain, no gain. Atlanta Olympics, 1996. *Courtesy of Getty Images*

*Below* Please keep that pail away from me. Helping out in Bosnia.

laughing. They knew I never got drunk normally because I was a PTI and they knew very well that nothing terrible had happened the night before. The whole thing had been a complete wind-up. Everyone had been in on it – even the police, who had faked an official notice of complaint. Because I'd been so shaken I hadn't listened properly to everything the CO was shouting so I'd missed all the words on the complaint that were obviously made up, such as 'PC Greenstuff'. There I was, believing I had let the unit down so badly, while they were all having the biggest laugh ever. While they were laughing, I was practically crying with relief.

However, the year wasn't without its real problems, particularly when I had a run-in with one of the sergeants. Two or three times a month, we'd have to go on guard duty between 6 p.m. and 6 a.m. It meant sleeping in the guardroom, operating a rota with the four or five others that were on, so that two of us would sleep while two would patrol the perimeter of the camp and one would stand on sentry duty. It could be so cold that we'd be wearing as many layers of clothing as possible, just longing for the night to end. Nobody was allowed to talk to us when we were on duty and we were forbidden to eat although the civvy security would sometimes sneak us a warm drink. I'd stand there, weapon in hand, freezing to death, watching all my mates going out for the night. Sometimes I would ask them to smuggle me a treat or two on their way out so that I could suck boiled sweets or munch away while no one was looking. I knew I'd be in deep trouble if I got caught.

Sure enough, one of the sergeants somehow got wind that I'd been given some sweets. He didn't know me because he was on a course at Beaconsfield and was new to the unit. He'd never been in the gym. If he had he probably wouldn't have been such an idiot because he would have realised that if I got him in there I could give him a lot of grief. He came charging down to where I was posted, and started yelling at me. Eventually I got so fed up, I decided I wasn't going to take it any longer. I stepped out towards him and shouted, 'Give me a break,' slamming down my weapon before walking off. That was a very bad thing to do. I was responsible for that weapon and if it had gone off and injured someone, I would have been court-martialled, jailed and stripped of my rank. As for walking away from a senior rank without waiting to be dismissed? That was another offence. But I couldn't have stopped myself even if I'd tried.

The sergeant came after me, absolutely furious. 'Corporal Holmes. Pick up your weapon.'

I knew he was in the right this time so I went back and retrieved it.

'Corporal Holmes. Report to the guardroom. Now.' He marched me up there, keeping right behind me as various officers stopped to watch the drama. I stood to attention and saluted the officer in charge while the sergeant reeled off my offences, charging me with misconduct. Loads of us thought that he didn't do his share of the duty, and I couldn't keep my mouth shut. I decided to stick up for myself. I wasn't sure what would happen to me, but I told the officer my opinion of this sergeant. The officer put me on a warning. I was let off lightly and was just given a couple of extra duties.

I was furious over the incident and was determined to get my own back, although I hadn't a clue how I was going to do it. Then, a couple of weeks later, that same sergeant's unit was ordered to do the BFT (Basic Fitness Test). He and another guy failed so they were both sent to my gym for extra training. What a result. When he saw me standing there, waiting for them both, his mouth fell open. We both knew he was on my turf now and had to do whatever I ordered. This was my moment. Revenge will be sweet, I thought.

I considered what I should do very carefully. He was reliant on me if he wanted to pass his Basic Fitness Test, essential if he was to pass his course. I had two options. Either I could totally beast him, working him to exhaustion point – which is what he was expecting. Or I could play mind-games with him. The first would have an effect while he was in the gym and would doubtless have given me great pleasure, but the second would have much more of a long-term effect by making him feel guilty about the way he had behaved towards me. I decided to go for the second. I was completely professional and trained him properly. I took him out on the BFT course just outside the medical centre. It was a loop around a large playing field where we used to play mixed hockey. I structured the course so it was a gradual build up of their endurance, like run/walk/run for twenty minutes, or fartleks. After the first retake the other guy passed, leaving only my failed 'friend' to continue with the training. He probably sank to the ground when he knew he would be on his own from then on. The temptation to beast him was great, but I didn't. Don't get me wrong though. He had to train very hard. Progress wasn't easy as he was very unfit and quite a way off completing the course in the nine and a half minutes he needed to pass. But he and I stuck at it. In the gym I had to work him hard with running circuits to improve his strength and endurance. Press-ups, sit-ups, squats – you name it, he did it! It wasn't easy for him but the work paid off and he eventually passed his fitness test.

To my surprise, after he'd passed, he came and found me in the gym one day to apologise for what he had done in the guardroom and to say that he totally respected me as a person and as a PTI because of the way I had conducted myself with him. He knew how unpleasant I could have made the training for him but he said that he would never forget what had happened and how I had helped him pass. Hearing him say all that made me feel great, much better than if I'd taken physical revenge on him in the gym. I think we both learned a big lesson from each other.

It was in 1993, while I was at Beaconsfield, that a stomach problem I had first experienced with Dave recurred. Years before I had once collapsed with a painful tearing sensation in my stomach when we were training. Neither of us had any idea of the cause but I remember him rubbing my back and stomach to ease the pain. We dismissed the episode as something associated with puberty. This time though, I had to take it more seriously. I'd set up an indoor assault course, using the beams, ropes and poles, making little tunnels and placing the boxes to jump over. For safety reasons, the PTI always had to go round the entire course, checking everything was working properly, before potential officers could use it. I got round it fine until I jumped off the box and I felt a deep sharp pain in my stomach. I had to go straight to my room where I lay in agony until one of the girls in my block, who knew I should have been taking a class, came to find me. They called a doctor and I was immediately taken to the local hospital. The first thing the consultant said to me was, 'God, you look grey.' I must have looked bad. During keyhole surgery he found that I had a burst cyst on my ovaries. I had treatment to reduce it, and was told it was nothing serious. However, this incident was the real start to a problem that has bugged me all my life.

I returned to the camp, relieved and excited about the possibility of competing in the World Championships in Stuttgart – I didn't want anything to get in my way.

# 9. BACK ON TRACK

At the gun, Paula Fryer, the 1991 UK Champion, took off like a bullet, flying round the first lap way ahead of the rest of us. I was way, way back, running with the pack and not sure quite what to do. We were bunching up and watching Paula go. This, the UK Championships' 800 metres at Crystal Palace, was my first championship race since I'd been a junior and I still had a lot to learn about how to race properly. I began to respond and took off after her. I wasn't going to let her get away. I had to catch her. I gave it everything, overtaking her at the 400-metre mark and running in the front from then on. Wes was standing at the top corner, shouting, 'Go, Kel. Go on, Kel.'

I could hear my friends and family in the stands yelling loudly as I came down the home straight. They could see the race clock and knew that I could meet the qualifying time for the World Championships if I didn't let up. To everyone's delight, I won quite easily, with Linda Keough, a top 400-metre runner, making a late break and coming second. I shaved a fraction of a second off the qualifying time, running it in 2:00.86 – a personal best. I had done it. I was going to run in Stuttgart in August. Now all I had to do was qualify officially at the AAA Championships in Birmingham a month later. I was so chuffed.

I knew the race had gone against all the pundits' expectations. As far as most of them knew, I had come from nowhere, but in fact I had won all my major services competitions that winter. The start of the summer season had gone well for me when I won the Middlesex County Championships and the Inter-Counties Championships. I also won the Army Championships 400- and 1500-metre titles, and three days later I made a shock breakthrough on the civilian scene when I won the UK Championships. I must have looked pretty intimidating to the other competitors because, thanks to all my PT training, I was very fit and muscular with well-developed shoulders, something that wasn't common then in British women runners. I was running in the green and white colours of Middlesex Ladies AC. I'd got rid of my Afro some time ago and had my hair cropped up the sides and longer on top to conform to the Army's regulation about hair not touching the collar.

For me, winning the UK Championships was a massive achievement. What's more, it looked as if I was on the verge of running the 800 metres in under two minutes, a world-class time for female athletes.

One of the major race meets in 1993 was the Europa Cup Championships in Rome. There was only one athlete chosen to represent their country in each event. I was chosen as the reserve runner to Diane Modahl. She was already an established 800-metre runner and English record holder with a career best of 1:58.65, who had also qualified for the World Champs. I remember sitting high up in the stands watching her race, wishing so much that it was me down there on the track. She didn't win but she ran a great race. She also ran in the 4 x 400-metre relay. As an 800-metre runner, she knew she wasn't fast enough. Middle-distance runners don't always have that necessary speed. As the 400-metre specialists overtook her it almost looked as if she was running backwards. She must have felt terrible, as if she'd let her team down, although it wasn't her fault. I felt so sorry for her. She, like me, had the strength and endurance necessary for a longer race, but not the speed that enables you to sprint the shorter distances. Watching that race made me vow that I would never allow myself to get into the same position. Unlike Diane, I've never had the guts to put myself into a team race over that distance in Civvy Street.

After the Inter-Counties Championships in May, I had been approached by Andy Norman, a race agent. Wes and I were both pretty ignorant about the international racing circuit. Wes was a London club coach with little experience of international athletics and of course it was a whole new world to me. So I thought, Why not? As a race agent, it was Andy's job to get me entered into races on the international grand prix circuit.

The first grand prix I ran was the 800 metres at the D N Galan meet in Stockholm that year. I was incredibly nervous at the idea of running against world-class athletes but as I hadn't really a clue who any of the other runners were, I was less scared than I might have been. I just had to run the very best I could. At 120 metres, a tall Russian girl leading the field started going ahead. I was tailing her as she pulled away, but then I made a last supreme effort. I don't know how I did it but in the last thirty or forty metres I gained on her and ended up going past her to win in a personal best time of 2:00.45. Apart from giving me more confidence, that race also made me swear that I would never wear racing knickers again. That was the first and last time I wore them as a senior. I felt as if I was racing in a bikini. I've always worn Lycra shorts ever since.

Sometimes too much knowledge can be a dangerous thing. Instinct is everything. The naivety I had in those early races was a great help to me because I ran without worrying about my opponents' form or about which tactics to adopt. During the Oslo Grand Prix, the only thing I remember Andy saying to me before the race was, 'Follow the black girl.' That was all. So I thought, Right, that's what I'll do. I'll follow the black girl. I had no idea who she was but, in the absence of any better advice, I thought I'd go with it. As we came off the top bend, she pulled away, lengthening the gap between us. I managed to come second. That was brilliant. It was only later that I found out she was none other than Maria Mutola, a young Mozambican runner, who was already making her mark on the athletics world. Andy told me she was the youngest athlete to have ever gone to the Olympics when she'd ran in the 800 metres in Seoul as a teenager in 1988 and was eliminated in the heats. Then, in the 1992 Barcelona Games, she came fifth in the 800 metres and ninth in the 1500 metres. For me to finish so close to such a superb athlete was a great boost and put me right on the map as far as the athletics' world was concerned. It was also the first time I had broken the two-minute barrier. Andy was incredibly pleased that I'd challenged Maria.

Next stop Birmingham. My main objective was to get in the first two to secure my place in the World Champs. I did by winning my first ever AAAs title in the 800 metres – the first of many. After a couple more races I was off to Stuttgart. I had to swap my guard duty so that I could be allowed to go.

The athletes' village was in an old army barracks out of town so I felt quite at home with the spartan accommodation it offered, although I know some of the other athletes were less happy. For me, metal bunk beds and a metal wardrobe in a room that was as plain as anything didn't seem so out of the ordinary or even particularly uncomfortable. I was so excited to be there that I didn't really take in my surroundings any more than that. All I wanted to do was race. All the races I had run that year had contributed to my growing ability as a tactician. I needed to draw on all of my experiences in my heat.

As we broke from our lanes at the beginning of the back straight I took my place in third position. By the bell I had taken the lead with Natalya Dukhnova from Belarus and Yuan Wang, the Chinese girl, close behind. I hung on as Yuan Wang challenged me but then the Mozambican girl, Tina Paulino, charged past with a tremendous burst of speed with Dukhnova hot on her heels. As we got to the final bend, I was boxed in with Paulino in front and Dukhnova running at my side. There was only one thing I could do. I slowed momentarily so that I could then move out, coming down the outside and overtaking Dukhnova to bag second place. I had done it. I was in the semi-finals. I couldn't believe it.

The next day, I had a lie in and then went for a short jog to loosen up the legs, had breakfast and relaxed. To get a place in this final, I only had to come in the first four. I was drawn on the inside so I had the choice of running out fast to the front and placing myself or starting off slowly and coming from the back. I was very nervous about what to do, only too aware that this was now the big league. We were called to the start and as the gun fired I stormed off to take the lead. As we broke lanes, the American Meredith Rainey and Tina Paulino crossed to the inside, running in front of me. As we came into the final lap, I was blocked in fourth place with Ella Kovacs from Romania challenging me for the last qualifying place to for the finals. I dropped back into fifth place behind Lyubov Gurina, as Kovacs raced ahead of us. But I wasn't done yet and came up on the outside to challenge her. I couldn't make it. It had been a fast race and I had to pay for my very fast start. But I was happy all the same. I had run in the semi-final of the World Championships and although I was placed fifth, I had also set a new English record of 1:58.64

When the race was over I went down to get my kit from the holding room. About ten minutes later I began to feel a sharp, stabbing pain low down in my stomach again. I had assumed that the treatment I'd had on my ovaries would put a stop to anything like this. It quickly became excruciating. I found a toilet, somewhere underneath the grandstand. By this time I was sweating buckets so I took off every single item of my clothing. The pain was so bad that I think I must have been slightly delirious as I lay on the filthy concrete floor in one of the cubicles, terrified that there was something badly wrong with me. Nobody knew I was there so I lay alone, curled up in agony for at least half an hour, not knowing what to do, praying someone would come and find me soon. Then, Bridie Roach, another middle-distance runner with the Middlesex Ladies AC and Tracy 'D', a friend from Beaconsfield, came looking for me. By the time they eventually found me the pain was easing and I got dressed. The attack had lasted over fifty minutes. As suddenly as it had begun, the pain disappeared and I was able to carry on as if nothing had happened. Unaware that this would continue as a problem throughout my racing career, I dismissed the incident and got on with enjoying myself at the Championships.

I watched Sally Gunnell, the captain of the women's team, break the world record as she romped home to victory in the 400 metres hurdles, as well as Colin Jackson, who won the 110 metres hurdles in a world record time, and Linford Christie, who established a new European record in the 100 metres in his fastest time ever. These people were the big stars of athletics. It was a great experience to be a part of that atmosphere and to be on the same team as all these world-class athletes. I couldn't get over the fact that I was there competing in the same team as them.

Watching the final of the 800 metres from the stands was exciting. Diane Modahl had qualified from her semi-final and was the British hope. The race didn't go as predicted because on the final bend four of the girls fell, including the Russian favourite, and Diane finished fourth. Maria Mutola had run the best race and won. It was her first World Championship title. I won't ever forget the way her face lit up as she crossed the line to win, showing exactly how much it meant to her. It made me think about how athletes respond to victory. It doesn't seem natural to me not to be ecstatic when all your passion for the sport, hard work and training has paid off. From that day to this, I've always wondered about winners who show no emotion as they cross the line.

I was really pleased for Diane but, if I'm honest, I have to admit to feeling a bit disappointed, because I had run faster than her in the semis and couldn't help thinking how fantastic it would have been to run in the final. Diane is a calm, genuine person, quite naive in her outlook on life, and with such a lovely personality that I couldn't possibly begrudge her the race. She was my team-mate and has only ever been a rival when we've been competing in the same race. Then, everyone is my rival.

Before I knew it, I was back on guard duty in Beaconsfield, standing there, freezing cold, shaking like a leaf in the pitch darkness with the fog coming down, no-one to talk to and hating every moment. What a kick down to earth it was. While I'd been going through so many new experiences, and for a sports person they were such significant ones, everyone else had been getting on with their normal day-to-day life in the Army, oblivious to what I'd been through. It was such a bizarre feeling. Two such different worlds. Suddenly I'd gone from having given up athletics altogether to being a semi-finalist in the World Championships with an English record. The feeling was the same after every race I ran. One day, I was in the racing world competing with the very best, the next I was back in the barracks as if nothing had happened. Strange as it was, I always quickly slotted back into my normal everyday life. Although I would think about where I'd been and what I'd achieved, I was totally dedicated to my job. As far as I was concerned, the Army was still where my future lay.

# 10. MEDALS OR MONEY?

'Are you out for medals or for money?'

I didn't have to hesitate. 'Medals,' I replied.

'Fair enough,' said Dave. 'What's your ultimate ambition?'

Again, I knew the answer immediately. 'To win a gold medal at the Olympics.'

The ambition that I had once had as a junior athlete had resurfaced. Despite my passion for being in the Army, I couldn't ignore my competitive attitude to racing. Now that I was on the international scene, I realised that I had a talent I couldn't ignore. I thought I should make a serious attempt to achieve the best I could.

Seeing Lisa York running in Barcelona and then winning myself in Stockholm, coming second in Oslo and reaching the semi-final of the Stuttgart World Champs had made me realise that I might have a real chance of achieving my dream one day. This would be my driving force for the next ten years of my life. But if I was going to do it, I needed Dave Arnold back in my life to help me. I felt that he was the one person who really knew me as an athlete. Although we'd lost touch while I was in the Army, we had spent the six years before with him as my coach. Six years is a long time in an athlete's life. I liked the way he worked, I knew his training plans were effective and I believed he would be able to progress me as an athlete.

I had written to him to ask if he would consider taking me on again. He had agreed, so I'd driven over to Hildenborough to visit him and his wife Carol. We were in their living room talking about everything that had happened since I had left him to join the Army. Although he'd seen the civilian races I'd run on TV, I wanted to bring him up to speed on how well I'd been running and training in the Army too. It was so good to see him and I was thrilled that he seemed so excited about the prospect of coaching me again. Wes and I both agreed that getting back in touch with Dave to see if he would coach me at this stage in my career was the best way to go. Wes didn't know me nearly as well as an athlete and his experience as a club coach was more limited. He had been so fantastic, dragging me kicking and screaming back on to the athletics scene, but he recognised that I was moving beyond his capabilities. However I did want Wes to remain involved with me so he happily agreed to act as my manager instead. Since I had made a small breakthrough in the sporting world I had begun to receive various requests to do things, such as visiting schools and appearing on a couple of TV programmes. I needed someone to field them for me and Wes was the man for that. He also put in a great deal of work getting my first sponsorship deal with Asics. He has been a huge friend to me ever since – a really good guy, very passionate about me and another of my biggest supporters. He has always treated me as one of his own, while to me he is one of my closest friends and confidantes.

So Dave and I were back together again. Only this time, instead of training on the Tonbridge track and in the surrounding fields, Dave usually came to me. By early 1994 I had been posted back to Duchess of Kent Barracks in Aldershot. It was hard to get away as often as I needed so we'd use the track at the PT school. I can picture Dave now, wearing his wellies with his floppy green hat protecting him against the weather, standing in the middle, whistle at his lips. As far as I was concerned, his method of training had only changed in its intensity. I trained every day, sometimes twice a day. Normally he'd set me a week-long programme that involved all the different kinds of training – hill training, circuit training, weight training, repetitions round the track and long runs. Somewhere within the following couple of weeks, he'd repeat some of the sessions so I could monitor how I'd progressed. In the middle of a session, I'd be on my hands and knees, exhausted. Then, over he'd come to check my recovery rate, making sure my pulse was low enough before setting me another repetition. It was a good way for him to know how well I was coping with each session too. The quicker my pulse rate came down, the better I was adapting to that rate of running.

When I first got back together with Dave, the sessions weren't too successful. I felt that he sometimes treated me just like the teenager I used to be. But I was 24 years old and a corporal in the Army, for God's sake. I had completely changed as a person. I was more outspoken and confident. Also, as a PTI, I had had plenty of experience of circuit training so we would often clash over the best way of doing things. I used to stick up for my ideas if I didn't agree with him and, to begin with, I think he found that hard to handle. I remember we had some big arguments on the track, although he prefers to remember them as 'discussions', when I would scream at him, 'Stop treating me like a kid.' He always remained very calm and, most of the time, just took my outbursts on the chin. Then we'd get on with the training and forget about whatever had caused our differences. As time went by, we got used to one another again and things settled down.

Meanwhile my life in the Army demanded as much of my time as ever. At Duchess of Kent Barracks I was one of the PTIs for 251 Signal Regiment which, like 2 Signal Regiment at York, was now made up of men and women but was much smaller. Because the WRAC PTIs were disbanding as part of the general amalgamation of the WRAC and the Army, there were no more promotional roles within the WRAC, so I had been given the title of Acting Sergeant. In Aldershot we'd have tournaments that brought women's army teams from stations all over the world to compete. It was always great fun. They'd take place over long weekends and turned into big social events. Often people I'd been with on a previous posting would turn up so there were plenty of opportunities to catch up. In the evenings we'd hit the town and visit the different London clubs. The tournaments were brilliant. Hundreds of WRAC ladies all there for one purpose – to have fun! If anyone asked me I would say volleyball and judo were my favourite sports apart from athletics. I eventually had to give them up in 1996 when my athletics became serious.

Life was good. The only blot on the horizon for us women PTIs, assuming we didn't want to change trades, was the six-month selection course we would have to pass to join the Physical Training Corps. Otherwise we'd be forced to look for other jobs. We were all incensed at being made to qualify for and then complete a second six-month training course when we'd already spent nine months in training to be Women's Royal Army Corps PTIs. Most of us felt that at least corporals and upwards should be entitled to an automatic transfer while lance corporals would benefit from another year of experience. But we had no choice. We knew it was going to be incredibly tough. We'd be in direct competition with the men and would be expected to excel in all the physical tests just as they would.

The pre-selection course was even harder than I expected. Out of the thirty of us on it only five were women. In every exercise we were ordered to complete, I kept pushing myself on, repeating, 'I can do it. I can do it.' I was not going to be beaten. We completed all the physical fitness tests from heaves (straight-arm chin-ups), rope climbing, runs, gymnastics and command task skills. But the worst was the log run. With eight to a team, we had to complete a three-mile run, each of us placed at intervals along a large log that we had to carry from Aldershot to some sand dunes nearby. The difficulty the teams experienced was down to everyone being different heights. Because we all had to make allowances for that, the logs were all over the place. The instructors were screaming and giving us hell as we sprinted our very uneven way to the dunes. Running up and down them was physically the hardest thing I ever had to do in the Army. When we'd finished, we dropped the log, exchanged our boots for our trainers and ran back to camp. I was absolutely wasted but still determined not to give in. I ran so hard that I beat everyone back – everyone. I stood alone in a car park in Aldershot, the meeting point, waiting for the others, feeling completely out of it. My legs were dead. Every muscle in my body was screaming and my back was killing me. My head felt as if it was going to burst. I hadn't realised how hard I'd pushed my body over those dunes. That exercise marked the start of recurring lower back problems that have dogged my career. But all I cared about then was that my efforts paid off. I was one of the five people from our group that were accepted on to the training course – and the only woman.

After the pre-selection course, I was given the date for the next stage – April 1994, four months before the Commonwealth Games in August. It couldn't have been at a worse time for me. I knew I couldn't combine the PT Corps' training course with the level of training Dave would expect if I was going to meet the qualifying standard. Unfortunately, I had no choice but to defer my entry. For the rest of the year, I was hungry to see what I could achieve with my running.

After watching me in training, Dave thought I had the strength and endurance to be successful at the 1500 metres. I went into the year with a best time of only 4:17.3. I had improved on that when I won the Middlesex Championships in May in a new personal best of 4:10.2. But I wanted to see if I could achieve something faster so the Army agreed to enter me in the men's 1500 metres at the Army Championships to see if I could improve on my time. Men and women don't normally compete against one another. If they do then the women's time will not be ratified, under International Amateur Athletics Federation (IAAF) rules, on the women's racing lists. The men were fine with me entering it because they realised it was my only chance to compete in a fast race. Running against such tough competition was brilliant. I ended up beating a lot of the field in another personal best time of 4:07.7. I was over the moon as it qualified me for the AAA's Championships in Birmingham three days later where I was to come up against the Scottish runner Yvonne Murray, who was firm favourite to win. She was an established long-distance runner and medallist, most recently having won a gold in the 1990 European Championships 3000 metres.

After qualifying for the final, I knew that competing against Yvonne would be tough, but what a race it was! We got out there and battled the whole way round. She was in the lead; then I was. Then she came back and overtook me. The crowd was going mad with excitement as the new girl on the block challenged the very best out there. As we came down the home straight, we were neck and neck all the way. I was determined not to give her an inch. Being so close, it was a photo finish and the judges had to check to determine the winner. I won with a time of 4:01.41 – a worldclass time. I couldn't believe it. I had gone down from 4:10 to 4:01 in three races. But, more importantly, it was another massive breakthrough in the racing world, qualifying me to run in the European Championships in Helsinki and the Commonwealth Games in Canada. Winning that race in that time put me in the public eye for the first time.

The races in the European Championships were certainly up to

World Championship and Olympic standards, largely because a number of Russians were entered. They have always been dominant in women's 800 and 1500 metres. There were three Russian girls running in the 1500 metres so I knew that it wasn't going to be easy. The night before the race, Dave and I had sat down as usual and had discussed the race plan, going through who I should watch out for, what strengths and weaknesses had been shown by the other runners in their heats and semi-finals. We would rehearse various possible scenarios so that I went into the race with more than one plan. You have to be able to adapt when you race simply because you can't control what the other runners might do. He was always careful to say only what was appropriate, going through the tactics that I needed to win, then leaving me to dream about them. I know some trainers talk frantically to their runners right up to the last minute but Dave always left me alone as much as possible on the day of the race, believing it was the best way to keep my focus without any unnecessary distractions. This way of doing things was to become a habit before every major race. In Helsinki, his advice was not to let anyone get too much of a lead.

But funnily enough it was Mum's words that stayed with me. While I had been training so intensively, we had tried to speak more and more on the telephone as I kept her up to speed with what I was doing and feeling. She always cheered me up if things were going badly and was pleased when things went well. I realised that, almost without noticing we had gradually become close again. Before I'd left for the championships, we'd been looking through the competition I'd be facing. She noticed that one of the Russians, Yekaterina Podkopayeva, was about the same age as her. We were talking about if I got into the final and about Podkopayeva when she said, 'If she beats you, it'll be as if I did.' We laughed at the idea but it must have stuck somewhere in the recesses of my memory.

Two hours before the final, I got to the warm-up area, found a spot, lay down on my towel and relaxed until it was time to warm up. I never really talk to anyone before a race but prefer to be in my own little world, focusing on the race to come. Dave was there to take the pressure off me by checking my spikes and to sort out any small problem that might unexpectedly arise. We hardly spoke to one another. When the time came, I did my drills. Dave patted me on the back and said, 'Go for it.'

The race started slowly almost at a jogging pace. We were all nearly tripping over one other. Without a pacemaker to set the speed, everyone was running a tactical race. This was all about winning the championship, not about running the fastest. I was so aware of where all the other runners were, who was behind and who was in front of me, and how they were pacing themselves. I knew I couldn't afford to make a single mistake. Like the others, I didn't want to put myself in the front because then everyone would be running off me. I wanted to be able to see what was happening and judge my run from that. The runners leading the field obviously didn't want to be there either and were hanging back as much as they could. The noise of the crowd booing broke through my concentration but didn't alter my focus. They wanted to see something more exciting than this unadventurous trot round the track. Then, as we completed the third lap, all the runners began to move and push forward, positioning themselves. We all must have had the same thought running through our heads, It's only 400 metres to go. I've got to get myself into the best position.

Until then we'd been bunched up together but now I knew it was time to move, making sure I wasn't going to get boxed in so that I'd be able to move forward when I had to. As the bell went, Lyudmila Rogachova, Yekaterina Podkopayeva and Lyubov Kremlyova picked up the pace and when they hit the 300-metre mark, they and Geraldine Nolan or Ireland went off like rockets, tearing ahead of the rest of us. I switched on immediately and charged off after them. By this time, Rogachova had got well away with Podkopayeva and Kremlyova racing behind her. Nolan and I were close on their tail. As I came up behind Nolan, she slowed down unexpectedly and I momentarily lost my footing. I regained it and as we came round the bend, I overtook her and Kremlyova running in third place. Only Rogachova and Podkopayeva were in front of me. I came into the home straight with Mum's words ringing in my ears: 'If she beats you, it'll be as if I did.' I couldn't let that happen. I put on the most almighty charge, gritting my teeth and grimacing like anything. I was closing them down, but Rogachova was too far ahead and crossed the line. Podkopayeva was right behind her. She must have thought she had second place in the bag because she slowed down a fraction just before the line and ... I just dived past her. A silver medal for me and the British team. In fact the race was one of the slowest-run 1500-metre races at a major championship in recent times. I came second with a time of 4:19.30 but that was irrelevant as I had won a medal.

I joined Andy Norman in the stands. He gave me his mobile so I could speak to Mum who was screaming down the line, 'You beat her. You beat her. You've done it.' We were laughing as I told her how my vision of her being in front of me had been such a terrifying thought. The only person to then spoil the moment was Andy. One of the bluntest people I know, all he could say was, 'Yeah, well. It's not a gold.' I could have bloody punched him.

At the end of the Helsinki Championships I went back to Aldershot and proudly showed off my medal to the girls and the officers, who I think were very proud of me. It was a short visit because it was then the turn of the Commonwealth Games. The other PTIs I left behind in the gym were very understanding; I think they realised that I certainly didn't take them or their support for granted. I flew out to Canada with the rest of the English team, the fact that I'd pocketed a silver medal the previous week boosting my confidence, making me believe I really had a good chance of winning a medal in Victoria. We were taken to our accommodation in a brand new 'village' built specifically for the Games, which would later be passed on to the University of Victoria as student accommodation. The accommodation blocks were made up of flats, each with its own kitchen, bathroom and living room. In the same block as me were Sharon Gibson and Myrtle Augee, two big black ladies who did the throws and who could have been a comedy act together. Myrtle was a shot-putter and was one of the funniest people I have ever met. She would keep us in stitches, regaling us with stories that she told with the voice of a black mama, using all the slang. I was incredibly lucky to meet the two of them but particularly Myrtle, who took me under her wing. It was great to relax with them although I wasn't too good at the card games they always played. I was so thrilled for Myrtle when she came home with a gold. Sharon was successful too and won the bronze for the women's javelin.

I didn't really make any firm friends at the time because I was still in the Army and that's where I would be the moment the Games ended – back in barracks, almost as if none of this had happened. So the people I met remained more athletics acquaintances than close friends at that time. I sometimes hung out with a couple of the 400-metre guys, becoming close to David McKenzie, a 400-metre hurdler and a sweet man. We'd often all go into town together. One time, I was sitting with a group of girls, including Denise Lewis and Diane Modahl as well as triple-jumpers Michelle Griffith, Ashia

Hanson and Connie Henry, another good friend, when we got talking about colour. For me, it was quite a weird conversation but it did bring up issues about our different backgrounds. We asked each other whether we felt black or white. After thinking for a while, I said, 'I don't know. I'm just me. All I know is the environment I grew up in. I don't distinguish between different races and feel uncomfortable when these issues come up.' Throughout my life, I've never worried about people's race, colour or religion. I just take people for who they are. My only concern is that they should respect each other when respect is deserved.

The big shock of the Games for the English team was when, on 24 August, the day of the heats for the 800 metres, Diane Modahl was told she had tested positive for testosterone. In June, she had run in Lisbon where she had been selected for a random drug test. There's nothing unusual in that. One of the things professional athletes have to accept is that they can be called upon to undergo a drug test at any time. What was extraordinary was that Diane's had tested positive. Like the rest of the English team, I knew that one of the last people on earth to be guilty of drug-taking would be Diane.

The first I knew of it was when I was looking through the names of the runners in the 800 metres on the computers in a tent in the village and noticed Diane's name had been scratched. There had been some speculation that one of the runners had tested positive, but I couldn't believe it would be her. For Diane, it was the start of a nightmare few years, in which she and her husband and manager, Vicente, fought to clear her name. All we knew then was what we saw on TV. The shot-putter Paul Edwards, who had also tested positive, flew home to England in a plane with Diane to face the waiting paparazzi. He was carried off first shrouded in blankets. She eventually followed, walking down the steps with her head held high to face the cameras. She was innocent and wasn't going to return home as if she was ashamed of anything. I remember feeling so sorry for her. I had heard how distraught she had been when Susan Deaves, the team manager, had to break the news and withdraw her from the Games. Now, with her eyes hidden behind her dark specs, she looked lost and bewildered. To be robbed of her chances after all those months and years of preparation – it was a terrible thing to happen to her.

Later I was more than happy to be one of those asked by Vicente to write a character reference for Diane to help them in their fight.

Until then, not many athletes accused of drug-taking had succeeded in clearing their name, but Vicente and Diane felt they had no alternative but to try everything to save her reputation and to enable her to race again. Years later, after a number of hearings and appeals, her name was finally cleared when serious flaws were found in the way her urine sample had been stored and analysed.

Despite the big shock of Diane's removal from the Games and the blow to the team's morale in general, the rest of us had to keep going. When it came to the 1500 metres, I ran it with the confidence of a European silver medallist and won quite comfortably, using the speed I had from being an 800-metre runner to beat the Canadian Paula Schnurr into second place, and the South African Gwen Griffiths into third. I was so happy when I crossed the line, winning my second medal and my first title.

At the end of the games, a big group of us went into town to celebrate. Down at Victoria's Inner Harbour where the city curls around the waterside, we partied in one of the many restaurants while fireworks blazed into the sky from one of the ships anchored there.

I was brought back down to earth with a bump. Within forty-eight hours I was walking into a rounders tournament in Aldershot. I sat down to watch unable to get my head round the idea of having won two medals and now being bounced back to where I belonged. There was only one thing I could do. I joined in the game. As I've always said, succeeding at something and satisfying my own sense of personal achievement doesn't make me a better person than anyone else. When the racing is over, I just carry on as me.

# 11. DECISION TIME

I had always thought of my athletics as coming second to my career in the Army. Whatever my other childhood dreams, I hadn't dared believe they might really come true. But without being 100 per cent committed to my training, I had won two prestigious international medals. What if I gave more to my athletics? How much more could I achieve? The more experienced I became as a runner, the more motivated and confident I became. I began to follow my training programme rigorously, although I made sure to fit it round my job. I wanted to run internationally and to see if I could be selected for the World Championships that were coming up in Gothenburg in August, 1995. At the same time, I was only twenty-four years old and was very conscious that I wanted to continue committing myself to my job until I had decided where my future lay.

When I heard the deferred date for my PTI training course was to be early in 1995, I realised for the first time that I was going to have to make a choice. All I'd ever wanted was to be a PTI and, until now, I wanted to join the PT Corps more than anything, but if I went on the six-month course, which I knew was extremely demanding, it would mean that I wouldn't be able to train properly.

I talked to Dave and to the officers in charge of me at Aldershot. I tried to work out with them whether I'd be able to fit in enough athletics training during the course to be able to come out of it in June and still qualify for the World Championships in August. Everybody agreed that the training course would be too intense for me to be able to do that. Finally I decided that I would defer going on the course for a second time. That way, I could train for the Championships but if I did badly I would be able to complete my PTI training afterwards. Everyone seemed happy with that solution, so I continued as Acting Sergeant but put my head down and began to train.

Gothenburg and the World Championships beckoned. I won every race that I entered that year, including the European Cup, all the grand prix, the Inter-Services Championships and finally the AAA Championships in Birmingham again, with a personal best for the 800 metres of 1:57.56. I approached the World Championships with confidence, determined to go for gold. I knew I had a good chance of winning and perhaps naively told the press so. I was already under pressure from myself, but by telling them of my hopes, I increased the weight of expectation from the media as well. It was perhaps not the wisest thing I could have done. Some people were waiting to see me fail.

The only runner in the competition that I hadn't been up against during the season was Hassiba Boulmerka. World champion in 1991 and Algeria's first ever Olympic champion in 1992, she had been laid low with injury problems this season. Gothenburg was her first time out, so effectively she was an unknown quantity. We were drawn in the same heat but I wasn't too worried because the first six out of a field of ten went through to the semis. We ran quite different races, with Boulmerka running close to the front from the start while I stayed at the back waiting my moment. I moved to the outside in the third lap and at the bell I hit third place behind Boulmerka and Lyudmila Borisova from Russia. In the last 200 metres, it was Boulmerka who took the lead and I came in a comfortable second behind her. When the draw for the semi-finals was announced we were racing against each other again. Dave was incensed, saying how outrageous it was that we were drawn together twice before the final. But there was nothing we could do about it. This time I really gave her a run for her money and we battled it out down the finishing straight, shoulder to shoulder, with Boulmerka just inching ahead in the last moment to beat me by 0:00.2 seconds. We had both easily made it through.

Things were looking good but, come the day of the final, a very weird thing happened to me. From the moment I woke up, all I could think about was the race. I couldn't get it out of my mind. Normally, I try not to think about an imminent race too much. I know it's coming but I don't want to waste too much nervous energy thinking about it. I wasn't racing until 5.25 p.m. but when I woke up at 7 a.m., I found myself thinking, Only ten and a half hours to go and it will be over. I registered every hour throughout the day. Eight hours and it will be over. Seven hours and it will be over. I couldn't stop the thought going round and round my head, not realising how much nervous energy I was using up. Six hours and it will be over. Every time I picked up a magazine, all I could see was the track with Boulmerka and me in a titanic struggle to win. I went to lunch still counting. I had a rest in the afternoon, but every time I shut my eyes all I could see was the damn track. Friends kept telling me to relax but I found it impossible. Two hours before the race I went down to the warm-up area – but I was still counting. Then with twenty minutes to go I went to the call room. By now I was counting the minutes. Even when I stood on the line, waiting for the gun, I remember looking at the clock at the end of the stadium and thinking, Four minutes and it will be over.

Before we even started the crowd was booing. Some kind of equipment failure meant the gun sounded twice and we'd had two false starts. That's so unusual in middle-distance races that it was momentarily distracting. Third time lucky. We were off. Nobody wanted to take the race on so there was a lot of pushing as we all bunched together, with Yvonne Graham, the Jamaican, reluctantly going into the lead. At the 400-metre mark we were all still bunching, although I was careful to keep on the outside in fourth place, avoiding trouble and remaining in a position where I could accelerate fast when I needed to. Three laps to go, two laps to go, there was a lot of talent running in this race and I couldn't afford to make a mistake. Boulmerka was running second to Graham until the last lap when she overtook her and slowed the race right down. It was dirty racing really because she made everyone bunch and trip in a matter of seconds, causing a complete rhythm change. It wasn't against the rules but it's certainly not considered good sportsmanship. By then I was right behind her. As we went round the top bend, she made her break. I thought I'd wait till we were round it before I attacked, but I left it a fraction too late and couldn't quite catch her.

At 200 metres Boulmerka was leading, with me on the outside, but then she pulled out to the side so that I would have to run that little bit further if I was to get round her, forcing me to switch to the inside lane. But I couldn't get through there either. In the last few seconds of the race, my legs had gone and she proved herself the stronger of the two of us as she stormed home the winner. I was absolutely gutted. I knew I could have won and that I'd messed up the entire thing by worrying about it the whole damn day. I was in the best shape of my life and I should have beaten her. I had lost before I had started!

Looking back I can see that it was my lack of experience that let me down. That race taught me a big lesson about adrenalin and controlling my nerves. An athlete needs adrenalin to gear them up for the race, but too much of it and they're lost. I hadn't learnt to control my nerves in the way that I can now. Years of racing have taught me to try and switch off during the day of a championship race by chatting to other people, reading magazines or listening to music. I get through the day being as relaxed as I can, then when I leave the athletes' village, I step into a totally different zone. I don't talk much to people, I just acknowledge them. Instead I watch people warming up and try to detach myself a little bit from the fact that I'm about to race. It's only when I start my own warm-up that I focus 100 per cent on what's about to happen. That's the point when there's no going back. The other lesson I learned that day was never to underestimate an opponent. Boulmerka may not have been racing all season but it didn't mean that she wasn't in peak condition and able to use all her years of experience to run an excellent race.

For me the championships are the be all and end all. All the other races of the season offer chances to achieve certain targets, whether establishing a record or a personal best, beating a particularly strong opponent or by getting race sharp. But the Championships are what it's all about. That's what all the year's training and hard graft are geared towards. They're where you get your medals or you don't. Nineteen ninety-five was the first year that a Mercedes car was presented along with the gold medal. At the press conference afterwards, a reporter asked me what it was like to have lost the car. What an idiot, I thought. All I wanted was the medal and the sense of personal achievement that went with it. I lost the gold, not the bloody Mercedes.

Dave had been waiting for me when I came off the track. He knew exactly what it meant to me to lose that race but he wasn't going to let me lose sight of why we were there. I was so upset that, at that moment, I felt like packing up and going home. In fact that's what I told him.

'I'm not going to run the eight hundred.'

'What do you mean?' Dave was astounded.

'I'm not running it.'

'Don't be ridiculous, Kelly. You can't give up now,' he insisted. 'You've just won a silver medal. You're in top form. Besides, you'd be letting yourself and all your supporters down if you dropped out now.'

We argued back and forth for almost an hour. Eventually he said, 'Come on, Kelly. You know you've got to race tomorrow.' I knew he was right. I did.

The next day I was running in the heats of the 800 metres. I was still so upset about losing the 1500, my head wasn't in it at all. I didn't automatically qualify in the first two so had a tense wait in the tunnel under the stadium until all the heats were over to see whether or not I got one of the places for fastest losers. I was on tenterhooks waiting for the results to come in. I scraped through. I was furious with myself, knowing I had been on the verge of not getting into the semis just because of what was going on in my head. That seriously made me buck up my ideas.

The semi-finals were something else. I just switched on. I think everyone had written me off as being physically and emotionally exhausted after the 1500 so this time, I was the one putting all the pressure on myself. To begin with the race didn't go my way. I got off quickly but as we broke lanes, I was blocked in so had to slow myself down and drop to the back, keeping close to the pack. I couldn't find a way through until the last bend, when I forged through to take second place to Cuba's Ana Quirot. I'd made it to the final.

Suddenly the whole picture changed when, in the other semi, the race favourite Maria Mutola was disqualified for stepping on the white line within the first 100 metres of the race. With her out, Ana Quirot was tipped to win. It was her first championship since being horrendously burned and losing her baby in a domestic fire two years earlier. The eyes of the world's press were on her and expectations were high. With Mutola out of the race, Dave and I knew we'd have to change my race plans.

After six races in almost as many days, I was exhausted, but I kept telling myself I had to run the best race I possibly could. This time I was totally focused, oblivious to the crowd as I lined up. Meredith Rainey from the US set the pace with me slotting in close behind, committing myself to that position for the rest of the race. I had expected the pace would be fast and it was. As we came round the final bend, Quirot overtook us, Rainey dropped back and Letitia Vriesde from Surinam shot past me on the inside. With 30 metres to go, I was in third place. Suddenly I was aware of Patricia Djate of France on my shoulder, attacking my position. I wasn't going to let go. I wanted another medal. I fought her all the way and in the last ten metres pushed forwards to take the bronze. I did it, and established a new British and Commonwealth record of 1:56.95. To come away from the World Championships with two medals in women's middle-distance running was fantastic and quite unusual, especially against such tough opposition.

I learned so much at Gothenburg. I went in thinking I could win the 1500. It didn't go the way I wanted and I was gutted. I went into the 800 without any expectations and ended up with a bronze, totally elated. Such different expectations and results added to my experience and helped me prepare for the biggest challenge so far – the following year's Olympic Games in Atlanta.

Coming home was wicked. My family came to meet me at the airport. Kevin and Stuart, still my 'little boys' although they towered above me, were so proud of me. By this time, Kevin was working as a printer in a Sevenoaks firm while Stuart was taking a carpentry course. It always amazed me how they'd grown up so fast. Typically, Mum had brought a bunch of flowers and some 'Congratulations' balloons for me as well as laying on a great family party back home to celebrate. I was so happy that our relationship was back on track again and that we were as close as we ever were. Soon after, I was back at work and getting more congratulations from all my colleagues. That feeling of success was immense and gave me the hunger to become the best athlete I could be.

But the year wasn't over yet. After a couple of smaller races, the toughest race was to come. The grand prix finals were held in Monaco that year. In those days, those finals were where the big prize money was and where the final world rankings were decided. This time Maria Mutola was racing, fired up for victory after her disqualification in Gothenburg. Since then, we'd run two races together and I'd come third to her in both of them, but I was determined to give this last race of the season my very best shot. She seemed invincible but a race is a race so I went in positive. All the top runners were there including Ana Quirot, Meredith Rainey and Patricia Djate. It was Djate who got off at the gun, setting a fast pace and keeping well in the lead. Unlike the World Championships' final, this time I kept to the back, moving up into third place by the bell. Ahead of me, Mutola was running Djate down, closing on her as she approached the last bend, and then streaking past her. I chased Mutola all the way and came second. Smashing the British record in a time of 1:56.21 was the icing on the cake. I was proud to set that record – one that still stands today – and very pleased to have challenged Maria all the way to the line.

It was achievements such as these that made me realise that my Olympic dream would always be with me. Somewhere deep down, I felt I had to get there, that it was the right thing to do. When I feel that strongly about something, it is very hard for me to let go. I believe in Fate, but I also believe that you must be passionate about your dreams and never give them up. I admit to being quite a stubborn person – it's my way of making sure that I am completely dedicated to everything I do. Life is never easy. There are always obstacles to overcome. But fighting for your dreams will make the eventual achievement of them all the more satisfying.

Back at barracks, I had to make a decision. If I was going to train hard enough to be selected to represent Britain in the 1996 Olympics, I knew I wasn't going to be able to dedicate myself totally to my job. Until now, I'd been able to commit myself right up to the day I left for a championship meet and immediately after I arrived back. I counted most of the time I took to attend race meetings as leave. Everything I had achieved so far had been fitted in round my job, but I recognised that, realistically, that couldn't last. If I were going to go for the Olympics, I would have to turn down my place on the PT Corps training course.

Nobody could believe it. Places on that course were like gold dust. You didn't say no to one. In fact, turning one down was so unheard of that it became my real claim to fame in the Army. Fortunately, I was able to approach Lieutenant Colonel McCord and discuss my options with her. She was extremely sympathetic to my dilemma and, after discussing the various possibilities, she arranged for my transfer to the Army Youth Team (AYT) based in Mill Hill, just north of London. It was the perfect solution. I could do my athletics and had a great new job where I would be helping teenagers to get the best out of themselves. I love being able to pass on my experience, whether it's to kids or to adults. It's just a question of changing my approach and applying the techniques appropriately. It was great news, but what it did mean was that I had to test my skills in the water again but this time not for life-saving, or was it . . . ?!

## 12. MEDAL HOPES

White water churned and thundered down over the man-made rapids. I stood on the bank beside them, took one look and said to myself, 'No way am I going down there.' The orange fibreglass canoe that I'd been given didn't look as though it would survive the course any better than I would. Even though we'd been practising turns, speed paddling and capsizing drills, and I had been told the water had been toned down for us, the idea of riding those rapids put the fear of God into me. Toned down? If that's what they called toned down, God knows what the full-blown experience would be like.

I wasn't the only one looking apprehensive. The four NCOs in our group seemed pretty unhappy about the prospect of testing their new-found skills too. Then two of them bottled out altogether. At that moment I realised that I could either follow their example, and then regret not having tried afterwards or I could go for it and risk the consequences. Sometimes in life, you have to face up to your fears to overcome them. Suddenly I found I had the guts to give it a go even though I was absolutely petrified. I'll show them, I thought.

Our captain went first, neatly slaloming his way through the poles, making it look so easy. He and his canoe appeared to be seamlessly joined together as he manoeuvred it down the course, almost playing in the raging water. One of the lance corporals followed him, successfully making it down to the end. Then it was my turn. I turned to one of the guys left waiting at the top with me. 'I'm going down but you've got to stay right beside me.' All my fears of drowning were welling unpleasantly close to the front of my mind. But I swallowed hard and forced myself into my canoe at the top of the run. I managed to get under the bridge, heading towards the first stopper (underwater obstacle) where the white water was churning furiously. My fellow canoeist was closely following me as I had begged him to.

As I hit the stopper, the force of the water capsized me, sucking me under. The words of our instructor rushed back to me. 'If you fall in, hang on to your canoe.' I managed to keep a grip on it for about ten seconds before my sense of self-preservation kicked in. Sod the canoe. 'I'm not hanging on to that damn thing,' I said to myself. 'I've got to help myself here.' I let go and the canoe shot off without me. I screamed for the other guy to help. He did try but then he capsized too and off he flew down the rapids. I didn't see him again until the end. As I got hurled down the course, I kept being sucked in by other stoppers. Each time, I thought, This is it. I'm going to drown. Then I hit a rock that threw me bolt upright out of the water before pulling me back under. How I didn't break my legs, I'll never know. At last I managed to grab hold of one of the slalom poles.

I could hear somebody yelling at me to let go. The poles were not all that secure, but this one was the only security I had. I grasped it for dear life with my legs flapping behind me in the rush of water. 'For God's sake get me out of here.' I screamed. The two guys who had bottled out were standing on the bridge above, yelling encouragement, but I couldn't keep my grip any longer and I let go. The next few minutes seemed like an eternity as I was swept the whole way down the rapids. One minute I was being pulled under, the next I was thrown out at a different spot, trying to get hold of a rock or another pole whichever was nearest, gasping for breath, then being dragged down again. When I was eventually tossed out at the bottom, I couldn't believe I'd survived in one piece. I had really thought it was The End, and a thousand times worse than even I had thought it would be. I was absolutely terrified, certain I was going to drown. There I was, spluttering and snatching breaths, looking more like a drowned rat than a well-trained and competent PTI, when our captain, Captain Lester Smith, strolled over with his canoe, oblivious to the hell I'd just been through. 'Kelly. Where's your canoe?' Not a word of sympathy, just laughter. I couldn't believe it. Hadn't he heard my desperate shouts or noticed my frantic struggle for survival? I was, however, very proud of myself for giving it a go, although I wouldn't repeat the experience in a hurry.

This session at Nottingham's International Water Sports Centre was all part of my initiation into the Army Youth Team. We had to be proficient in all disciplines so that we could take responsibility for the kids' welfare when they were on one of our camps. There was top rope, abseiling and learning more survival skills like bivouacking or coming up with good recipes when faced with the 24-hour ration packs we were given on expeditions. I could only pray that canoes and rapids wouldn't feature too often.

I soon got used to wearing the khaki beret with the red and blue stripes, colours of the AYT, instead of my green WRAC beret. I was the only woman in our unit. There was a major, a captain, a warrant officer and four other NCOs who were trained PTIs. We were in charge of setting up activity camps for young people, showing them what the Army was all about. We wanted them to see that it wasn't anything like the image many people have of soldiers getting up at the crack of dawn, having to scrub the parade square with a toothbrush or going to war as soon as they joined up. The purpose was to encourage them to look at the Army in a positive way, so they could see it offered a great career in which they would learn all sorts of different skills, discipline and self-respect. They could see what the challenges were for themselves.

The Army is a great institution. Apart from anything it instils respect, discipline and self-confidence. I've always thought that youngsters should be made to do National Service. It would teach them so many life skills: how to be independent, how to do a job and do it well, how to look after themselves, how to listen to what's being said to them before they act on it. Too many kids these days sit around playing computer games, hanging out on street corners with nothing to do, experimenting with drugs, and disrespecting other people. I think that being in the Services helps you grow up. It teaches you to fend for yourself and to conduct yourself properly. I am sure a lot of kids would disagree but I've experienced it for myself and have seen how much recruits get out of the training, so I really do believe it to be true.

The teenagers came from Combined Cadet Forces schools or from local schools – basically anyone who was interested in the Army. We took them on residential weekly camps, teaching them anything from tackling obstacle courses, first aid, map-reading and orienteering to field craft, command tasks, weapons handling and drill. Whatever we did, we'd instruct them about the safety issues, making sure no one did anything stupid. I wanted to encourage them to be as enthusiastic as I had been as a kid so that they would join up when they were old enough.

Sometimes we started our expeditions from a base just outside Purbright barracks, taking the youngsters into a field for a night or two, demonstrating how to put up bivvy tents, tying one end of a ground sheet round a tree trunk and hooking the other two corners over forked sticks, and then camouflaging it with twigs and leaves. Once I took my youngest brother Stuart with us. The idea was that all the kids, about twenty of them, would stay in their bivvies overnight. That was the whole point of the exercise. If they hadn't erected them properly, it would be a long, uncomfortable and possibly wet, night. But when we got up in the morning, some of the kids were in the hut we used as an HQ. Scared of being out in the dark, listening to the strange noises, they had crept back into the hut while the rest of us were sleeping. There were only five of them but one was Stuart, curled up in his sleeping bag. My own brother! The shame!

It was such a good period in my life. I had bought myself my first home so I didn't live in barracks. It was a semi-detached three-bedroom house in the bottom corner of an estate in Sevenoaks, not far from Hildenborough and close to Dave and the track. I didn't mind commuting to the AYT base in Mill Hill at all. If anything, it gave me a sense of freedom. As the year went by, I had to devote myself more and more to my training so I eventually moved into recruitment, working in central London. I enjoyed going into colleges and universities, talking about what the Army offered. Remembering my own experience, I found that explaining about Army life to the students was very rewarding. Telling them that there are over 144 jobs in the Army, only four or five of which are closed to women, opened many eyes to possibilities that the girls had probably never considered before. Talking to them about my own career showed how joining up had given me opportunities that I wouldn't have had otherwise. I had been able to choose the career that was ideal for me. I had never been discriminated against personally, either because of my colour or because of my sex. I had made plenty of friends and felt that I had benefited as a person from living within that environment.

As well as my army duties and my commitment to civilian athletics, I was heavily involved with army athletics too. Between 1989 and 1995 I had been Army or Inter-Services champion over the 200, 400, 800, 1500 and 3000 metres and been awarded Army Track Athlete of the Year for many of those years. Yet I had gradually come to realise that the structure of the athletics side of things left something to be desired. Among other established athletes on the team, my friends Jackie, Sue, Michelle, Steph, Dobo and I all felt that we didn't get the same support as was given to rugby and boxing. Yet we were always called upon to enter the Inter-Services or Combined Services Championships. The separate units would get a telephone call before the Championships and be expected to produce a team. That was never easy. Because I had been so involved in civilian athletics, I had seen that things could be organised more effectively and felt we could learn from that. We all felt that the way things were run wasn't conducive to giving good performances at the Championships, yet the Athletics Board always wanted us to win. In the end, we stood our ground. We insisted on a performance course for the athletes at Aldershot. So for a couple of weeks before the Championships they could train every day and concentrate 100 per cent on the events to come. Being given some quality time to train was extremely beneficial to all of them.

Now my commitment to being a PTI was over, the Army was very flexible about giving me time off to prepare for the major championships. The good thing about both the AYT and being involved with recruiting was that I had enough time to get on with my training with Dave. Our sights were firmly set on Atlanta and our preparations had to be as thorough and as rigorous as possible. We knew the conditions were going to be hot and humid, unlike anywhere I had run before, so towards the end of 1995, we had gone to a training camp in Tallahassee, staying in the local university. It was an ideal opportunity to experience jet lag and the climate.

Back in the UK, I lost two months of training thanks to another operation in November. My stomach pains had come back and were giving me a lot of trouble after every training session. I felt as though my insides were ripping apart, then, about forty minutes later, the agony would go away. It was decided that investigative surgery should be carried out again. This time I saw the consultant, Michael Dooley, at Northwick Park Hospital in Middlesex. He discovered that more cysts had grown back in my ovaries. For about six months, his treatment did relieve the pain after training but then it began to return. It was very frustrating for me that we couldn't find a permanent solution. I was prescribed hormone patches and various tablets but whatever I took only worked for a limited time. I began to recognise that I would have to put up with the stomach pains as part of my racing life and learn to deal with them by relying on regular medical help.

However, by 1996, I was ready. Dave and I went to South Africa for warm-weather training. We stayed in a farmhouse in Stellenbosch, one of the most beautiful places in the world. Blue, blue sky, vineyards stretching almost as far as the eye can see, interrupted by grand old homesteads, with blue-grey mountains rising up in the distance. After a frustrating end to 1995, when I had lost those two months of training to ill health, I needed some warm weather to lift my spirits and make outdoor training possible, and some time in which I could motivate myself again. We worked hard every day. I'd run in the morning, have breakfast, then rest. Later in the day I'd do a further session on the track and then run, or do a weights session in the evening. We had one strategic rest day a week.

I was also taking part in a BBC documentary called *Olympic Diaries* that followed the preparation of various sportsmen and women in the year leading up to the Atlanta Games. Apart from myself, there was the coxless pair crew of Steve Redgrave and Matthew Pinsent, sailor Shirley Robertson, young gymnast Annika Reeder, hurdler Tony Jarrett and Karen Dixon, a three-day event rider. The idea was that we were to video our training programmes, voicing our everyday hopes and fears as the Games drew closer. In South Africa, I wasn't at my most positive. I looked miserable and talked about all the negative thoughts I was having and the need to motivate myself if I was to fulfil my dream.

Just as I got back into training, I pulled a hamstring while running, putting my progress in jeopardy again. Had I rushed things too soon? Everything seemed to be going wrong. It looked as if I might lose another four weeks to injury. Normally a positive, upbeat sort of person, I confided to camera, 'I'm feeling very negative and being a moody cow. But nobody knows what I'm going through. I have so many thoughts going through my head. Is it worth it? Can I carry on doing what I'm doing? I know at the bottom of my heart that I want to. I want to do it for everybody that's supported me and for myself.'

Fortunately the injury wasn't as bad as we'd feared at first. Benita van Zijl – later Benita DeWitt after we celebrated her divorce – a very good local physiotherapist helped to sort the problem. She worked with me every single day, helping me get back to form so that I was eventually able to race locally. Comfortably winning a 1500-metre race in Port Elizabeth helped lift my spirits.

When we returned to the UK, Dave and I travelled to Aberdeen to consult Professor Ron Maughan, an expert at the university, for advice on training in hot and humid conditions. He arranged for me to go to Brighton University where the Department of Environmental Physiology had an acclimatisation chamber. The idea was for us to play around with the conditions inside it, altering the heat and humidity to see what effects it had on my performance. We weighed ourselves before entering the chamber. I took in two litres of water that I drank while I used the exercise bike. Dave took in nothing with him. The temperature was raised to 38°C and the humidity increased. The sweat was pouring off both of us, but particularly me as I biked away furiously. When we emerged almost an hour later, Dave had lost two kilos in weight, whereas I weighed practically the same as I had when I'd gone in because I took so much water on board. I felt extremely dizzy though. It certainly showed us the dehydrating effect of heat and humidity, as well as how careful we would have to be in those conditions. Dehydration impairs performance. I'm very bad at remembering to drink enough so am always have to be reminded by other people. It also proved to us the importance of rehydration drinks. It's vital to replace those essential minerals and salts. We were able to return for further sessions five or six times during the year so we could gauge how much better I was coping.

My race agent Andy Norman had arranged for me to run my first grand prix of the season in Atlanta at a meet on 18 May that was marking the opening of the Olympic Stadium. It was a disaster. I was up against American athletes, all of whom were already perfectly acclimatised, and Maria Mutola who had already set two world records in the indoor 1000 metres that season. The calibre of the competition was extremely high. It was an important test for me but I was scared. Dave was encouraging me all the way but when the race came I just wasn't ready. To race successfully, I need to feel that

I'm a cut above the rest but that month, although my times were good in training, I didn't feel good in myself. I was still having a lot of ups and downs. One minute, I'd be so focused that I felt positive and confident. The next, I'd be feeling vulnerable, thinking that I needed to do better, questioning why I didn't feel right.

When it came to the race, without having eased down for it, my legs were still heavy from training. I couldn't get to the front of the pack. Maria Mutola came second but I came way back in seventh place. I should never have run in it. I was devastated. My morale was stretched to breaking point. I had never come that far down in a race. What was happening to me? I could feel my medal chances slipping away. I knew that I had to focus myself utterly on the Olympics if I was to have a hope of being placed in the first three in my races. People could motivate me, help restore my belief in myself, give me confidence and hope, comfort and support me but, at the end of the day, I was the one on the track. I was the one who had to reach and maintain the right frame of mind.

Things began to improve once I was back in the UK. Two weeks later I was running in the European Cup. I had come second in 1994 and won in 1995, beating Gabriela Szabo from Romania. This year there was a Russian runner, Svetlana Masterkova, in the race. Andy warned me to watch out for her because she had made a name for herself some years earlier although she hadn't been on the racing scene recently. I soon discovered she was still a real force to be reckoned with as she powered down the track to take the 800 metres title. I couldn't catch her and came in second.

I won both the 800 and the 1500 metres at the AAA Championships in June, something that no runner had done before, or indeed since. I then went on to win the Inter-Services Championships again over 200 metres, 400 metres and 1500 metres, getting a new personal best in the 200 and 400 metres. My biggest show of form was when I came second to the Irish runner Sonia O'Sullivan at the Bislett Games in Oslo, achieving a personal best in the 1500 metres with a time of 4:01.13. I was running well and felt in great shape.

During this season I took on Barry Nevill as my manager. I needed someone to handle the increasing demands on my time. He handled various sporting personalities, including Teddy Sheringham, and seemed ideal. Within a short time, he had negotiated a great deal with Nike to sponsor me. By this time I was feeling good, I was hitting and even bettering my targets in training and running brilliantly. It was time for the Olympics. The only problem was my stomach. I was still racked with pain after finishing every race and many of my training sessions. The only solution I'd found was one that I have had to resort to until very recently in racing: immediately I reached the mixed zone, the area off the track where the press are waiting to interview athletes, I'd be whipped off by the medics to have muscle relaxant or painkilling injections that worked quickly to ease the intense spasm in my stomach.

Prior to the Olympics, I returned to Tallahassee with the rest of the British team for acclimatisation and for my final training. It all went superbly. At last I had the self-confidence I needed if I was going to have a good chance at winning. On the flight over, I noticed a bruise on my left shin which was still there and slightly painful when I went jogging the next day. I went to Malcolm Brown, the doctor for the British team, to see if he could find the cause of the continuing discomfort. After carrying out a few shin tests, he thought we should go to the hospital for a bone scan. The scan revealed a bright white hot spot over the tibia in my left leg, identifying a possible fracture.

'Have you fallen or banged your leg recently?' asked the consultant.

'No. My last session in Tonbridge went perfectly.' I remembered clearly. 'I just noticed something when I was on the plane flying here.'

'Well, I'm afraid it looks as if you've got a stress fracture.'

No way. This couldn't be happening. 'I can't have,' I protested. 'It's impossible. I'm running in a couple of weeks.'

'You need to think very carefully about what you want to do,' he advised. 'You're the athlete and you're the one who makes the decisions. We're here to support whatever decision you make, but I have to say that my advice would be for you not to run.'

'Not run?' I couldn't believe my ears. I seemed to have ridden such a rollercoaster through the year to get here. They couldn't take my chance away now. 'I have to run. I want to run. I might not ever get to the Olympics again. This may be my one and only chance.'

'Well, as I said, it's your decision,' he repeated. 'We can work out a way of getting rid of the pain but as you run more intensively, the greater it will become and the more painkillers you'll need.'

'I have to run,' I insisted. 'We have to find a way to get over it.' I understood the risks involved. I knew that I might fracture my leg if

I fell or got bumped or kicked. 'As long as you're saying that it's my decision and you will support any decision I make, I want to run.' My mind was made up.

The doctors agreed to support me and to be certain that news of my injury didn't leak to the press. How I got the fracture I still can't be sure but it is possible that it was down to my footwear. I had changed sponsors halfway through the season after I had been offered my amazing four-year deal from Nike. I was so chuffed that the biggest sporting brand wanted to support me that I went for it. Instead of gradually changing over my running shoes so that my body had time to adjust to the new footwear, I just swapped my previous trainers for my new ones. Now I understand more about the intricacies of footwear and how careful one has to be, breaking in a new pair of shoes. My body doesn't adjust to new footwear at all well because of the way I run. I should have been much more careful, but at that stage I didn't know much about injury prevention.

We had two weeks of preparation ahead of us before the Games – the two most vital weeks there are. That's when you step right up to the plate: when an athlete has to keep sharp and everything has to be ready. Everything turns around in that crucial fortnight as you get your head straight and your confidence at its peak. My plans had to change at the last minute. I tried to jog but my leg was too painful. The medical team advised me and Dave that I should use it as little as possible, saving it for the Games themselves, so I had no alternative but to use the gym, go on the bike and exercise in the pool. One day, the press were being shown round the facilities and saw me in the pool. We didn't expect them to catch on that there was anything wrong but, because they never saw me on the track, they put two and two together and word went round that something was up. That was hard for me to deal with but I had to get over it and keep training as single-mindedly as I could.

Finally we left the holding camp and moved to the Olympic village in Atlanta. What a city! It was an enormous, characterless concrete jungle. It hosted the worst Olympics out of the three that I have been to. Elsewhere, I have experienced the Olympic spirit that everyone talks about and have felt that I am at the greatest show on earth. But it wasn't like that in Atlanta. The accommodation in the Olympic village was in tall high-rise blocks, rather like a university campus, with the British Olympic team being in the one furthest from the gate. There were a lot of complaints that we were miles from the dining hall so it took ages to get there and back, even in the little trams that circulated round the village. When a bomb exploded in Centennial Olympic Park on 27 July, killing two bystanders and injuring about one hundred people, the atmosphere understandably deteriorated. It was a terrible thing to happen. Of course we were all very aware of it and not surprisingly became a little nervous about the security in the village.

I had been allocated a room with Tessa Sanderson, the 1984 Olympic javelin champion. She was competing in her fifth Olympics, mainly to raise money for a charity she supported. At the time, she had a job with the BBC and had to keep sneaking out to do her broadcasts at some God-awful hour because of the time difference between the States and the UK. She wanted to enjoy the Games as much as she could so we had a real laugh together. Some of the other athletes would come to our room and we'd play cards and pretend to flirt with Jamie Baulch and Darren Campbell. All this helped take my mind off having to compete with an injury.

Before the Games opened, team management got all the British athletics team together for a team talk. We were given an address by Malcolm Arnold, head of British Athletics, but we also wanted to create a more motivational mood. I kept turning to Colin Jackson, Sally Gunnell and Tessa, encouraging them to speak up and get some atmosphere going. Eventually they turned on me and said, 'If you're so keen, you say something.' As bold as anything, I stood up. My army background meant that I wasn't at all intimidated as I took over, encouraging all the others to give their best and never give up. I tried to keep it all on a positive note, saying I was there to do the best I possibly could. In the back of my head, I kept thinking of my own situation. It wasn't ideal but I had to tell them to be as positive as possible. In the end it dissolved into good-humoured banter with the others, making a really enjoyable team occasion.

The Olympics themselves went as expected as far as the British team was concerned. Denise Lewis excelled herself and took away a bronze in the Heptathlon, which was brilliant, but our medal count was low overall. For the entire time, I had to concentrate on overcoming my own problem. On the day of my first 800-metre heat, I prepared myself for the injection that Malcolm Brown had said he would give me in the site of the stress fracture to help numb the pain. In the warm-up area, there were Portakabins, one of which served as the medical centre. He injected me just before the race. It stung a little but I knew I wouldn't feel the pain when I ran so I ignored it.

Despite everything, I had remained confident and I got through to the semi-finals, making my mark by qualifying easily in first place. The next day, Malcolm repeated the procedure before the race. It was more painful this time but I wasn't going to give up now. Again it worked. I couldn't feel any pain when running and I won my place in the final, coming third to Maria Mutola and Ana Quirot.

Two days later my leg was really sore. I gritted my teeth and went for the injection, but this time it was agony. The needle hit the bone in my leg. I could feel it scratching along as Malcolm injected the anti-inflammatory. At that point, I broke down, sobbing uncontrollably. The stress fracture, the injections, the pain and the emotional strain were all too much, but I still had to run.

On the bus from the warm-up area to the stadium, I was trying to focus on the race, although it was hard after suffering the trauma of the injection. Once I was out on the track, I could hear the expectant murmur of the crowd, the cheers as they spotted their favourites. This was the Olympic final I had dreamed of for so long. The gun sounded and we were off. Masterkova shot to the front quickly, only to slow the race right down, running with Mutola and the Russian, Yelena Afanasyeva up there with her. I held my own round the first lap but found myself trapped just before the bell. I pulled back and moved to the outside, forced to run wide. At 200 metres I was neck and neck with Masterkova with Quirot and Mutola right behind me. As we came round the top bend, Masterkova, Quirot and I were battling it out, with Mutola right behind us. As we came down the last straight, I remember Masterkova looking over at the rest of us as if we were club runners, then streaking ahead to win. Ana Quirot came storming past me then, and just as I was a fraction from the line, Mutola put in a last-minute spurt and took third place. I didn't have that last bit of sharpness I needed to fight back so she just dipped past me, beating me by a tenth of a second. I had missed out on the bronze by a whisker. I remember Maria sitting on the track after the race with Ana bent over nearby with her hands on her hips. I was crouching down, with the realisation dawning on me that I had just missed out on a medal. Meanwhile Masterkova was off running the fastest lap of honour I have ever seen. Vrooooom. It was as if she was still racing. Usually on that triumphant lap, the winner goes mad for the first fifty metres and then they hit that brick wall and either can hardly walk, or end up jogging very slowly. But she didn't.

Given my stress fracture, the one thing I shouldn't have done at those Games was run in the 1500 metres as well. It put too many demands on my injured leg. I had come to the Games feeling that I should try for a medal in both races. Having come fourth in the 800, I couldn't give up the chance of being placed in the 1500. At that time, I didn't know whether I'd ever get to another Olympics so I wanted to give everything I could at Atlanta. At least I could go home without regrets, knowing I had tried.

Just as I had in the 800, I got through the heats and the semis into the final, coming second in the heat to Gabriela Szabo and taking the semi from the American Regina Jacobs. The injections and willpower carried me through. But by this time, every step was jarring my leg. I thought of nothing but winning. Blocking out the pain, I gave the final everything I'd got and took the lead from Masterkova after 300 metres. I wanted to try to disturb her rhythm and stop her controlling the race in the way she had the 800 metres. I pulled everyone else round in an incredibly fast time with Masterkova at my shoulder every step of the way. Probably if I had been more relaxed, I would have run differently and got myself into a better position. With a lap to go, I was still leading. But I had given too much too soon. With 250 metres left, they all stormed past me with Masterkova repeating her victory in the 800, and Szabo just behind her. I ended up jogging across the line last in eleventh place.

Dave had gone home after the 800 metres final so wasn't there when I was taken straight to the doctors and my leg put in plaster after the 1500 metres. I came home on crutches. I knew I'd come so close to a bronze but there's no getting away from the fact that a medal is a medal. If you enter a race with a chance of a medal, fourth is an awful place to come in a championship. It's so close and yet nowhere near.

For once, I wasn't able to go straight back to work. I went home to Sevenoaks to convalesce. However, I didn't stop training with Dave. Even when injured, I could always train. I just had a more limited number of resources. I could use the exercise bike because it didn't put any pressure on the injured leg but gave me a cardiovascular workout. I could still do weight training. One thing I did do while rehabilitating was to go to Bosnia as part of a PR event to start the Bosnian Marathon. I thought it would be a good thing to do to keep my mind off athletics for a while. I never got posted abroad when I was in the Army but going to Bosnia helped me appreciate what a lot of the soldiers do. I felt very lucky to be in my position. The energy over there was fantastic. I still wasn't able to run so I went around on a bike encouraging the competitors. I have a great picture of me with a Bosnian lady. Just before it was taken, she gestured that she had just skinned a rabbit and was carrying it in a pail, which she kindly moved away from me when I asked her to! It was a short trip but it did wonders to boost my morale.

Although things hadn't gone as I had hoped, I was far from abandoning my dream. What had happened made me much more determined. If I could come fourth with a stress fracture... As soon as that plaster was off, my mind was on the 1997 World Championships in Athens. I knew exactly what I was going to do. In 1997, I was going to come back flying.

# 13. BREAKING THE BRITISH RECORD

As I warmed up for the 1500 metres in the Sheffield Grand Prix in June 1997, I felt as if I was floating. It was a bizarre feeling, one that I've experienced perhaps only three times in my career. At the time, I didn't realise its significance. It was as though someone was picking me up off the ground and letting my legs do their work so smoothly. I looked over at the other runners, among them Sonia O'Sullivan and Suzy Hamilton. These were world-class athletes, many of them having won major championships. But as I watched them preparing for the race, I suddenly knew I was going to beat them all. I could feel it in my head and my body. I was going to break the British record. I knew it.

Andy had suggested that we get Yelena Nikolayeva, one of the Russian middle-distance runners, to pace me just as she had in other races. The British record that had stood for twelve years at 3:59.96 was held by the South African Zola Budd. Dave and I set the time: 64 seconds a lap, making a four-minute 1500-metre race.

I went off with the pacemaker leading the field, but the race was very erratic. I was aiming to run sub four minutes – a world-class time back then and a very hard thing to do although these days it's a time that's more consistently achieved. The first lap was run in

62.32 seconds, then went up to 68.29 for the second while the third came back down to 62.66. The pacemaker and I were well ahead of the rest when at 500 metres, I made my break, getting to the bell in about 2.59 minutes. I was watching the clock and knew that to set a new record, I would have to break 60 seconds for the last lap. I went for it. Going down the back straight it was really windy. I was alone, charging into the wind, pushing as hard as I could. The crowd was going wild and the commentator was getting more and more excited as he saw me going for the British record. As I went through with 200 metres to go, I was just up on the record and I was aware of all the cheers and screaming, encouraging me on. The commentator was going crazy. As I came off the top bend, I shouted to myself, 'Come on.' I wanted it so badly. I could see the clock and knew the last 100 metres had to be fast. I ran as hard as I knew how and crossed the line, my mouth wide open, at 3:58.07. I had broken the British and Commonwealth records. I went absolutely mad with delight.

Obviously winning all the major championships was my annual goal, but this had been one of my other targets that year. It was a major achievement for me. I felt like a superstar. As I ran my lap of honour to a massive ovation, the only person I saw was Benita my physiotherapist and friend from South Africa. My mum, dad, brothers and sister Penny were there too, with Jason and my manager, Barry. But I didn't see any of them. I just took in the atmosphere and enjoyed the fantastic feeling of achievement.

Breaking the British 1500 metres record was not the only reason that week was a momentous one for me. I also finally announced my retirement from the Army. At twenty-seven years old I had served in the forces for nearly ten years and it was time. I put the wheels in motion back in January when I had written a letter, with the help of Dave, to Lieutenant Colonel McCord, who was now Chief of Staff at Adjutant General Corps at Worthy Down.

> 8 January 1997
>
> Ma'am,
> Following my personal disappointment in relation to my results at the Olympic Games and the overall results of the British Athletics Team in Atlanta, I have carefully analysed the situation.

My individual events were dominated by a Russian, Svetlana Masterkova, who won both the 800 metres and the 1500 metres Olympic titles.

Masterkova – like the majority of Olympic Champions – carefully and ruthlessly prepared for Atlanta by isolating herself from everything except preparing to win at least one Olympic Gold Medal.

Both Masterkova (although she is Russian, she resides in Spain during the winter and spring) and Michael Johnson (an American who won the men's 200 metres and 400 metres) are both ultimate examples of this method of preparation.

I am positive with the right preparation both mentally and physically, I can beat Masterkova at this year's World Athletics Championships which will be held in Athens during August.

My wish is to go to South Africa at the beginning of February, returning in May. I would spend a period in Pretoria at altitude and then Stellenbosch (in the Cape) to finalise my preparations at sea level.

When I return from South Africa in May, I will immediately enter into a carefully structured competitive programme which coupled with training will lead me to win at Athens...

Unfortunately, we live in a world where success is the criterion and I believe I can win a Gold Medal in Athens, but this will entail me embarking on programme I have outlined.

I would be grateful if the Army would consider my needs in my aim to become the World's number one middle-distance runner.

I am Ma'am
Sgt K Holmes
WO804968

To my delight she had agreed, so I had been able to join Andy Norman, Fatima Whitbread, world javelin champion and a few other athletes who were going to Pretoria, South Africa, to compete in the ABSA series. One of the races was in Potchefstroom, a small university town south-west of Johannesburg, so I went to race there, staying at the Elgro Hotel in Wolmarans Street. After a couple of days, I moved out to stay briefly with Jean and Alta Verster, who became great friends then and have remained so ever since. Jean had been a well-established South African athlete himself, his chances of international success crippled by the South African government's apartheid policies, as were the chances of so many of his country's sportsmen in those days.

He remembers being a white guy in an otherwise mainly black training group. There was no colour distinction as far as they were concerned. Yet, during the 1980s, politicians in the rest of the world decided that sport would be one of the ways of putting pressure on South Africa to remove its apartheid policies. Although these runners had no problems with anybody, they effectively ended up being the ones who were discriminated against no matter whether they were black or white. All they wanted to do was run. There were extremely talented athletes such as Johan Fourie, who still holds the South African record for the Mile and would have challenged Seb Coe and Steve Ovett in those days, Matthew Temane, the former world-record holder for the Half Marathon, and Evette de Klerk, who is still the national record holder for 100 metres and 200 metres, but none of them could compete anywhere outside their own country. They had to make do with the many meetings held in South Africa where they achieved times without the normal help of quality pacemakers.

The only person who found a loophole was Zola Budd. Her grandfather had been born in Britain. That was enough to make her eligible for citizenship, even though neither she nor her parents had set foot on British soil. Although there were a lot of protestors who objected to her running for Britain, she made it to the 1984 Los Angeles Olympics where she ran in the controversial race against Mary Decker, the American favourite, who fell and was carried sobbing from the track. Budd managed to continue the race, to the boos of the crowd who blamed her for tripping Decker. She finished seventh. She was an amazing young runner who went on to establish numerous British records as well as winning two World Cross-Country titles, but she was always dogged by controversy. She returned to her home country in 1988.

In 1992, two years after Nelson Mandela's release from prison, South African sportsmen and women were at last allowed to compete outside their country in time for the Barcelona Olympics. But by then Jean had retired from the scene. Keen to remain involved with athletics, he began to promote Potchefstroom (Potch) as a training base for athletes from all over the world. There are fantastic training facilities there including a good grass track for running without impact, a good hard track, great gyms and really nice runs for a middle-distance runner. The altitude isn't too high and the weather is wonderful during the British winter. The town has a busy centre but is generally a sleepy, quite old-fashioned residential place with wide, quiet streets that feel very African to me. It wasn't long before I felt completely at home there.

To begin with, I was one of the only British athletes training in Potch until I was joined by Tony Whiteman, Marcus Harrop, Glen Stewart and a few other runners. I knew a couple of these guys from racing over the years so I was able to run with them. For three months, I got my head down and trained hard until I was extremely fit. Dave sent me weekly training schedules from the UK but I added on extra weights, circuits and runs because I wanted to get so strong. I was determined that 1997 would be my year.

June was the month that everything started falling into place. Dave and I went to Barcelona where we got in some fantastic training. I was hitting and exceeding his targets and I felt strong and fit. I was ready for anything. The season began amazingly well as I came storming out to win everything I entered. Prior to breaking the British and Commonwealth records at Sheffield, I had a remarkable number of wins. In particular, on 15 June, I ran the 1,000 metres at a small meeting in Leeds, setting new British and Commonwealth records of 2:32.55 despite the terrible cold and windy weather. I then went on to win the European Cup in Munich as well as winning at the Bislett Games in Stockholm, where I defeated Ana Quirot for the first time. My form was amazing. I also went on to win the 800 metres at the British Championships.

It was during this summer that I finally decided to make the break with the Army. I knew that any career in athletics was a short one and I wanted to dedicate myself to achieving my dream of winning an Olympic gold. I wanted to be the best. Although the Army had been extremely accommodating in allowing me to change my role within it so that I could meet the demands of civilian racing, I was struggling to do both as well as I could. I had reached a point where one of them had to give, and it wasn't going to be my athletics. What finally made me decide was a stupid little incident – the straw that broke the camel's back.

For ages I had been bugging my sponsors Nike to make a new strip for the Army athletics team. They eventually had generously agreed to provide everything – tracksuits, sports kit, the lot – for free. Naturally, they expected some sort of exposure in return so I had been hurrying them to provide the kit in time for a civilian meet held at Loughborough University in which the Army was competing. I knew that Nike would be happy about the publicity generated by us wearing the kit there. Jackie and I got the kit and were so excited about it. The old kit was just that. Old. It had been worn time and time again by so many people. Items were missing and what was there was well past its best. The new kit was in the army colours, red with a white panel, the army logo and a Nike swoosh. It looked the business. But as we started giving it out, Major Lyons, the officer in charge of the Army Athletics Control Board (AACB) stopped us. He was adamant that we should save it all for the Inter-Services Championships a few weeks later. I refused, explaining the situation with Nike. Major Lyons still wouldn't alter his position. He didn't seem to understand the way civilian life worked. It hadn't been my job to get the new kit but I had thought I'd use the fact that I had a sponsor behind me. The AACB hadn't had to pay a penny. The least we could do was wear it where it would be seen. We had a big row over it. That was it. I went over to Lieutenant Colonel McCord. 'Ma'am,' I said. 'I'm sorry but I think it's time for me to leave the Army.' I was losing respect for rank and couldn't deal with someone who didn't seem to understand the effort I had put in and how important giving back is.

She didn't want me to go but understood that I couldn't be disciplined in that way any more. I had stepped over the line between being a PTI in the Army and being a civilian athlete. Leaving the army wasn't an enormous risk for me to take. I was hardly jumping into the unknown after all. Winning the races that I had, meant that I was already in the middle of my second career. I knew exactly what I was doing although I was sad to have to make the decision.

On that occasion, all the girls and a few of the guys eventually wore the Nike kit at Loughborough anyway. But my mind was made up at last. After 9 years and 257 days precisely, I was out of there. On my final report, Lieutenant Colonel McCord gave her assessment of my military conduct as 'exemplary'. I couldn't have asked for a better parting gift.

I was in the best shape of my life. I had been unbeaten all year and I felt completely geared up for the 1500 metre World Championships in Athens. Shortly before we were due to leave, Dave and I were having a training session on Tonbridge track just before a small athletics meet was to be held there. I preferred to be on my own when I trained, to be somewhere without people watching. I concentrate better when there's no one around. Some kids were already there and asking for autographs. I didn't want to be unpleasant to them but I did want to focus on the session; I asked Dave if we could cut it down so that I ran for less time than was originally planned but faster. Then we would be finished before too many people had arrived. I finished off with a 200-metre sprint. I was absolutely flying. Suddenly I felt a slight pull in the back of my left heel. Nothing major. I stopped running. Dave was staring at his watch in disbelief. 'No way.'

'What? What? What?' I was dying to know the time.

'You have just run 00:23.7.'

Because I was so fit and was pushing myself that little bit harder so I could get off the track sooner, I had run an incredibly fast time. I went to get some ice to put on the heel before I went home. The next day, I did an hour's run and the heel didn't seem so bad. It wasn't until the next day that we really knew it was a problem. Dave had suggested that I did the next training session with Allen and Andy Graffin, twin brothers he knew who came from Tonbridge. They were both up-and-coming middle-distance runners. I wasn't sure. I wasn't used to training with other people. Until then I had mainly trained on my own, a good thing for building up strength and character. Even when I was younger, I'd preferred it.

Years ago Mum had followed me running on her bike but she fell off in the middle of the road. I was so annoyed that she'd messed up my run that I didn't even ask her how she was. The training partner who had cut it for me was Harley, my mother's dog, who'd come with me around Hildenborough whenever I was at home. He'd come on my forty-minute runs and had absolutely loved it at the same time as getting really fit. I don't have much patience during training and get so frustrated if it gets mucked up. I remember effing and blinding one day when Harley was lagging behind me and having to drag him around the run. It was only afterwards that we discovered he had arthritis in his hips and his running days were over. He still remembers them though. Even though he is twelve now, every time he sees me put on my trainers, his tail starts to wag and you can tell he thinks he's about to go running.

However, it can be very hard trying to achieve your targets alone, and one of the last sessions Dave and I had planned before Athens was particularly tough – 800-metre repetitions. Having the Graffins there made the reps a bit easier for me. One of them would run beside me while the other one paced me. I discovered the great thing about training this way is that although I'm still doing the running, I'm more relaxed because I'm not thinking about the clock all the time and fighting against it. Dave would tell them the pace at which I had to run the repetitions and it was up to them to get me there. The first repetition went great, 2:03 minutes, the second the same, 2:03. It was going amazingly well when, on my way to an even faster time, I had to pull up on the third repetition. My heel was flaring up again.

We only had a couple of weeks before we were due to leave for Athens, so we went immediately to Thurrock to see my physio, Kevin Lidlow. He did everything he could but my ankle kept on nagging me during my training. One minute it would hurt, the next the pain had gone. A telephone call to Sue Barrett, the manager of Linford Christie's management group Nuff Respect, put us on to Dr Hans Muller Wolfhart, a renowned specialist in sports injuries in Munich. I didn't want to risk anything major happening to my leg, so I went to see him on my own. By this time my Achilles tendon had become so stressed he gave me some injections in my calf to relieve it. After that I was in agony, as if my leg was on fire, leaving on crutches. I remember calling Mum at 2 a.m., unable to sleep, crying with pain, not knowing what to do. I was alone in a tiny room at an Institute of sport, unable to speak German and petrified something was very wrong with my leg. She was the great support that she's always been, reassuring me and wishing she could be there with me. She'd had so many telephone calls from me in floods of tears when things had gone wrong. She hated me suffering from these injuries, knowing that there was nothing she could do about it. Talking to her calmed me down and restored my confidence that I would be all right by the time of the race.

The next morning, I woke after five hours sleep to find the pain had completely disappeared. I got on the plane to Athens and arrived at the Championships feeling positive. Everything had gone wrong in Atlanta. That couldn't happen to me again. Could it? I was in the first heat on the first morning of the Championships. I woke up in the hotel at 5 a.m., in time for breakfast and to prepare for the race. I was incredibly tired, because my flight had been delayed the day before and had only got in at one or two in the morning. I kept repeating to myself that I was five seconds faster than anyone else in the world. I was favourite to win. I was going to do it. During my warm-up, my calf felt tight so I asked for a massage from one of the physios at the track to release it. After that, I did my drills and everything seemed to be fine.

As the race set off, I was aware that I was half trying to protect my leg so that I would be ready for the semi-finals. If there was a problem, I didn't want to aggravate it too much. The heat should have been a jog for me but I was running erratically as I worried about my calf, wondering whether I would be able to deal with it before my next race. We'd been round two laps and were going down the back straight, round the top bend, when suddenly I felt the most excruciating pain in my left leg. It was as if a golf ball was exploding out of it. It was so unexpected that I shot up into the air in shock. It was impossible to carry on running. I had to hobble off to the side of the track where I crouched down, holding my leg. I was devastated. I was out of the race, my World Championship goal in tatters.

Normally a stretcher or a medic should have come for me immediately. Perhaps it was because it was the first day and they hadn't organised things properly but nothing came. The British medics weren't allowed to run on so I had to hobble down the home straight, absolutely devastated. I couldn't believe that this could have happened after what had occurred in Atlanta the year before. As I came off the track, I was taken straight down to the medical centre as I cried on Julie Asgill's, one of the team officials, shoulder. There was nothing anyone could do except give me some pain relief.

Back at the hotel, I saw some of the British team physios, who very quickly realised that something major was wrong. They referred me immediately to Roland Bidert, a sports injury specialist in Zurich. I was flown out later that day. After putting me through various scans, he came to see me.

'It's good news and bad news,' he announced. 'The good news is that you haven't ruptured your Achilles tendon; you've only torn it. However you have ruptured your calf.' He showed me the MRI scans, pointing out where the muscle was torn from side to side.

The upshot was that I had to remain in Zurich for the duration of the Championships while I received treatment. Kevin Lidlow kindly flew out to find out what kind of work was recommended for my leg so that we could continue with it when I eventually got home. One of the worst moments while I was there was when I watched TV to see Carla Sacramento romp home to victory ahead of Regina Jacobs in the 1500 metres in Athens. I was so gutted I wasn't there and although I like Carla enormously and was pleased to see her victory, I admit I was envious that she had won the medal that I had so badly wanted.

After Athens, one of the golden league races (a series of elite athletics meets) was held in Zurich. The doctor and masseur of the meet took me down to the stadium to watch. I could get around unsteadily with the help of crutches. Being there gave me goose-bumps. What the Zurich stadium lacks in size, it more than makes up for in excitement. It's one of the best meets for atmosphere and is always absolutely packed. The crowd hang over the sides of the stands, banging their support on the promotional boards. It was the first time I had ever been purely a spectator at my own sport and I found the experience completely thrilling. There was a real buzz with all the newly crowned world champions competing with one another again. Maria won the 800 metres in Zurich for the fourth time in a row. Nobody could have predicted that she would go on to win that same race eleven times in a row.

When I got home, my leg was in plaster and I was unable to do much, although I did my best to stay as fit as I could. Claire, an old army friend whom I had first met in Guildford, invited me to go on holiday with her and two of her friends. At the time, I had no idea when, or indeed whether, my leg was going to get back to normal. My year had turned catastrophically on its head. I was desperate to get away from everything so gratefully accepted. We stayed on a caravan site somewhere by the sea. I don't remember much about the holiday itself except for one thing. I was sitting on the floor of the caravan one morning, doing my sit-ups, when the door burst open. The granddad of one of the girls ran in, saying, 'Turn on the news. Turn on the news.' He sounded as if something terrible had happened, so we switched on to hear that Princess Diana had died in a car crash in Paris. I can remember the moment so clearly. We were all distraught, sitting watching the footage in shock. Like the rest of the world we couldn't believe what had happened. Despite all her problems, Princess Diana was an amazing woman who really was the people's princess. Everybody loved her. Her death was a terrible thing that shook us all. I thought that this was a year that had started with so much promise and had ended in differing degrees of disaster. How would it be possible to pull back from it?

# 14. INJURY TIME

The rehabilitation of my leg went badly. So much scar tissue had formed round my Achilles tendon that Kevin Lidlow recommended an operation to remove it. Given an epidural in my spine to numb my leg, I was awake throughout the entire procedure, able to see only too clearly when the surgeon dangled bits of fatty white scar tissue in front of my eyes, explaining what it was that they'd removed and why. I appreciated their informing me of what was going on but it was gross – not a sight that I enjoyed much. Apparently the surgeon needed me to be awake in case he found any additional tears and they needed instant permission from me to do any other major surgery.

A tourniquet was put around my leg to prevent the blood flowing to the area while they sewed everything back up. As the epidural wore off, the surgeon was desperately stitching away as quickly as he could because, gradually, the sensation was returning and with it came the most terrible pain. At last he finished and they untied the tourniquet. The pain was excruciating as the blood flowed down into my leg, bringing it back to life. That was an experience I never want to repeat.

Afterwards, I continued working with Kevin and Dave, trying to get my leg functioning properly and to get myself back to some level of fitness. I maintained fitness by doing cardiovascular work in the gym and aqua-jogging in the pool. But progress was slow.

Without the Army and without the track, I had to have something else to do. I can't bear sitting doing nothing. My mind is always busy working overtime so whenever I was injured I'd spend hours thinking about what I could do instead of athletics. As a result, in 1996, I had decided to set up my own company, Dynamic Energy, so that I could run my own events. I'd been lying in bed with my leg in plaster after the Olympics when I dreamed up my first concept. I wanted to work out a way of relating the potted sports we did in the Army to children in schools, putting together a competition that would be fun but active and not the normal run-of-the-mill school routine. Children seemed to pay attention to me, probably because I'd made a name for myself especially in my home town. Writing all my ideas down and finding a picture of a cartoon character jumping up and down on a trampoline that I used as my logo, I came up with the idea of the Kelly Holmes School Challenge. My plan was to involve 25 different Kent schools, including my own old school, Hugh Christie in Tonbridge. I would hold heats at all of them in which the kids would have to complete ten different tasks, scoring points in each one. The ten best-scoring schools would all come to a grand final.

I'd turn up at the schools in a Volvo estate, loaned to me by a local Hildenborough garage that had agreed to sponsor the project. It would be loaded down with all the equipment that my dad and granddad had helped me collect – tyres and planks painted in bright colours kids would like – bright yellow, green, red and blue – which were used as part of a mini assault course. As I was funding the challenge myself, I had to use whatever odds and ends I could lay my hands on and be as inventive as possible. There was a supermarket shopping trolley for the 'Trolley Push', in which someone would be pushed down to one end of the hall where there were apples in water and sweets buried in flour. After they'd struggled to take a bite out of the apple, they had to get a sweet with their teeth – no hands allowed. They got into a fantastic mess and loved every minute. There were basketballs for 'Basketball Dribble', hockey sticks, footballs, a mixture of sports clothing and my army gas mask for a fancy dress game. Once I'd unpacked, I'd brief the teachers and helpers who were going to be working with me and we'd get the whole thing going. My mum and brothers always remind me how cold they were standing out in a playground with their feet like ice blocks as they helped with the setting up and the scoring.

At Christmas, it was time for the final. It turned into a real family affair. Mum had various cleaning jobs at the time so I employed her as company secretary to take charge of the administrative side of things. We set up an office in the front room of her house in Hildenborough. She was living on her own with Penny by this time so our relationship was right back on track, often having a real laugh together as well as the rows if I didn't think she was working hard enough! After all the times she had supported me, I was able to give her a bit of support back – even when we were mistaken for sisters! She loved that. There was also a lady called Maxine who worked for me. I managed to con my brothers and their girlfriends into helping me run some of the events while my granddad was brilliant on more practical matters, helping make the more complicated props. Some of my local friends came along to help out too. I hired the Angel Leisure Centre in Tonbridge, where I had done my weight training with Dave when I was at home, and we prepared it for the arrival of the ten winning teams from the twenty-five schools we'd visited. We had huge balloons all over the place so that it looked like a Christmas party.

The Santa's Grotto was squashed into a store cupboard. It was decked out with an old army camouflage net while outside there was a little picket fence made by Granddad with the outside covered in fake snow. My manager, Barry, made a great Father Christmas. The kids went inside for a musical challenge. I'd made a tape of songs in the charts that they would all know. When the music stopped, there would be a question about the singer or the song. If they got it wrong, Barry would spray them with silly string and fake snow. They loved it.

Granddad made a huge snowman out of board. It was about six feet tall and very fat with holes down his front that got bigger the lower they were. We painted him all white, gave him a black hat and an orange wooden nose that looked like a carrot. This was the 'Throwing Challenge'. The idea was to throw as many tennis balls as possible through the holes, scoring the highest number of points for each throw: the smaller the hole the more points the children got. Santa's sleigh was Granddad's masterpiece. Using bits and pieces from his work as a painter and decorator, he made a huge sledge complete with runners, high sides and with a seat inside. The clever thing was that he made it with pegs and string so it could easily be dismantled. I gift-wrapped cardboard boxes so they looked like huge presents. What the children had to do was take the whole thing to bits, presents, runners and all, and run with one piece at a time to the top of the sports hall and put it all together again as fast as they could, just like the cannon run at the Earl's Court Military Tattoo.

There were ten different stations to complete that were either command tasks or tasks that each involved some sporting element such as skills, balance, co-ordination, endurance or speed. My sponsor, Nike, provided T-shirts for the judges as well as caps, T-shirts, key rings, bags and stickers for the kids' prizes; another company from Scotland provided the drinks; the local council gave me a small amount of funding for the final that I used to pay the DJ and to give something to the helpers; various manufacturers gave me freebies for the kids' prizes; Timson's engravers gave us trophies and medals for the winners. I was in charge of making sure everything ran on time, keeping the scoreboard up to date and running around shouting encouragement and checking no one was cheating. The whole project took off really well. The days were great successes with the children and I kept the school challenge going for three years.

The other thing I did under Dynamic Energy was to set up a series of athletics and cross-country performance days at Tonbridge School and at Knole Park near Sevenoaks, the scene of my Sunday runs and dreaded hill training with Dave. I charged about a fiver to the participants but they'd get lunch, drinks and a weekend of athletics or cross-country, depending on the time of the year.

Although I kept myself busy setting up and carrying out these projects, I was always itching to get back on the track and the winter of 1997 was no exception. I also felt I needed some extra comfort so decided to get a dog. I had always wanted one but it was never the right time. I now have two but because I'm always travelling so much they live with my dad in Hildenborough. I got my first one from the RSPCA near Maidstone, Kent. She is a cross between an Alsatian and a Lurcher. She was totally different from what I had hoped to find – I wanted a big, butch, stocky boy-dog with short ginger hair, but ended up with a skinny, small, grey/black/tan cross named Shelly. I felt so sorry for her that I kept going back to see her every day until I finally decided to take her home. I renamed her Whitney after Whitney Houston. Three years later, I got my second dog from a rescue home – God knows what type he is. But his brindle colouring makes him look like a scruffy stocky bear and that's why I named him Barney. What I like most about dogs is that they give you unconditional love and never answer back. What bliss!

My leg seemed to be taking a terribly long time to heal and I often felt Kevin and I were getting nowhere. I wanted to run again so badly but by the end of the year, it was still out of the question. At some stage during my recuperation I had a conversation with Paula Radcliffe, whom I'd known from athletics for years. We'd often competed at the same meets and occasionally ran together in 1500-metre races. She told me about Gerard Hartmann, a physiotherapist she visited in Limerick, southern Ireland. She absolutely swore by him, the man with magic hands. He had been seven times Irish triathlon champion between 1984 and 1991 before he trained as a physio. He specialised in treating sports injuries, with overseas clients flying in to see him from all over the world.

So it was that in May 1998, I made my trip to Limerick, in the hope that Gerard would be able to help speed up my recovery. When I arrived, the weather matched my mood: grey with storms threatening. I felt awkward going to see Gerard because up to this point in my career, I had remained loyal to everyone who had contributed something to my success so far. I didn't want to leave Kevin but I had to try a new approach to my injury. Sometimes when you've tried every way you know how to solve a problem, it's time to hand it on to someone who can look at it with a fresh eye and tackle it from a new angle. Kevin and I agreed that he had tried everything he could. I had to recover if I was going to be fit enough to compete in the 1998 Commonwealth Games that were due to take place in Kuala Lumpur in September. It was time to try a new approach.

Gerard and I hit it off right away. He's got a strong Irish accent and a good sense of humour so we were always joking together. As a physio, he has a reputation for being one of the toughest in terms of his methods of treatment. I couldn't begin to count the number of times I cried on his bed and tried to pull myself off it in an attempt to crawl to the door and escape. It was all a bit of a roller-coaster ride: joking one minute, tears the next. But he got stuck straight into the problem. By that time, I could only manage a hobbling kind of run. My foot seemed to be locked in one position that made it virtually impossible to use. Gerard came on a run one day with two male international athletes who were also there to receive treatment. He was amazed that I was still trying to run on my leg at all. He got going with ankle mobilisation, friction on the tendons, using his elbows to massage my calves which were very, very painful. The treatment was necessary but it was hell to go through.

During the six weeks I stayed there, he got me running again. Really running. It was extraordinary. Dave came over to see me because Gerard had effectively taken over my training while he was treating me. They worked together on a training programme to suit the circumstances, involving a gradual increase in both the volume and intensity of repetitions on the track. I always ran in trainers so as not to put too much strain on my damaged Achilles. My hopes began to rise again. I missed the AAA Championships that year as well as the European Championships because I simply wasn't ready, but I was still determined to have my chance at the Commonwealth Games in September. Throughout 1998, I went back and forth to Limerick. I continued with the rehab programmes when I was back home, going for a change of scenery to the Larkfield Leisure Centre near Maidstone, where I did weights and circuit training – something I missed from my days as a PTI. Although my physical recovery was slow, my spirit remained as determined as ever. Despite the frustration and disappointment I felt at not being able to race, my previous achievements continued to motivate me. I knew how important it was for me to remain positive and to trust Gerard to get me back where I wanted to be. Without him, I suspect I wouldn't have had a season at all.

As it was my season was very short. Apart from the difficulties with my leg I was beset with other recurring health problems. I became anaemic and my stomach pains flared up again, both of them making it difficult for me to run well. However, eventually I managed to win a 3000 metres race in the Southern Women's League and a mile race in Glasgow. I wasn't race fit for those first races of the season but they proved to me that I had the endurance I needed for competing in the 1500 metres in Kuala Lumpur. For me, that was like coming back into the land of the living at last. Fortunately the Commonwealth Games were late that year and not held until mid-September. Although I hadn't been able to run at any of the qualifying meets, I was selected to run for England on the strength of my previous year's performances and because I was the reigning Commonwealth 1500-metre champion.

I had to fly out to Kuala Lumpur soon after I had competed in Glasgow so that there would be time to recover from jet lag and to get acclimatised. Apart from that, because I'd only been in spikes about three times that year and it was going to be only my third race of the season, I needed the time to focus hard on my training in the two weeks leading up to the Games. My fitness level was low. I hadn't been able to do any speed training that year and had only run the mile, a slow race, with no 800-metre races at all. However much training an athlete puts in, we can only get our real competitive edge from racing. That's where we put our tactics into place and learn how to best adapt them.

In the event, the 1,500 metres was a tight run thing. My biggest rivals were the new Commonwealth record-holder Jackline Maranga from Kenya, and her team-mate Naomi Mugo, both of them in peak condition. Maranga had achieved the fastest time over the distance in the whole world that year. The two Kenyans went straight to the front of the pack, but after the first lap I had moved from the middle on the outside right up to their shoulders. The pace was steady, nobody was attacking as we made our way round. With one lap to go, I was still in a perfect position, lying third. Then Maranga took off on the back straight, but I wasn't going to let her go and I chased her all the way. I did my best, gritting my teeth, but she was too strong for me and won. Nonetheless I was really happy because winning the silver saved my season. After such a stressful year, it was great to know that I could still run and to imagine that, with more training, I could have made it to gold.

The other great aspect of those Games was that they marked Diane Modahl's return to running after four years of battling to clear her name. It was great to see her there and to see her win the bronze in the 800 metres. She must have been so determined to stick it out and show everyone how mistaken the accusations about her were. The competition was hot with Maria Mutola and Tina Paulino hitting first and second places, and with Diane coming in only a fraction behind Tina in one of her fastest times ever. What a moment that was. Fantastic. I admired her so much for coming back after all she'd been put through.

For me, the highlight of 1998 was receiving an MBE for services to the British Army, the career that I had dedicated myself to so far. Lieutenant Colonel McCord had called me when I was in Limerick to tell me that my name had been put forward. I was thrilled to go along to Buckingham Palace and took my mum, dad and Wes. Wes was as proud of me as they were. I was so glad that he could come with us because he had continued to support me and said prayers for me every night in the hope that one day I would be an Olympic champion. We were taken to the Palace by a driver from Tonbridge who kindly lent us his services for my special day. I didn't have to wear military uniform because I had left the Forces, as I told Prince Charles when he questioned me about it. I wasn't much into fashion then and had never had the luxury of being dressed by the best designers in town. Instead I wore a nice cream suit from one of the high street shops and a blue bowl hat – big mistake. Looking back, the hat looked terrible, although I thought it suited me at the time. Because I received my MBE under the name of Sergeant Holmes, it counts as a military award rather than a civilian one, so that when I was invested as a Dame I didn't have to give the honour up – something I was really pleased about.

The one thing I was not prepared for that year was my falling out with Dave. Up until then, we had always had a solid professional relationship. He understood my drive to succeed and sympathised when things went wrong. He had been supportive, tolerant of my moods and, most importantly, always there for me. Then, out of the blue, he gave me a draft contract intended to formalise our relationship, which specified I should give him a percentage of everything I earned. Given I had earned hardly anything that year, it didn't seem like the best moment to produce it. I had no idea that he wasn't happy with our existing arrangement and wished he had just spoken to me about wanting more money so that we could have worked something out between us. If he had tried to approach me beforehand, I didn't remember.

The problem was that the face of athletics was changing at this time. Many people involved with athletes' careers, including coaches, who saw that their athletes were sometimes making money on the circuit, felt left out. I can understand that, but as an athlete you only earn money if you are among the cream of the crop and then you get appearance money by racing regularly on the circuit and getting to a top position. But that's it. Over the years, although I had been winning medals, they didn't reflect the number of times I was unable to race on the circuit. My view was that we were representing UK Athletics for our country, so they had a responsibility for helping with the coaching costs.

I think that perhaps Dave had been badly advised and that the subject probably could have been handled a bit better by both of us. I would have preferred matters to have been kept between the two of us and was irritated that someone else had been involved. I think it's hard for a coach to see a middleman who gets races for an athlete taking a cut of their earnings, when it's the coach who has put in all the work and commitment. I see that much more clearly now than I did then. I really wasn't wised up to it at all because, up until the end of 1997, I had relied on my army wage to fund most of my expenses. It was at that stage that I realised that it wasn't going to work between us any more. The trust had gone. So I decided to leave him.

My physiologist at the time was Joe Dunbar, who also worked at the British Olympic Medical Centre in Northwick Park. He had been a long-distance athlete and had represented England and Britain. He was very supportive and knew my body from a physiological point of view and how it coped with the stresses of racing. It made sense to ask him if he could oversee my training. Of course, Wes was still around too. By this time I had encouraged him to leave his job as an insurance salesman and embark on a new career. He had started taking a number of courses to become a professional sports masseur. I felt sure that, between the three of us, we'd manage.

My training didn't go well in 1999 though. The same old problems kept on recurring, preventing me from competing as much as I would have liked. However I was fit enough to win the AAA Championships 800 metres for the fourth time (my sixth AAA's title) and so qualify for the World Championships that were coming up in Seville at the end of August. They were the last major checkpoint before the 2000 Sydney Olympics so it was important for me to do well there. I went with Wes to a training camp in Madrid where I rented a flat so that we could settle in for a very intense couple of weeks' training. Wes was terrific, giving me massages as I put everything into reaching my best form for the Championships. It was good to have him there as a support and friend too. We'd sit together and talk for hours. Matt Skelton, a middle-distance runner from Tonbridge AC (and a great friend of Joe's) had come over to be my training partner, but my training wasn't going well. For some reason I couldn't adapt. It could have been down to the heat or the fact that I missed the structure I had with Dave. Whichever it was, it meant I was terribly lacking in confidence. In between sessions, Wes and I would go out for walks together, eat out or watch videos. But however hard I tried, I wasn't going to get into shape in time. I knew in my heart that 1999 was not the year it was going to happen for me.

Wes came with me to Seville as well as two friends, Sarah and Sandra Whitlock, who came to cheer me on. I had met Sarah when I went on the caravan holiday after the 1997 World Championships. Their other sister, Jane Basham, her husband Peter and their children Daniel and Sarah, as well as their mum and dad Shirley and Alan, had become part of my family since then. We had become such close friends that Sarah and Sandra had come to share my house in Hildenborough after a short stay with me in Sevenoaks. They were everything I needed to keep my life on track over the next five years. They gave me loads of support, comfort, a shoulder to cry on and acted as a sounding board for all my injury problems and the resulting ups and downs. They probably were the two people who helped me most through those five tough years.

By coincidence, my mum had won a newspaper competition with a trip to Seville as the first prize so she was there too, with her friend Sue. My main memory of the Championships was that the hot weather did its best to sap everyone's energy. The sun beat down relentlessly every day. Because my training had had so many ups and downs, I only ran in the 800 metres. The heat went well and I qualified for the semis, but that was as far as it went. When it came to the semi-final, I couldn't quite make it. As we came down the home straight I was battling for third place, but in the last twenty or so metres I faded as the Russian, Natalia Tsyganova, shot through on the inside. My performance was not good enough to make it through to the final. I was quite disappointed but I had had too many problems to overcome – general lack of good health, injuries and the change of coaches. It was too much for me to contend with and I recognised that I wasn't able to focus properly. Simple as that. This was only the second time I didn't make it to a final in a major championship, the first was in 1993, and it still bugs me.

For the rest of those championships, I went around with my friends and watched the athletics, disappointed for Denise being narrowly defeated in the Heptathlon by the favourite Eunice Barber, sympathetic to Marion Jones who pulled up in the 200 metres, and angry that Fiona May was cruelly robbed of the world long jump title because the field judges controversially gave it to the Spaniard, Niurka Montalvo. By then I was far from the naive runner who had started out in 1993, oblivious to the competition, not having a clue who the other runners were or anything about their form. Now, I knew everyone so I was interested to see how they did and to gauge how they were shaping up for the next year's Olympics. The 800 metres had an incredibly exciting finish as I watched my usual rivals battling it out to win. The Czech, Ludmila Formanova, just pipped Maria Mutola, overtaking her in the last fifty metres, with the Olympic champion Svetlana Masterkova making it into third place just a fraction of a second behind them. Five days later, Masterkova powered to success in the 1500 metres (her last major victory as it was to turn out) with the American Regina Jacobs and Kutre Dulecha of Ethiopia in her wake.

I rounded off the year with a holiday in the Maldives. It made a positive end to an otherwise disappointing year. I'm not a lie-by the-pool sort of person but at least it gave me the chance to take stock and move forward. What it made me realise was that holidaying was not something I wanted on my agenda until I had finished with my athletics altogether, hopefully having achieved all my goals. What I needed to do was put my injury problems in the past and get myself into the right frame of mind to approach the next year's Olympics.

# 15. OLYMPIC FEVER

It was no good. I knew that I needed Dave if I was going to succeed in the 2000 Sydney Olympics. His experience and dedication counted for a lot. He was the only one who knew what I was really capable of and how I could achieve it. At the end of 1999, I contacted him and asked him whether he would consider coaching me again. I explained that I thought the way he'd presented me with the contract wasn't good and that if he wanted to get paid for coaching me then of course we could discuss it. So that's what we did. By this time I had started receiving funding from UK Athletics so I was able to talk it all through with the technical director for endurance there, Zara Hyde Peters. I'd known her slightly over the years because she was a runner herself and we had competed against each other in track races, road races and cross-country not so long before. At the end of every year since I've been funded, I've sat down with her and gone through the following year's budget, deciding how it should be split over coaching expenses, physiotherapy, warm-weather training trips, and so on. On this occasion, she was incredibly helpful in sorting out the financial arrangements between Dave and me, and added to the payments I started making to Dave.

So, with Dave happily back in the picture, I began my training for the Olympics in earnest. But almost as soon as I started, I was in trouble again. Even though I really hated running cross-country, I had agreed to run the British Inter-Counties in Nottingham. I did absolutely dismally. I remember the race vividly because Mick was with me and we got a message saying that Charlie, his polar bear of a dog that we all loved so much, had had to be put down. Charlie had been ill; Mum and Kevin had been looking after him but had had to take him to the vet's for the last time. Mick and I were both so upset. The state of play in Nottingham didn't make me feel any better. The weather was awful and it was horribly muddy and slippery underfoot. Whenever I hit mud, the conditions completely change the way that I run and don't allow me to get on my toes and use my stride. By the end of the race, because of straining to keep my balance and continue running, I had damaged my back badly enough to affect the femoral nerve running down my right leg. For the next five months, I lost all the sensation in it from the hip to the knee, which inevitably affected the way I trained and ran. It didn't stop me running completely but the lower-back pain did give me problems over the next few months.

There was only one place I wanted to go that winter for warm-weather training and that was back to Potchefstroom, although I didn't realise that I would be spending quite as much training time there as I eventually did. The pinched nerve prevented me from entering any races during the first part of the year but I would not be deflected. I was absolutely determined that I would be ready for the Olympics. My prospects looked less rosy when, thanks to my overcompensating for my injured leg and putting too much stress on my lower limbs, I got a tear in my right calf muscle. Among other treatments, Burt Hattingh, one of the physios in Potch, used acupuncture to try to release blood into the area that was hurting, but nothing seemed to work. Regardless, I kept on going to the Health and Racquet Gym to do two hours of cardiovascular work a day, spending an hour on the stepper and splitting the other hour between the rowing machine and the bike. I kept up my weight training and pool training everyday too. I knew that if I kept really fit, I'd be able to step back into my training quite easily once I could start running again.

There were plenty of other athletes out in Potch putting in all the training and dedication and commitment required to qualify for the Games. Our only major lapse was on my 30th birthday, when some of us hit Castilians, one of the bars, a small place with a pool table at the front and mainly used by university students. A few of the French athletes came, Jean and Alta, Alan Smith, a running manager for a shoe company in South Africa, and Jeina Mitchell and Jason Dupuy, two athletes also coached by Dave at the time. After various shot-drinking competitions, we went to Bourbons, a small club that's like a Wild-West saloon, where we took over the karaoke – I can't sing to save my life but that night I thought I was Whitney Houston. I pulled Alta up on to the table to dance but she ended up falling off thanks to all the banging and barging that went on as everyone tried to clamber onto the table to join us. There we were, a bunch of super-fit athletes who supposedly live quietly and don't party, absolutely hammered and making complete prats of ourselves. I should have known. I'd already proved to myself years earlier that I can't take my drink. But it was a brilliant night.

Other than that, I completely concentrated on my training, despite the fact that my calf was not recovering. Reaching the age of thirty did make me start to question how much longer I would have in athletics. But for now I stuck with my goals. When eventually I tried to run on the calf properly, it went altogether and I had no choice but to return to the UK and get a second opinion. The one good thing about my visit was that the celebrations for my birthday didn't stop. I was taken out by Sarah and Sandra, their sister Jane, Kerrie and my sister Lisa to celebrate with a Spanish meal. To top it off, after we'd arrived by train in London, Sarah had organised a limousine to take us all back to my house in Hildenborough.

Eventually I went for a scan that revealed a twelve-centimetre tear in my calf muscle. With the Olympics only three months away, I flew to Limerick for more treatment from Gerard. I remember being in his gym with Paula Radcliffe, who was recovering from a knee operation. She'd be working away on the Nordic ski machine while I pedalled hell for leather on the bike. Neither of us was going to give up our dreams without a damn good fight.

Once again, Gerard worked his magic and I was running again within a few weeks. Thanks to all my manic cross-training, when I went back to the track I was in reasonable shape. My spirits however were not so high. Sometimes I'd cry myself to sleep, believing I was never going to fulfil my dream. All the ups and downs of the past couple of years were really getting to me but I did my best not to let it show and tried to pick myself up. I knew that if I gave in to them, I'd be finished. I would not let them stop me. I was going to go to the Olympics and I was going to do well. So I used the setbacks to my advantage, forcing myself to be more determined than ever. I only had six weeks of track preparation but I would make them count. It was all a question of gearing up to peak at the Olympics, so I mainly focused on the speed and speed-endurance sessions worked out between Gerard and Dave.

My first major race of the season was in August at the AAA Olympic trials in Birmingham. I won the 800 metres easily, taking the lead from the moment we broke lanes and keeping it right to the end when I managed to get about fifteen metres ahead of the field. But my time was 2:02.08 – almost two seconds slower than the qualifying standard. I hadn't made it. But there was a ray of hope. Normally UK Athletics specify that a runner must finish in the first two of the final within the qualifying time to be selected for a championship. But there is a third discretionary place that can be granted in exceptional circumstances. Dave wrote asking UK Athletics to look at my circumstances and to take into account the fact that it was only the second time that I'd had my spikes on that season. To my delight, they gave me the discretionary place in both the 800 and 1500, based on my previous qualifying times and on them knowing my form. I was entering the 800 with Diane Modahl as well as the 1500 with Helen Pattinson (now Clitheroe) and Hayley Tullett. I did three races after the AAA and felt I was getting better with each race and things were definitely improving for me. Before leaving for Australia I ran in a grand prix in Gateshead where I was beaten by Letitia Vriesde and Hasna Benhassi but nonetheless I was pleased with the way I ran.

Next stop: Australia's Gold Coast, only three weeks before the Games opened on 15 September, and counting. The Radisson Resort Gold Coast was the business. Surrounded by five championship golf courses and close to the athletics track, it was perfectly located for training. I had managed to avoid the worst of the jetlag by switching off from everyone on the team who I was travelling with on the flight out. I slept for the first half of the flight and stayed awake for the second. It worked brilliantly so I adjusted to the time difference very quickly and was able to get straight into training. I carried on with the intensive training I'd begun in the UK, including runs at Pooh Park, a nearby nature reserve. Most mornings the endurance athletes were driven either there or to Pissey Park. Of course we joked about the names. One bonus about training there was that we came across some of the wildlife. One morning, I especially remember, we were running on the forest trails in Pooh when suddenly there were wallabies bounding through the trees at the side of us. It was an amazing sight. Another time, when I was being interviewed for TV, to our surprise we spotted a furry ball of a koala bear making its television debut behind us as I talked.

The good thing about the resort was that, apart from having great facilities for training, it also gave us plenty of chances to relax. It somehow didn't feel as though we all had as much at stake as we did. Although we were all busy getting ready for the most important moment of our athletics careers, the atmosphere was so upbeat that everyone gelled quickly. Many of the British team were staying there, including the judo players. I often took my mind off the Games by watching Kate Howey, a very distinguished member of the judo squad, and the rest of the team in training. I had got to know a few of them. Andy Graffin had qualified for his first Olympics in the men's 1500. It was good see him there. Unfortunately his brother Allen hadn't made the team and I think that was quite hard for both of them. Andy seemed quite shy, probably because it was his first Olympics and also because he and Allen are used to being together and are very supportive of one another. It was only during and after these Games that Andy and I became friends; today he is one of my best mates and training partner in the UK. I nicknamed hammer-thrower Lorraine Shaw 'Cleo' because she reminded me of the larger-than-life character in the film *Set It Off*. In return she called me Super Star Babe.

Relaxation is so important. Being comfortable among my teammates meant that although I was playing catch-up in my training, I wasn't sitting around feeling anxious about how well I was doing. The other thing that helped me relax was sharing a room with my good friend Jo Pavey, the long-distance runner. We had met in 1997 when she had made a massive breakthrough on the athletics scene by qualifying for the World Championships in Athens that year. We had shared a room at the European Cup and met again at a road race in London. Later I was to ask her if she fancied sharing in Brisbane. I get on really well with her and with Gav, her husband, training partner and coach. They're completely inseparable. Jo came into athletics in 1997 after they'd spent four years travelling round the world together. Gav had been an athlete too but he put his career to one side to devote himself to coaching Jo, the more promising of the two of them. Despite her frequent injury problems, she is a superb athlete. They have become very good friends of mine and between them they always manage to crack me up. We're always laughing together. Jo can never find anything, whether it's her spikes, her purse or her water bottle – even when they're right under her nose. Whenever we share a room, something always happens.

One night in Brisbane, I woke up to hear rustling, munching and a soft mysterious hum. I switched on the light to find Jo sitting in the middle of the room, with a TENS machine, the small black pads on her knee vibrating to keep down some inflammation, while she was chomping her way through the freebie nutritional crunchy bars we'd been given.

'Jo. What the hell are you doing? It's two in the morning.'

'I was so hungry, I couldn't sleep,' she explained, a bit embarrassed. 'So I thought I might as well use my TENS machine. I really wanted a cup of coffee but I thought I'd wake you up.'

'But you've woken me up anyway. For Christ's sake, go to sleep, will ya?' We laughed for ages in the dark. It hadn't crossed her mind that slight noise of the TENS machine on its own might be enough to wake Sleeping Beauty, never mind the sound of her munching.

My last training session in Brisbane went really well. Gav had helped me with a couple of sessions earlier but this time Paula Radcliffe's husband and training partner, Gary Lough, helped me out. Having a pacemaker really helped at this stage in my preparation. Over the years, at certain stages in my career, I've had many who have been a great help to me, including Gav Pavey and Andy Graffin. Dave and I had gone down to the track and Gary had agreed to help pace me for 500 metres of my 600-metre repetition. After only sixty seconds' rest, I ran a fast 200 metres – the session was much faster than Dave had envisaged. For the second time in my life, I got that winning feeling again. I knew I could run 1:56. I was racing round the track, arms in the air, yelling, 'Yeeeeeeah. I'm ready.' After running like an elephant a few weeks earlier at the trials, my head had at last moved into a totally different zone. I had reached the mind-set I needed for the Games, or any championship. It gave me the huge amount of confidence that I needed. Dave knew I was ready at last and we left the track in a really positive mood.

It was a very relaxed and good-humoured team who arrived in the amazing Olympic Village in Sydney. Built specially for the athletes, it was a green village near Homebush Bay, in keeping with the spirit of the Games. The houses had all sorts of energy-saving features, including solar heating, with cycle-ways, walkways and bus routes that connected it with the Olympic Park in Homebush and the rest of the city. When we eventually left, the houses were sold off to private buyers. So as far as we were concerned, everything was sparkling new. There were eleven of us to a house and each house flew its nation's flag. There was a fantastic friendly atmosphere with athletes from all over the world going round in their team uniforms. Everyone was respectful of one another while operating in that peculiar half-focused state you reach before an all-important event, aware that everyone else was also there to do their best in their competition.

Our house was shared by Helen Pattinson (1500 metres), Hayley Tullett (1500), Marian Sutton (marathon), Andrea Whitcome (5000) and Sam Davies (sprinter), with Paula Radcliffe (5000), Alison Curbishley (400), Lorraine Shaw (hammer) and Janine Whitlock (pole vault) upstairs. Once again, Jo and I were together, first in a tiny room at the back of the house. There was no way we could stay there with all our luggage so we asked the team management if we could change. The only option was through the back door and into the garden where a Portakabin stood. Great, we thought. An adventure. Our Portakabin was totally empty apart from two beds, one at either end, two bedside cabinets, a wardrobe, no carpet and a small shower room at one end. Once we'd pinned up our cards and the faxes wishing us luck, we thought it was quite homely. By the side of my bed, I had a stack of chocolate bars because Colin Jackson had told me that he ate a 200-gram bar of chocolate before every race. It seemed to work for him. Right, I thought. I'll try it. Good excuse! It was much less painful than the tip I had taken from Sally Gunnell in 1994, when I copied her winning routine of taking a cold shower just before every race.

The whole atmosphere at the house was more like a holiday camp than anything else. We seemed to laugh all the time, even when Jo came in on the morning of my 1500 heats having slept on the floor in the lounge so as not to disturb me by coming in late.

'Kel, I think there might be a bomb in the house.'

'What do you mean? Where?' The bomb in Atlanta was still something that occasionally nagged at the back of our minds.

'There's a box outside the lounge. I'm sure it wasn't there before.'

'Why do you think it's a bomb?' Me, keeping as calm as I could.

'I don't know. But it looks the sort of size a bomb might be.'

I followed her to take a look. Thank God we didn't call security first. There was a box all right but it was the box containing Lorraine's hammer. I could not believe that Jo had spent a sleepless night, worrying that we might all be about to be blown to smithereens without even thinking to wake any of us up to check if we knew what was in the box. So luckily we all survived!

One other thing that sticks in my mind was the huge canteen that was open almost 24 hours a day where you could get dishes from all over the world. The food was amazing, with every kind of salad leaf or cheese right down to McDonald's and Magnum ice creams. When the racing was over, everyone went mad in there. We'd had to be so strict with ourselves up until then.

Luckily for me, the final of the 800 metres wasn't until 25 September, so I had a chance to get ready for it. On the day before the first 800 heat, I was given the start list as usual. Because of my qualifying time, I was down as something like the twenty-fifth fastest in the world. I remember thinking, How the hell am I going to do it? Dave was there, keeping me calm, encouraging me, convincing me I could as he always did. I had to be in the first two of the heat to go through to the semis. I went into the heat as positive as I could be.

As always, I'd gone through my ritual of laying out my kit the night before and I came into the packed stadium looking for the British flag that would tell me I really was at the Olympics. The atmosphere in the huge stadium was incredible. We could all feel the Olympic spirit. The Australians are such friendly, sports-loving people that made it very special for us. It was all I needed. I ran a great race, coming in first. I approached the semi-final feeling good and strong, aware that I had to get through. At the Olympics, you're not really in the race until you get to the final. That's the only way you have a chance of getting a medal. I had to get through. I was 100 per cent focused and utterly determined. Again, I ran well, staying at the back, pacing myself because I knew it would be a fast race, then moving into sixth place and not letting the front five get away. At the bend I kicked for home and finished second to the Austrian Stephanie Graf, with a season's best, shaving nearly two seconds off my previous one. Only six weeks of training and I was in the final of the Olympic women's 800 metres

The night before the race, Dave and I went through my tactics – even though they all went out the window when the time came.

There's a difference between running a race and racing a race. When you're running, you might be lagging behind or staying up at the front, but when you're racing, you have to adapt your tactics to the circumstances. I had to be prepared for anything that might happen. So we went through a number of possible scenarios based on the other runners' previous performances and considered the best way for me to react to them. The favourites were Maria Mutola and Stephanie Graf but, after my non-existent season, I had nothing to lose. Thanks to my injuries, I wasn't a medal contender so all I had to do was go out and race. Dave gave me all the encouragement I needed and then it was up to me.

The 800-metre final took place on the same night that Cathy Freeman, the Australian 400-metre runner, was running in her final. It was a sell-out crowd. The pressure she had on her must have been fantastic. She was the biggest name Australia had in track and field events and as an Aborigine, competing for her country against the world, she symbolised so much to her countrymen. As she walked into the stadium, it lit up with the popping of thousands of flash bulbs. It was as if royalty was making an entrance. The atmosphere was electric. She took off her tracksuit bottoms and long-sleeved T-shirt to reveal the all-in-one swift suit, specially designed for her by her sponsor. In the Australian colours of green, white and yellow, it covered everything except her head, hands and feet. Then she pulled the hood on, to more camera flashing. She stood out a mile. I'll never forget the moment after she'd won the race, when the crowd were going wild. She didn't celebrate but sat down with the most enormous look of relief on her face, just shaking her head as if she couldn't believe it. So many other athletes would have cracked under the sort of pressure she had been under but she had stayed so strong. The Brits were celebrating too as our two runners had done brilliantly, with Katherine Merry winning a bronze and Donna Fraser getting fourth place in the same race, and Jonathan Edwards winning a gold in the triple jump.

Two hours later, as I walked into the stadium again, I was aware of the sense of anticipation and the noise. Keeping it in the background, I focused on the race, controlling the adrenalin that is so essential to victory. Ignoring the sick feeling in the pit of my stomach, I prepared myself for the race, doing my strides round the bend. In the distance I could hear another country's national anthem being played as athletes received their medals, so momentarily slowed down to be respectful. I looked at the British flag again, smiled and told myself to relax.

At the gun, Helena Fuchsova from Czechoslovakia took the race on and set a very fast pace. I tried to take the first lap easy so stayed a way back, knowing that it meant I would be running more consistently. Then for some reason, as we were going round the last bend, I overtook everyone. Why I did that, I do not know. Going round the bend, I was leading. Going into the home straight, I was leading. I was leading in the Olympics and I shouldn't even have been in the damn final. But I was so shocked to be in that position, I didn't run for the line. Instead I kept my eye on the big screen, watching to see who was going to come past me and to see whether or not I was still in contention for a medal. I was running hard all right but not fighting. Because I hadn't been running for most of the year, I hadn't built up that competitive edge that I needed. Sure enough, at about sixty metres, Maria came past me. That's one, I thought. As we got close to the line, instead of battling for it, I saw Stephanie come past and cross it behind Maria. That's two. And then I went over the line. I'd got the bronze medal. I was in shock, like a kid who can't believe her luck. My grin was set to split my face. All I could say over and over again when I was interviewed after the race, was, 'I can't believe it.' I must have said it at least thirty times. After a year of struggle, that bronze was like a gold to me. I couldn't have been more chuffed.

It was a great, great night. By the time I got back to the house, everyone else was asleep. So far all I'd been able to do was join Jonathan in eating as much as we could in the canteen. Embarrassingly we had been spotted by a TV crew who broadcast the fact that they had seen us wolfing down chocolate cake and as many sandwiches as we could manage. I tiptoed in, wishing I could celebrate my victory properly. But we were all competing at different times, so it was difficult. Everyone else seemed to be in bed. Then I saw someone was in the shower room so tentatively knocked on the door. Alison put her head out. She had been in the middle of making a call on her mobile but when she saw my bronze medal, she started screaming and jumping up and down. I was on such a high from the whole evening that we chatted for ages into the night. All I wanted to do was party and that was my downfall.

When it came to the 1500 metres, my mind was somewhere else. Hayley and I both got through to the semi-finals and from there we made it to the finals. I knew I had to run the races but I really wanted it all to be over. I wanted to go out and celebrate winning my bronze properly. Dave tried to keep me focused but he had a hard job. He was very encouraging, as he always is, discussing possible tactics, trying to get me to relax and assuring me that I had it in me to win. But try as he did, I didn't really take in what he was saying. Instead of my mind being on the race and that finishing line, it was on what I was going to get up to afterwards.

That lack of focus cost me the the chance of a medal. From the beginning, the pace was slow, I was baulked and barged so much that I lost my rhythm. I was too aware of what was happening, seeing every bit of pushing and pulling. Then, with 300 metres to go, Hayley was running behind me and she fell. I was so aware of her going that I didn't concentrate on my positioning and kept getting pushed around by the other runners. Without the ability to focus solely on what I was doing, where I was going and where I had to be, I was lost. The other runners legged it towards the finishing line, with Nouria Merah-Benida of Algeria taking the gold. I didn't react fast enough and ended up coming seventh.

Did I care? Not one bit. I still had my bronze. But Dave was upset because he really thought I could have won a medal. I guess I did let him down but now I think it wasn't meant to be. My time was yet to come. As it was, there was a lot of celebrating to do. The British Olympic team did incredibly well bringing home eleven gold, ten silver and seven bronze medals. Denise Lewis had become Olympic Champion for the heptathlon after an amazing battle to overcome injury, Darren Campbell had run one of the best races of his life to get silver behind the Greek athlete Costas Kenteris, and Steve Backley, our amazing javelin thrower, had again struck silver too. Kate won silver in the judo, the only event I did go and watch to take a break from the village. Steve Redgrave won his fifth Olympic gold, this time in the coxless fours. He went on to win the BBC TV Sports Personality of the Year while the whole team won Sports Team of the Year. The British Olympic Association keeps the main trophy but we were offered a chance to buy a replica. 'It's probably the only chance I'll ever get to have one of these,' I thought, so I bought one, never dreaming I would one day get one of my own.

# 16. CURSED

At the end of every outdoor season, I treat myself to a three or four week break from the track. Three weeks when I hardly run at all and when my diet goes completely to pot. At last I can eat all my favourite things that I rarely eat while I'm in training: Chinese, chocolate, Indian, chocolate, pizzas and . . . chocolate. I spend hours catching up with all my friends and going out for meals with them, making up for lost time. Then by the end of the third week, I feel as if I've been transformed from a fit and healthy person into a total slob. I usually feel so terrible that I have to do something about it by eating properly and starting training again.

So, having eaten myself stupid and celebrated my Olympic bronze until I was partied out, in January 2001 I headed back to Potch. It was time to refocus and to set my sights on the season ahead. In 2001, the racing season would culminate in the World Championships in Edmonton, Canada. I knew that the best athletes in the world would have their sights set on them too and that they, like me, would be embarking on their training programmes with the aim of reaching their peak in August.

But, once again, things started badly. In Potch, I found it increasingly hard to do the endurance work. I went back and forth to the

UK for the AAA Indoor Championships, which I won but I didn't enjoy it at all. Later, I went on to win a three-kilometre road race in the beautiful setting of Balmoral, Scotland. I constantly felt very tired and so lethargic, in training, that I couldn't achieve the times on the track and felt sluggish when I had weights sessions. My glands were swollen and I had occasional fevers. In the end I visited the local doctor in Potch who ran some blood tests which revealed a form of glandular fever.

When I spoke to Dave, who had stayed in England this time, he immediately suggested I come home to see the British Olympic doctors who had experience in treating over-training syndromes as well as chronic fatigue and glandular fever. I went to see Dr Richard Budget of the British Olympic Medical Centre in Northwick Park, who was very sympathetic. He explained that normally after intensive training, an athlete's energy dips so they need a break to recover. After more exercise, there's another dip. After a rest the body is ready for another level of training, helping you move up the fitness levels. That's why rest days are so essential to an athlete's regime. In my case, my body had gone into reverse. Instead of recovering, I simply became more exhausted. He diagnosed chronic fatigue syndrome and told me that the only way to get better was to stop my training. 'You have got to let your body recover totally,' he explained. 'Otherwise you will never get out of the cycle.' Of course he realised that as a professional athlete, I couldn't stop training altogether, so he suggested we took things down to zero and then started to build them up again really slowly. I would have to do a maximum of ten minutes' easy jogging a day without my heartbeat going above 130 beats a minute or just do hard 100-metre sprints with a long rest from which I would recover very quickly.

This was terrible news for me. Every time I began to recover from injury, it seemed as if I was always knocked back again by something else. My morale was at an all-time low. Instead of returning to Potch, I went with Dave to do some warm-weather training at sea level in Stellenbosch. We rented a house there and embarked on a regime of careful preparation that involved sprinting with long recoveries, as the doctor had advised, as well as some weight training. As ever, Dave was an amazing support to me during this incredibly difficult and frustrating time, helping me judge exactly how much I should do and when I should do it. But even though I wasn't training much, I started getting various minor lower-limb injuries. I went to see Benita, the physio, again. I liked her scientific approach to balancing the body by looking at the individual muscle groups. She worked really hard with me and I came to trust her implicitly as we worked on building up my core muscle stability.

After a couple of weeks, I moved up to some very, very slow runs as well as repetitions on the track, building them up from 50 to 100 to 200-metre-sprints and so on until I had reached 800 metres, all the time shortening my recovery times. We monitored everything carefully, making absolutely certain I wasn't overdoing things. Even though the sessions went well, another problem surfaced. This time, within myself. Although I was recovering physically, instead of getting the confidence to fight back I was getting more and more depressed. I couldn't help asking myself why I kept getting all these problems. It was as if I was cursed. A lot of the time I was in tears about my future in athletics. I was thirty-two years old and had no idea how long I had left in my career or what I would be doing when it came to an end. I wanted to achieve my dream of Olympic gold so badly but it sometimes felt like an impossible challenge. I was scared by the thought of the unknown. It must have been a difficult time for Dave too as, like me, he was away from home with no one else to turn to for advice or company.

My morale was knocked back even more when I lost my Nike contract. At the Olympic Games they had been singing my praises as we discussed its re-negotiation. Although my career was rife with problems, I was still producing some great results, so obviously I expected them to be supportive – but I was wrong. I went to the Nike headquarters in London for a meeting with Dave Scott, the head of running. I had been given an amazing deal when I first signed with them in 1996, thanks to my then manager Barry Nevill. However at this point I was between managers so had no one to help. To my astonishment I was offered what I thought was an insulting contract. This was a real kick in the teeth for me. They had supported me handsomely until then but it looked to me as if they didn't put any value on my winning the Olympic bronze medal. However, I had returned from the Olympics feeling very positive about my performance. I was careful not to leak anything of this to the press, but they got wind of the story, misrepresented the facts and made it look as if I was really critical of Nike. Not so. I was only very disappointed that we couldn't keep our relationship on the same footing. I loved being with them, but neither was I going to accept an offer I believed was inadequate. Andy Norman sorted out sponsorship from Brendan Foster's company View From, which made clothing but not footwear. I was nervous about changing the make of my shoes after all my leg injuries so I decided to carry on running in my Nikes but without the swoosh. I carefully removed it from a few of my trainers.

Dave and I returned to the UK after about a month in Stellenbosch. I was due to run in the trials for the World Championships and had reached a point in my training where we felt it would be possible. As an athlete, I have always managed to rise to the occasion when it comes to the major championships, whatever obstacles have been in my way. I won my ninth AAA title (which was also my eleventh British title). The following week, in the grand prix at Crystal Palace, I did far better in the 800 metres than I'd expected given my lack of preparation. Although I came second, I ran 1:58.85. This proved to me that sometimes quality is better than quantity when it comes to training. But I did know that without the necessary endurance base I was going to have problems in the Championships themselves because of the rounds.

The Edmonton World Championships were memorable for a couple of reasons. One was the protest staged by Paula Radcliffe and Hayley Yelling who, during one of the heats for the women's 5000 metres, stood in the stands with a sign that read EPO CHEATS OUT. They were protesting about the inadequacy of drug testing in athletics. They were incensed that the Russian athlete Olga Yegorova had tested positive for the performance-boosting drug EPO shortly before arriving in Canada but had got off because the French testing authorities had failed to carry out the required blood test as well. I didn't join their protest because I was preparing for my races.

In my view, people who take drugs are just cheating themselves and their sport. Sport is about passion, determination to be the best, training, effort and dedication. What is the point of having a dream that involves personal physical achievement and then taking some drug to make it happen? It seems to me there isn't one. Over the years the drug-testing protocol has become much more watertight, making it increasingly difficult for athletes to cheat. Yet we know there are pharmacists and doctors working hard to keep one step ahead of the system, to produce performance-enhancing drugs that will be undetectable. As a result, it's an accepted part of an athlete's life to be subjected to random drug testing, whether after a race or when the tester arrives on your doorstep without warning. We are all governed by the IAAF governing law that dictates what drugs you can and can't take.

I made it through to the finals of the 800 metres, coming second in my heat to Mutola, and second to Graf in the semi-final, but on the morning of the race, even after the rest day after the semis, I didn't feel right. I could feel that I hadn't recovered as well as I should have so knew I was going to struggle. In the final, Mutola and Graf went off quickly, under pressure from Vriesde and Diane Cummins of Canada on the inside, with Vriesde settling in the lead, looking very strong. I picked my way through from the back and for the first 550 metres I was challenging the rest of the field, lying in fourth position at the bell. On the final bend, I became detached from the front-runners as Vriesde, Graf and Mutola battled it out ahead. I didn't have the extra speed and endurance needed to keep going after the heats and the semis. My legs turned to lead and I ended up coming sixth after my old rivals, Mutola just beating Graf into second place and Vriesde, who ran brilliantly, into third. Considering what I'd been through that year, it wasn't such a bad result. I was very disappointed but I consoled myself with the fact that I had the rest of the grand prix season ahead of me. I was confident that with another two weeks of training, I would at least make my mark on them.

First up was the golden league in Zurich. I expected that in a one-off race I would stand a very good chance of doing well however tough the opposition. I was relaxed going into the race and, instead of using my usual tactics, I decided to run in the middle of the pack on the inside, but got trapped in fifth place on the back straight. Then I saw a gap and kicked forward as hard as I could. I went past Graf for the first time in four years, although I couldn't catch Mutola who got well away, so I took second place.

Two days later, I flew into Gateshead for another meet, although my luggage didn't make the journey with me. I waited at the carousel, watching everyone claiming their bags, with a nasty feeling in the pit of my stomach as I realised that mine weren't there. For me, that was a catastrophe. I had stupidly forgotten to pack my spikes in my hand luggage. My missing clothes were also difficult to replace because not many sports shops stocked View From clothing. Luckily Gateshead is near Newcastle where the brand was mainly sold. My race was that evening, so I spent the morning trying to find View From clothing and the right trainers and spikes. I wasn't too worried about the kit because I knew I could always borrow a tracksuit from someone else at the meet, but shoes are very personal and crucial to the way an athlete performs. By the time I'd finished running around town, I was exhausted, having missed my usual pre-race rest and having failed to eat properly. However, the fact that I hadn't had time to worry about the race did me a favour.

I turned up at the track an hour before my race, still without any spikes. Before I'd set off on my hunt, I'd asked Jo Pavey what size feet she had. As hers were the same as mine, I had no alternative but to ask her if she'd lend me her spikes. She agreed quite happily. The one thing we hadn't bargained for was that her race was the one immediately before mine. As soon as the 5000 metres finished she jogged over and gave me her shoes, nicely warm and sweaty. Anybody watching must have thought it was very bizarre as I quickly put them on and lined up for the race. I ran a great race, moving into second place at the bell, running at Vriesde's shoulder, and then going flat out down the home straight to win. Against all expectations, I won it in 1:58.10 – the fastest time I'd run that season as well as getting the award for Performance of the Meet, beating Vriesde, Cummins and Jolanda Ceplak. Jo was astonished, 'Wow. That's the fastest my shoes have ever run an 800 metres,' she said as we were laughing about it afterwards. 'They'll never do that again.'

After that the season went superbly well. I came second in the Brussels league, my first defeat of Maria Mutola in the 800 metres, and then fourth in Berlin. At the beginning of September, I returned to Brisbane, Australia, for the Goodwill Games. Kathy Butler, Jo Pavey and I were the three women on the athletics team representing Great Britain. I was running the 800 against pretty much the same opposition I had faced in the World Championships earlier in the year. I went in very positively and decided just to go for it. I got stuck into the race, passing Stephanie Graf on the home straight, but had left a bit too much of a gap for me to be able to catch Mutola.

I was so pleased to have taken home a silver medal. I then went to the grand prix final in Melbourne, where I came up between Graf and Mutola on the home straight to take second place from Graf. I ended up being ranked third in the world. The final race of the season was the Great North Mile, when the runners were to be the first people to officially cross the Millennium Bridge in Newcastle. I was quite tired from the season by then but thought it would be fun to run, although it was twice as long as all the races I'd entered that year. The quayside area was packed so there was a great atmosphere as we set off. Helen Pattinson took the lead from me as we left the bridge with a bunch of six of us, close behind her. As we dropped down to the river under the Tyne Bridge, I took the lead again and struck for home. It was a long way to keep the lead, but I managed it. It was a great end to one of the best racing years I'd had so far. It just hadn't happened for me at the World Championships as they had come too soon after my bad start to the year. What I needed now was a consistent winter so that I could come out strong on the other side, ready to race a full season and achieve what I knew I was capable of achieving.

By this stage in my career, I was beginning to feel that I perhaps wasn't being paid as well as I might be. I had reached a point where I was thinking, Hang on a minute. I'm thirty-one years old and my career won't last forever. I'm not getting the kind of money I think I should be but I don't want to leave my race manager, Andy. But if I haven't got that many races left, then I need to have my appearance fees renegotiated. I was hopelessly undecided about what to do for the best. Although I had experience of racing, thanks to my injuries it had been pretty inconsistent, so I was very naive when it came to the circuit and the race managers. But during my time on the circuit that year, I had met Robert Wagner.

Robert represented, among others, Colin Jackson, Stephanie Graf and Jolanda Ceplak. In Berlin, I mentioned to him that I was having problems with my travel plans to Australia for the Goodwill Games, so he offered to sort them out for me. Not only did he sort them out, I ended up flying Business Class from Berlin to London, London to Brisbane, Brisbane to Melbourne and Melbourne to London. Wicked! That's the way to travel, I thought. What a difference from my usual seat in Economy. The space, the comfort. All I could think was, Wow! This is brilliant. I need to be with this guy. An athlete's lifestyle is hardly glamorous at the best of times: fly to the venue; get picked up and taken to hotel; get taken from hotel to track; run the race; return to hotel bedroom; back on the bus; back on another flight. We don't get to see much of the country we're in or meet its people. So getting Business-Class tickets may not sound like much but it does make a big difference to anyone who spends their life in this mad way.

After the grand prix final, Robert made it clear that he would like to manage me. I was so torn between whether to go with him or stay with Andy, where my loyalties lay, because he was the first person to give me a chance in athletics and I respected him for that. In the end, I wrote to Andy, telling him how much I appreciated what he had done for me but explaining that I felt it was time to move on. It was such a hard letter to write but, for the first time in my life, I started to stick up for myself. I decided that if I didn't start doing something about making a living out of athletics, I was going to end up going nowhere.

# 17. ON HOME TURF

The high point of 2002 was the Commonwealth Games. Being in Manchester was fantastic for all the British athletes taking part because it meant all our friends and family could come and support us. Going into the Games, I was in pretty good shape having won in the AAA 1500 in Birmingham a couple of weeks earlier.

Once again, I'd had a slow start to the year, having had to recuperate from a stomach operation at the end of 2001. I had still been getting horrendous stomach pains that had to be relieved with muscle relaxant injections after every race. The tablets I'd also been given to help seemed to be less and less effective, so Dave and I decided something had to be done. I went back to see Michael Dooley, the consultant who had treated me before at Northwick Park, and was admitted to Winterbourne Hospital in Dorchester. This time he performed a laparotomy and found a large fimeral cyst that he removed along with one of my ovaries because it had twisted around my fallopian tube as well as signs of endometriosis and severe infection. Because I am an athlete, Michael was careful to push all the muscle away from the site of the operation to avoid any long-term delays in my recovery. After the operation, I went to Tonbridge Cottage Hospital to have treatment to minimise the amount of scar tissue that might form. I wasn't able to train for a few weeks because I had staples put along the incision in my stomach. I was very lucky to have Sarah with me to drive me and help back at home. As usual, when I did get back I suffered a few problems with my calves and my Achilles. But Dave was there to help guide me through his meticulous training schedule. It was another real low point in my life. How could I be up against yet another setback?

Despite these problems, I did run in six European races at the beginning of the season, including the European Cup in Annecy where, because of being one of the oldest on the team, I was asked to be team captain for the first time. I took the job very seriously. I wanted to live up to the title, so I ran around making sure everyone was fine, chatting to them and making sure I got to know the younger members of the team whom I hadn't met before. I even organised a team photo. Everyone was really pleased because it was the first time we'd had one. I had a great weekend, loving being involved with making sure the girls didn't miss out on the photo by pushing a note under everyone's door with the help of a couple of the admin staff, and being interested in everybody else's performance. Normally, I would only be concentrating on my own, so it was a great change for me. The only snag was that by the time it came to my race I was absolutely exhausted and trailed in fourth, having died in the last 100 metres or so. Ever since, I've thought that the role of captain would probably be better given to a non-participant.

When it came to the Commonwealth Games, I was ready. In Manchester, accommodation was in the University student halls. Once again I shared with Jo and once again it was an eventful night. We'd been chatting in our bunks and had just turned the light off when suddenly she let out a great scream. I jumped off the top bunk, thinking something terrible had happened to her. I switched on the light to find her sitting up, screaming that she couldn't get the wax earplug out of her ear. She was tugging away at it, making the suction pull at her eardrum. I tried to calm her down as I gently twisted it – it came out straight away. But poor Jo had such bad earache afterwards she later went to the doctor, who diagnosed a haematoma on her eardrum from where she had yanked too hard and the wax had stuck to it. The great thing about sharing with Jo is that, despite the odd drama, it's not at all stressful and we can laugh and feel relaxed in each other's company.

The atmosphere at the Games was fantastic because of the massive home crowd. Among the red and white sea of English flags were pockets of Welsh and Scottish flags too. Dave came up to help me with my final preparations, and he was joined by my mum and dad and my brothers and sister Penny, along with Kerrie, her brother and her son Louis, Jackie and her mother, Sarah, Sandra and few other friends. I got through the heats of the 1500 with no bother but in the final I was facing the British runner also representing England, Helen Pattinson, at that time the number one in the Commonwealth, having run a fantastic race in a personal best time of 4:01.1 in Monaco.

Helen went out hard and took over the race quite early, really trying to pick up the pace. She knew I was a threat but that my performances were erratic, thanks to my various niggling injuries. I knew she was trying to drop me by making it a fast race. I was aware of the shouts of the crowd and the mass of red and white flags. I cannot lose this, I repeated to myself. My championship head was screwed back on and I was totally focused on what I was doing. As we were going down the back straight, I managed to get past Helen and I kicked for home with Hayley Tullett, running for Wales, in my wake. Before I even came up to the line, I was grinning broadly as I realised I was going to win the title again, eight years after I had first won it. Running my lap of honour to the roar of the crowd was amazing. There's nothing like winning in front of your home crowd to lift your spirits sky high. At the end of the day I was a British athlete, so it didn't matter that I was representing my home nation of England. Everyone was supporting me. I picked out my family and friends in the crowd and waved to them. The only thing that bettered that feeling was when Helen, Hayley and I were standing on the rostrum receiving our medals. Then, for the first time, the words of *Land of Hope and Glory* were displayed. It was as if the stadium came alive with a massive, bellowing roar as everyone burst into song. I will never forget that moment.

Apart from our own successes, we had plenty of others to celebrate. Lorraine 'Cleo' Shaw won the first gold medal for England in the hammer. She was so carried away by the moment that she took a lap of honour, jumping up and down as she went. We were all thrilled for her and laughing because we'd never seen a thrower take a lap of honour before. Paula took the gold in the 5000 with Jo in fifth place. Marlon Devenish and Darren Campbell took the silver and bronze in the men's 200 metres, Mike East won the

1500, Chris Rawlinson the 400 hurdles and Jonathan Edwards won the triple jump, among many other victories.

The other memorable aspect of those Games was the presence of WADA, the World Anti Doping Agency, who carried out the largest programme of testing that had ever been carried out in the UK or at a Commonwealth Games. They had a large tent that was very prominent in the athletes' village. Many athletes, including me, signed up to their athletes' passport programme there, which gave you a certificate showing your commitment and support to doping-free sport and a record of your testing history.

Six days after the Commonwealth Games, the European Championships took place in Munich. I was anxious about competing in both distances, having put so much focus into the Commonwealth Games, and had discussed with Dave whether or not I should. I was entered in both the 800 and the 1500 metres for the first time that season, and was worried that running both of them would be too much, but Dave reassured me. My worry also stemmed from the fact that I was running terribly over 800 metres, unable even to break two minutes. I found it very hard to push my body to the limit. Something always seemed to be holding me back. Maybe it was to do with what was going on in my head or maybe it was the recurrence of the chronic fatigue syndrome. I was aware that it could resurface at any stage but I didn't go as far as having tests for it. Nonetheless, I went to Munich with a positive mindset.

The athletes were all staying in big university accommodation blocks that were heavily guarded. Such tight security was the legacy of the terrible events at the 1972 Munich Olympics, when Palestinian terrorists scaled the boundary fence of the Olympic village to kill two of the Israeli Olympic team and take another nine hostage. They were demanding the release of Palestinian prisoners and safe passage out of Germany. All the hostages were killed in a gun battle at a nearby airbase. Even though it all happened so many years earlier, I could understand only too well why the Germans might have been jumpy, particularly since the events of 9/11. I think a lot of the athletes found the presence of the guards with their weapons quite intimidating.

As at most international meetings, drug issues were prominent on the agenda as we were more and more aware of athletes who managed to circumvent the testing and the efforts made by WADA to stop them. I remember a group of us, including Paula, Jo Fenn, Jo

Pavey, Hayley Yelling, Helen Pattinson, a couple of others and myself, sitting in the corridor discussing doping. As usual, there was speculation about whether one athlete or another's performance had been helped by performance-enhancing drugs. Whenever any of us think about another runner cheating we all get extremely wound up, especially if that runner has been in one of our races. To know that you've worked your guts out to get your place in a race while the possibility exists that someone else may have cheated their way there is something that infuriates us all. Of course, what is frustrating is that there is absolutely nothing any of us can do about specific cases. Without a positive drug test, speculation about a particular performance can only remain speculation and no more. Every runner is innocent until they are proven guilty.

I went into my next race, the final of the 800 metres, a bit weary. I didn't feel that I was at my best, having just peaked at the Commonwealth Games, but I was determined to give it my best. I was up against it though as that year Jolanda Ceplak from Slovenia had set the fastest time for the 800 metres in five years, winning the indoor title and breaking the world indoor record. At the gun she went straight to the front of the race, setting a blistering pace. By the 500-metre mark she was way ahead of the rest of the pack, leaving us to fight it out for silver and bronze. Jolanda crossed the line to take her first outdoor title. Coming into the last 100 metres, I was in second place but struggling, and the Spanish runner Mayte Martinez charged past me to take silver. I came off the track and went up to Sally Gunnell for the post-race interview and said something to the effect of, 'I just had to go for it. I've been running well over fifteen-hundred metres but the eight-hundred metres has been hard for me this year. I've got to be pleased with a medal. I got one last week and another one this week. I'm doing it cleanly and freely and I couldn't ask for any more.' I had managed to break two minutes but again thought my performance could have been better.

The comment about doing it cleanly caused a terrible controversy. I had the conversation from the previous evening running around my head and was simply saying I was proud of what I had achieved coming back from injury and that I was doing it cleanly. The press twisted my comment and made it look as if I had implied that there was something wrong with Jolanda's win. I would never have done that during an interview. I am always very cautious about what I say, especially to the press. She was reported as saying that she had run the race fairly too, that she considered me a friend and had never heard me say anything like that before, while Robert, our mutual agent, was reported as being baffled by my comments. I couldn't understand the fuss. If I'd come second then I could have understood my remarks being construed as sour grapes, but as it was ... why wasn't it taken that I was criticising Martinez as well? After all, she was the one who had passed me. Apparently I had made the remark as Ceplak was walking past me and I had looked meaningfully in her direction at that moment. What absolute rubbish!

That was when I learned how easily journalists can twist your words and insinuate meanings that aren't there. Since then, I have been very careful about what I say in case it can be misconstrued. More importantly, misinformed reports can cause terrible damage and hurt. By the time the medal ceremony came round, the press were buzzing everywhere like flies and I was aware of the fuss that was being stirred up. Afterwards I was having a massage in the warm-up area when the UK Athletics press officer, Emily Lewis, told me that all the press were waiting outside. By then I had a new manager, Jane Cowmeadow. I had met her through Andy Graffin after my arrangement with Barry Nevill had come to an end and I was on my own. She had only been my manager for two months when this happened and she seemed a bit shocked by the furore. There was only one thing to do. All right, I thought. I've just got to walk outside and confront them. I've nothing to be ashamed of. But when I stepped outside with Jane at my side we were amazed to find that instead of a few reporters, there were the world's paparazzi, camera and radio crews and press journalists waiting at the end of the pathway. We walked up, talking and laughing, unable to believe our eyes. It was like the scene from *Notting Hill* when the Rhys Ifans character, wearing only his underpants, opens the door of the flat to the world's press when they've got wind of the fact that Julia Roberts had been spotted visiting Hugh Grant there. There was no other news breaking at the Championships so they had all jumped on this snippet because it looked like something they could turn into a scandal. The whole episode gave me another view of how the media works. To be honest, I was totally fed up. I always felt that the press had never given me much respect or recognition for my achievements in the face of all the adversity over the years, and now they had this sudden great interest in me all for the wrong reasons.

My greatest worry was how it would affect my relationship with

Robert and Jolanda. Neither of them would know the truth because they hadn't been there and were unaware of the conversation I'd been involved in on the previous evening. When I got back to the village, no one could believe the fuss that had been made. The athletes I spoke to all said that they felt I had been made a scapegoat by the press who were hungry for a story. I knew that Robert had been very discreet and had not risen to the bait offered by the media but I was anxious that he'd think I was a complete coward because I hadn't gone to explain to him that evening.

It was impossible to sleep that night. Anxieties were whirring round my head as I worried what people, especially Robert and Jolanda, might be thinking about me. I didn't want to fall out with them because I really liked Robert and didn't want to lose him as an agent. The other reason I couldn't sleep was because I had to race again the next day. In the morning, I dragged myself out of bed, exhausted. I texted Robert, explaining the truth of what had happened. To my relief, he replied, saying that he believed me and that we would sort things out between ourselves. I had my first heat for the 1500 metres that morning. I knew I wasn't strong enough to be racing again. I was drained by the 800-metre races but had to go through with it. Sure enough, I didn't even get through the heat to qualify for the semis. I remember the final when Sureyya Ayhan, a relative newcomer from Turkey, swept to victory. She ran like a bat out of hell, leading all the way round, with Gabriela Szabo taking the silver and Tatyana Tomashova taking the bronze.

It was at these Championships that I met Gareth Davies from Reebok. Jane had been talking to him, but he approached us to ask whether we'd be interested in discussing possible sponsorship. It was to be the start of a good, long-lasting relationship between me and the company. In January 2003, Reebok took over from Asics who had sponsored me over the previous year after I had moved to them from View From, and they have backed me ever since.

The press were still obsessed by this non-story they'd got hold of, forcing me to take a different flight home from the rest of the team so that I didn't have to face them again. They continued to try to stir things up but I realised that I had to let whatever they wrote flow over my head. I couldn't turn back time and change what I had said to Sally. Neither could I change what people thought. If people were going to accuse me of sour grapes then I would just have to take it. I accept that not everyone will like me as a person and they may make harsh comments against me. I can only respond by being who I am and not pretending to be anyone different. But it was a very unpleasant way to approach the end of the season.

The last meet that year was at Crystal Palace but I was forced to withdraw because I had a really bad cold. My doctor had contacted the officials to confirm that, in his opinion, I wasn't fit to compete. The next thing was that, I got wind of the fact that the race organisers didn't really believe me. I was told that Jolanda was racing and some people saw my withdrawal as a way of avoiding a confrontation between us. I was furious. I wasn't going to have people think I was lying. I asked Andy Graffin to take me up there so that I could show everyone that I was ill and couldn't race.

When I got there, I saw Robert and Jolanda sitting in the bar area. This was the first chance I'd had to speak to them both after Munich, so I immediately took the opportunity to put matters right. I was absolutely honest and told them the truth behind what happened. 'I am so sorry that what I said got twisted in the way that it did. There is nothing I can do about it. If you accept my apology, we can get through it. Otherwise you can think what you like about me, but it won't be based on the truth.' They were both very gracious in accepting my apology and I think they realised how everything had been blown completely out of proportion. It was a huge relief to be able to clear the air.

Nonetheless, after everything that had gone on in 2002, I was feeling very unmotivated. The idea of going back to Hildenborough, doing the same old training and maybe having to face 2003 fighting to get fit for another championship was an all-too-familiar scenario. I knew that something had to change. I couldn't go through another winter, hoping to be injury free, and then, possibly get injured again and end up having to work exclusively in the pool and gym, wondering if I was going to make it. I hadn't the heart to go through it all again.

Sitting near Robert and Jolanda was Jeff Fund, Maria Mutola's race agent/manager and the ex-husband of her coach, Margo Jennings. I'd met him before on the circuit but it was at Crystal Palace that we got chatting properly for the first time. Maria is so focused on her running that she and her team always keep very much to themselves and I had never got to know any of them socially before. I'd heard Maria was training in Johannesburg so I was telling Jeff about my own training arrangements in

Potchefstroom. While we were talking, it suddenly occurred to me that some of my old enthusiasm might be kick-started if I were to train occasionally with Maria. She was always so focused and motivated in what she did that it might bring out my own motivation and give me the spur I needed. After all, Potch is only an hour's drive from Johannesburg. It would be a complete change of environment, scenery and training. It would be different. I asked Jeff whether he thought Maria would mind. She was in her room at the time, preparing to race, so he took my contact details and promised to talk to her about it and let me know what she said.

Not surprisingly, Dave wasn't too keen on the idea. He had my winter training mapped out and felt it might upset my routine. He worried that training on a different programme with one of my rivals might not be the ideal set-up. I explained that I was only hoping to go for three weeks, just enough to change my mind-set. We couldn't resolve anything until the idea became concrete. Later, Bryan English had referred me to Barry Salisbury, an osteopath in Harley Street for further treatment on my back. While I was there, Maria called me herself. Sure enough, Jeff had passed on my message and she was happy for me to come over. We fixed dates that suited us both. At the time, I had no idea that this proposed short training stint was what would make all the difference to my racing career.

# 18. REACHING ROCK BOTTOM

After twenty minutes of hill running, I was dead. Apart from the effect of the change of altitude, my stomach had seized up with a horribly familiar pain. I had no choice but to stop, doubled over in agony. I had set out in the sunshine feeling so positive with Maria on her moped beside me, showing me the area, as I ran up and down the hills that are a guaranteed part of any run in Johannesburg. I had to stop in at a nearby office and ask if I could use their toilet. As I lay on the floor in there, willing the pain to go away, I could imagine Maria wondering who this lightweight was who had come to train with her and who couldn't even get beyond doing a short run. When I eventually came out twenty minutes later there was a mixture of concern and bewilderment on her face. Of course, she had no idea about the stomach problems that had plagued me during my career. I had always kept them to myself and to my immediate team. In any case, I don't think Maria would have been particularly aware of me as a competitor. I had never been a major threat to her on the circuit in the way that Stephanie Graf was. The two of them would battle it out race after race. Whereas I, instead of being able to run as often as I would have liked, would appear, race well, then disappear from the picture.

Nor was I consistently competing against her in the 800 metres because I split between that race and the 1500.

As I walked and jogged back home under the cloudless sky, my only thoughts were of how useless Maria must think I was and how she must be wondering what she had let herself in for, inviting me to train with her. The next day didn't go much better when we did weight training. I was exhausted after the previous day's run and was out of form having had a few weeks break after the season.

Things picked up after that inauspicious start when a few days later, I asked if I could jump in with her training programme. My original plan had been to work with Dave's schedule, but it seemed a bit pointless being in Johannesburg if I didn't train properly with Maria. As I'd hoped, my motivation was returning with the change of environment so I was able to slot in quite easily, although the first couple of days were so intense I thought they would finish me off. The fact that Maria was so focused meant I found my own focus again. I also enjoyed the change in the training schedule. I liked the structure of Maria's coach Margo's training. It was different to Dave's because there was less volume to it but it was a bit more extreme. Instead of long runs and endurance work, I was now covering shorter distances faster, with longer rest periods between them. Her method involved different blocks of training that covered all the phases of preparations. The sessions were split up differently too so, for example, we would do two days of track, one of road repetitions and a few runs between the weight training. I responded well to the change. My positive response wasn't because Margo's methods were necessarily any better than Dave's; it was simply that they were different.

Within the first two weeks of being there, I felt a fantastic improvement. I was able to do everything that Maria did. I felt strong because of the hill running. I adapted very well to the altitude and my enthusiasm for training had come flooding back. I really didn't want to leave at the end of the following week. I had found the motivation that I needed and Maria and I got on really well. We seemed to approach things quite differently. She had the air of confidence of an athlete who had won six world indoor and outdoor championships by then, whereas I had totally lost my confidence after all the set-backs I had suffered. I only had the certainty of my belief in myself. I knew that I could do it. Maria was confident, strong, had no self-doubts and had years of consistent training

*Right* On top of the world. British 1500 metre record. Sheffield, 1997.
*Courtesy of Getty Images*

*Below left* Going for success is often painful. Athens World Championships, 1997.

*Below right* Not a pretty sight after my ruptured calf and torn Achilles, 1997.
*Courtesy of Mark Shearman*

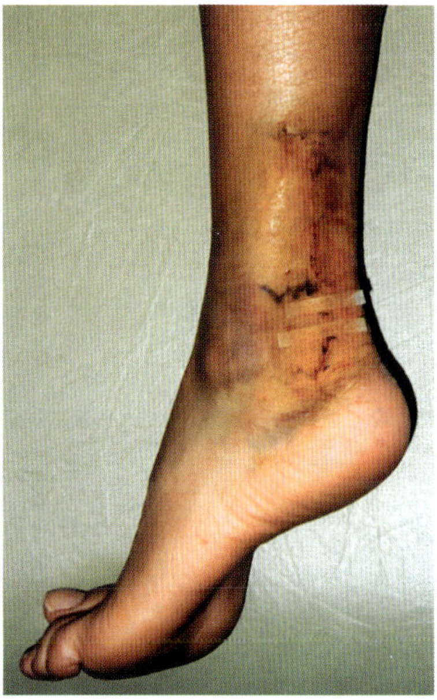

*Above* It's worth all the pain. Sydney Olympics, 2000.
*Courtesy of Getty Images*

*Top right* A year when things ended up right. Commonwealth Games, 2002.
*Courtesy of Empics*

*Middle right* United Nations – me with the amazing athlete Maria Mutola. Now I can smile. World Championships, 2003.
*Courtesy of Getty Images*

*Bottom right* Down and out with a bang . . . cursed? World Indoor Championships, 2004.
*Courtesy of Empics*

*Above left* If I keep kicking my legs, I might not drown!

*Above right* I do train, you know.

*Right* The dreaded ice bath.

*Below left* Can't you go harder, Ali?

*Below right* Margo made the difference.

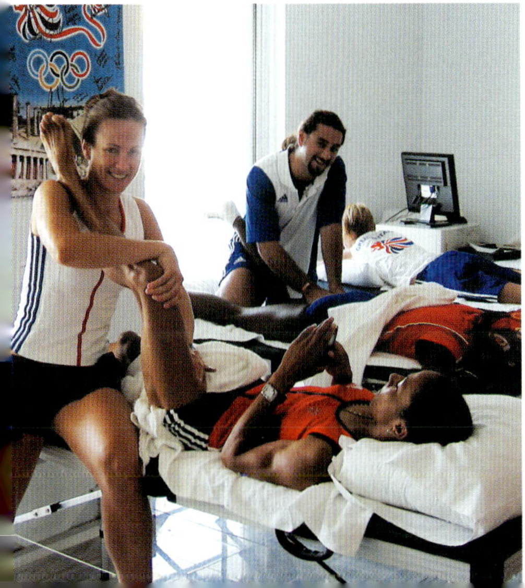

*Above* The photographer knew I'd won. Athens Olympics, 2004.

*Below* I did it! 800 metres gold.
*Courtesy of Mark Shearman*

*Below* Oooh, so close.
*Courtesy of Getty Images*

*Above left* Keeping out of trouble. Athens Olympics, 2004.
*Courtesy of Empics*

*Above right* A dream come true. 1500 metres gold.
*Courtesy of Empics*

*Right* A British record. I wasn't crying – honest.
*Courtesy of Getty Images*

*Left* You were my hero, Seb.
*Courtesy of Getty Images*

*Left* I still can't believe it was me.

*Below* The most amazing sight ever – Tonbridge homecoming parade.
*Courtesy of Empics*

*Left* Pinch me. With Prince Charles and Liza Minnelli at The Royal Variety Show, 2004.
*Courtesy of Empics*

*Below* Carry on smiling. With Barbara Windsor.
*Courtesy of Empics*

*Above* Proud to be an ambassador. With Sir Steve Redgrave, Amir Khan and Jonathan Edwards.
*Courtesy of Getty Images*

*Right* On camp with Kelly in South Africa. Handing over to the next generation.
*Courtesy of Getty Images*

*Left* Honoured by the public – Sports Personality of the Year, 2004. *Courtesy of Empics*

*Below* Becoming a godmother to Arcadia. With handsome Stu.

*Below* A very proud day. Granddad, Dad, Dame Kelly and Mum. *Courtesy of Getty Images*

behind her. All those things combined to make her a totally different class of athlete. It seemed I could only improve my mindset by working with her.

A couple of weeks after I had arrived, I spoke to Margo for the first time on the telephone. She lives in Eugene, Oregon, in the USA and keeps in contact with Maria through regular phone conversations and faxes. I found this way of doing things quite strange because I was so used to having Dave at most of my training sessions, standing there blowing his whistle in the middle of the track. I knew a little of what Margo was like because I remembered seeing her in the tunnel underneath the stadium at a grand prix in Rome. A small, feisty American woman, she was getting very upset because Maria, who had just won the women's 1500 metres (with me in third place), was not receiving a trophy although one was being awarded to the winner of the men's race. She struck me as someone who spoke her mind and stood up for her athlete. I liked both those things. She had been a high school coach in America for over twenty years and during twelve of them she had been involved in coaching Maria, who had moved there on a sports scholarship. I had a feeling that Margo may initially have been a little unsure about my being in Johannesburg with Maria given that we were potential rivals. However I explained to her that I felt the time had come for me to focus on racing in the 1500 metres. I thought it was my best event but I hadn't had a good chance at it because injury problems had always prevented me from doing enough endurance work.

'Maybe I could help you,' she replied, once she could see I wasn't going to be a direct threat to Maria. 'But if I help you, I need you to be in Johannesburg with Maria. You've got the altitude there and it will be much easier for me to work with you.' She did have to think about it but I think she knew that Maria and I would be able to help each other out in certain aspects of training, whether on the runs or with the base training on the track. I had a natural endurance ability whereas Maria was fast and powerful. It would also be easier for Margo to compile our complementary weekly training schedules if she knew how we were both responding to her targets and she could fax us together. Staying in South Africa and training in this way was what I wanted to do more than anything. I thought that, if I followed her programme rigorously, it was the one way that might lead me to achieve my dream of an Olympic gold. Time was getting shorter and I had to take every opportunity

I could to improve. But first I had to return to the UK to sort out my situation there. I had to talk to Dave.

Understandably Dave was disappointed by my decision. We had been together for a long time, with him supporting me every step of the way. However, I knew my career as an athlete was not going to last for much longer so I had to make this change for my own sake. To achieve my dream, I needed the motivation that I was finding in South Africa. He already knew I hadn't been following his training programme, because I'd been texting him the details of what I had been doing. Nonetheless, it was the hardest discussion I've ever had with him. We eventually agreed that although Margo would become my coach, Dave would still be there to give me advice.

When I returned to South Africa at the end of November, Agnes Samaria, a Namibian runner, had also arrived in Jo'burg to train with Maria. She had come into athletics quite late in her life and although very fit was at a different standard to Maria and me. Agnes and I got on very well because we both enjoy other people's company and can see the funny side of most things. I found her an interesting person whose strong religious beliefs made her very sympathetic. The three of us trained together following the weekly programmes that Margo faxed to us. They were always headed with an inspiring motivational words such as: I am strong, not tired; I am fast, not sluggish; I am an aggressive warrior, not an anxious wimp. She would put a positive spin on everything – a half-filled glass of water would always be half full, not half empty.

I started memorising our programmes to the point that I could list exactly what we had to do on each day of the week. I knew every repetition we had to do, the times in which we had to do them and the recoveries. The training was stepping up, getting harder, but I wasn't going to let it get the better of me. Meanwhile Agnes had nightmares about what she would have to do the following day. She often found herself hanging on for dear life to keep up. I was definitely improving but constantly anxious about meeting all the targets that Margo set. We'd laugh together about our reactions to the programme. Neither Agnes nor I liked the hill training because it is so hard on the body and tired us out for the whole day. Whenever we did a three-mile tempo run, sustaining a fast pace all the way, Agnes would lose sight of Maria and me as we charged off into the distance and she was left without a clue where she was going.

Agnes went home by Christmas but Maria and I were joined by

Margo. One of the first things Margo asked me to do was to write down a list of my strengths and weaknesses. The list of my strengths ran to two pages, including:

> *drive, determination, guts, ability to withstand pain, disciplined, experienced, intelligence, courageous, fearless, eye of the tiger mentality, ability to focus and concentrate, desire, hunger, commitment, trust, honesty, strong, good speed, excellent form, motivated, goal oriented, faith in coach's programme, willingness to learn, open-minded, flexible, good traveller, good friend ...*

But I could only list two weaknesses: *injuries and lack of confidence*. There was no doubt in my mind that my biggest weakness was my lack of confidence, which stemmed from my injury problems. My confidence had taken such a battering over the years as I'd ridden this switchback of hopes and disappointments. I had left my career in the Army and my career as an athlete was coming to an end. I had no idea what would happen next. That was a very scary thought.

When I told Margo my goal of becoming Olympic 1500 metre champion, she said, 'OK. I can help you, but first we have to deal with your injury problems.' I was heading back home for a couple of weeks so we discussed the possibility of getting a good team of people to help me and to re-evaluate everything that had happened to me so far. She thought that if we did that, she would be able to work with me to build up my confidence and to help to motivate me towards winning the Olympic gold. I was so happy. It felt like a new start, a new lease of life. I couldn't wait to get going.

My first job was to cook Maria and Margo a traditional Christmas dinner – turkey, stuffing, Christmas pudding, with crackers and party hats, the works. They loved it. Then in the evening we had a party with all Maria's friends, including lots of the guys who were athletes I already knew from the track. Her house is a beautiful modern two-storey building that's painted white and surrounded by lush gardens. It sits in a suburb of Johannesburg that is more like the Hollywood Hills than anywhere else, with its huge houses on massive plots of land. Sun streams into the rooms, which are kept very minimalist and elegant. I had a lovely room that overlooked the pool, with its own bathroom, and I felt at home straight away. It was quiet, relaxing and a beautiful place to stay. Maria had several dogs that were wonderful substitutes for my two dogs at home whom I couldn't help missing, even though I knew they were in the safe hands of my dad. I'd spend ages playing with them in the yard and taking them for walks. I was in my element there. It was the first time I had felt really happy for ages. I knew in my heart that I'd made the right decision and that I was in the right place to do what I wanted.

As the weeks went by the training became increasingly focused. Then Margo suggested I compete in the World Indoor Championships. Normally I was injured during the winter months so I had never been in a position to enter them. I was so used to spending the early months of the year preparing for the summer season, I couldn't believe I would be ready to race in a championship in March. But Margo was superb at giving me the necessary motivation and encouragement. 'Look at what you're doing here. The training is going brilliantly. So do it.' What she did was give me a new target and so succeeded in changing my focus. Although I was nervous, I was also unbelievably excited. I felt as though I had started my athletics career all over again. Everything was going so well that I asked Maria if I could stay for longer. Having such a big house meant that we could easily co-exist without getting in each other's way, so she agreed.

The indoor season kicked off well for me. I felt strong and powerful and I won my first race in a five nations match meeting in Glasgow, running the 1500 metres. Then, I raced the 800 metres in Ghent, Belgium, where I didn't get off very positively; however, when Agnes Samaria came storming past me on the first 200 metres I woke myself up and got back in the race. As I came up on to Maria's shoulder with ninety metres to go, a wire left across the track by a cameraman meant I had to check myself and lost my stride. At that moment, Maria went for it and won. I smashed the British indoor 800-metres record that had stood since 1977 with a time of 1:59.21. I was so pleased with my run and having come so close to Maria. It proved to me that I was running really well. It also proved to me that I had adapted to the very different demands of racing indoors. Because the laps are only 200 metres and it's difficult to overtake on the raised bends, I had to revise my tactics, sitting down to work out my best method of racing but, because I was in good shape, I was well equipped to tackle the new challenge.

During the season, Maria and I went to a training camp in

Barcelona with Jeff, Maria's agent. Jeff helped me there a great deal by organising my travel arrangements and by always timing me in training. He was always there supporting both of us. I felt very uncomfortable about the situation though because Robert Wagner was still my agent. Jeff was doing so much more for me because he was on the spot, yet I wasn't paying him. I decided that after the indoor season was over, I would look at the situation to try and make things easier for everyone. I had a couple more races before the World Championships but they didn't go very well, especially not the Norwich Union Grand Prix, where I ran an abysmal 1500-metre race. I was probably over confident and went out way too hard and then completely died in the final two laps. I was embarrassed and annoyed but it taught me a big lesson: always focus on winning, not on the clock. I returned to Jo'burg for my final preparations but, once again, I started to doubt my ability because I failed to achieve every training target. However I kept on plugging away at them.

The 2003 indoor circuit culminated in the World Indoor Championships back in Birmingham. The main opposition I faced in the 1500 metres was from the American Regina Jacobs. At the age of thirty-nine, she had just broken the World Indoor 1500 record in 3:59.98 at the Boston Indoor Games in February. The fact that she had never run the distance in under four minutes before had prompted all sorts of speculation about her performance but nothing had been confirmed. Maria ran to an easy victory and her fifth Indoor Championship gold in the 800 metres, with Stephanie Graf and Mayte Martinez right behind her. The final of the 1500 metres was half an hour later.

When it came to it, my inexperience at running indoors let me down. Although I knew what I had to do, I was still a little naive about tactics, so I misjudged when to make my move. I had it in my head that with a lap to go we had 400 metres left, when of course we only had 200. Just as we went round the bend, Regina made her break and kicked for home. I sat back a fraction too long as I came into the back straight with 110 metres to go when I suddenly realised, Oh God. We're finishing here. I managed to pass the Russian, Yekaterina Rozenberg, on the inside but I couldn't catch Regina who romped home to set a new championship record while I took the silver medal and set a new British indoor record of 4:02.66. It was a happy end to my first indoor season.

Everything had worked the way Margo had said it would. My decision to ask her to be my coach had been vindicated. I felt so confident with the new arrangement that, after a short break in Hildenborough, I returned to South Africa to get back into Margo's programme. But then disaster struck. After only three weeks of training, I got iliotibial band friction syndrome in my left leg, which meant my tibial band was rubbing against my knee. Every time I ran, the pain in my knee was excruciating. I'd try to carry on but after about twenty minutes into a run, I wouldn't be able to go any further and I'd have to limp home. I struggled through it and, me being me, decided that, in May, I would travel to Scotland to run in a mile road race at Balmoral, regardless. I won the race but I was in agony. I didn't let anyone there know about my leg and I refused to admit to myself that I was injured. However, after returning back to South Africa the pain during training was so bad that I eventually had to stop. I had started to overcompensate and overworked my right leg, damaging my right calf.

Benita, my physio from Stellenbosch, had been coming to see me all through the winter. Knowing how unmotivated I had been at the end of the 2002 season, she had been an enormous support and had wholeheartedly approved of my joining up with Maria, especially once she saw the improvement in me. With this latest setback, we realised that it wasn't feasible for her to fly to Johannesburg as often as I needed physiotherapy. Realistically, I needed someone closer to hand, so I started seeing Dr John Patricios and some of the physios at the Johannesburg Sports Medical Centre. I also saw a chiropractor, Renate Schubert, who was great because she hadn't worked with elite athletes before but was willing to go out of her area to treat me and also to give me physiotherapy sessions. Recovery from the ITBFS was a long-drawn-out process and my calf also took a long time to respond to treatment. I felt so dispirited as once again the outdoor season approached and I was stuck in the pool or in the gym but not on the track. Meanwhile, Maria was carrying on with the training, injury free and getting stronger and stronger. By watching her progress, I could see the point that I should have reached if things hadn't gone wrong. To say it was disheartening is an understatement. I was absolutely distraught. By mid-July, my leg recovered enough for me to compete in two races, but then in a race in Madrid I was forced to pull out because the pain in my calf was so bad. As I hobbled off the track, I felt so scared and uncertain. Once again, it looked as if my season was dangerously close to being over.

Despite my difficulties, and after yet more treatment, I accompanied Margo, her husband Bobby and Maria to Font Romeu, a mountain resort in the Pyrenees. It was an ideal place for high-altitude training with good, though very old, facilities set in beautiful scenery. We all shared an apartment in the town after we decided not to stay in the Institute of Sport because the rooms were tiny. We drove around looking for somewhere to stay and eventually found an apartment block that looked very modern from the outside. Margo ran in to find that there was an apartment that she thought was fine and big enough for us to all share. But when I walked inside I was shocked to see that it was like stepping back in time to the 1970s, with its orange curtains and carpet-like wallpaper. Training began in earnest immediately. Maria's was going amazingly well. But mine? I was in the pool. In the pool. In the gym. In the pool. That was it. I tried to jog but, despite the physiotherapy, my leg still wasn't getting much better. On the other hand, everything was going well for Maria and I'd often go down to the track to cheer her on. But inside, I felt so down. I was reaching a stage where I felt I couldn't take any more injuries and pain. My head felt as though it was on the point of exploding. All I wanted to do was erase everything that was going on in my life at the time.

After one particularly frustrating day, I suddenly felt as if I couldn't cope any longer. I stood in the bathroom of our room in the apartment, locked the door and stared in the mirror, feeling utterly miserable. I was crying uncontrollably but tried to drown out the sound by running the tap into the basin and keeping down the noise of my sobs. There was a pair of nail scissors in a cup on a shelf. To this day, I don't know what made me do this, but I picked them up, opened them and started to cut my left arm with one of the blades. One cut for every day that I had been injured. With each one, I felt I was punishing myself but at the same time I felt a sense of release that drove me to do it again. The pain was intense at first but then it seemed to numb as I went over the same area again and again. When the cuts bled I would stop, but I was still in tears and feeling as though I didn't want to be in this world. I stared at myself with hatred, wondering if anyone could have put a curse on me to cause this endless run of injuries, asking myself,

'Why me? What have I done to deserve all this hurt and disappointment?'

In the lounge, Maria, Margo and Bobby were chatting, oblivious to what I was doing. After that, whenever I felt low, I'd excuse myself and go to the bathroom where I would break down again and get out the scissors to mark yet another day of injury. Once I even cut my chest – a cut that became very sore when I wore a crop top in the swimming pool that kept rubbing right over it. I have a couple of small scars to this day, but I didn't damage myself badly enough for anyone who didn't know to be able to tell. I don't pretend to understand what I was doing, and I definitely knew it wasn't right, but I couldn't help myself. I had reached a place that I couldn't get out of. I have never felt so desperate. Nobody else knew and nobody noticed the telltale scars because I covered them with plasters, then with long sleeves or make-up. But I knew they were there, reminding me of every one of my days without proper training. I know the scars will fade but the memories of that time never will.

It was a very difficult period. Maria was totally focused on her training so naturally had her own preoccupations, while Margo preferred us not to do anything together in case maybe I brought Maria down too. So if Maria or I suggested she came to watch me train in the pool, Margo would discourage her. Looking back, I can understand Margo's reaction exactly but at the time I didn't feel I was getting the support I needed. I couldn't talk to them about the problems I was having because I felt that I would be putting an enormous burden on them at a time when Maria should not have been distracted. She was focused on winning all seven races in the golden league. It would be an astonishing achievement if she could pull it off. The work and concentration she had to put into her training was phenomenal. We were a very tight knit team but I felt a definite second best. Whatever Margo said to me, I never believed I could live up to expectations. It was hard. No one else could understand how I felt because they couldn't know how much my athletics meant to me. My determination not to live with regrets means I always at least try. Not to be able even to do that was killing me.

I knew I needed help, but I didn't know where to find it. I had to try to cope with my negative feelings on my own – one of the hardest things I've had to do. The one person who perhaps could have helped me was Agnes. She was staying at the Institute because the apartment wasn't quite big enough for all of us. I think Agnes could tell something wasn't right when I went to visit her one day. She asked me if she could put some ointment on my leg and say a prayer for me. I was so touched by the gesture. I never told her about the cutting although I desperately wanted to. A bit of me wished I had made the decision to stay at the Institute with her to escape the claustrophobia I was feeling at the apartment. Although we all stuck to the same line of saying we were on one team, training together, I had begun to feel like an outsider. I should have broken away to find some space for myself and for the morale of others, but I didn't. I kept returning to the apartment, and every day my leg wasn't better, I would cut myself again. Those were the days when I reached rock bottom.

Then, gradually my leg began to respond to treatment and I started running a little bit. As things improved I gradually stopped the cutting. Thank God, I no longer needed that outlet for my misery, but inside I still felt desperate. I was so low that I'd find myself starting to well up with tears for no reason and when I was least expecting it.

Things began to pick up a little more after Zara Hyde Peters, my technical director from UK Athletics, suggested that I return to the UK to get some treatment from their medical staff. I hadn't gone before because it was one of those times when I had been living in hope, thinking I'd wait a couple more days to see if it would get better. But time flew by and before I knew it, the weeks had passed. The British trials were up in Birmingham. I had written to say that I would appreciate it if the selectors would consider my championship history and look at my case favourably. I hoped that as long as I proved I was getting back to fitness they would consider my position. Fortunately, they agreed. Bryan English, the doctor, asked physio Alison Rose to start working on my calf while he proposed to try some mesotherapy: homeopathic anti-inflammatory injections into the calf area. I agreed to try it although I didn't think for a moment that it would work. I had reached the point of being willing to try anything that might help my injury problems. I also had a long discussion with Bryan about the continuing problems I'd had with my back since my army days, my stomach and why he thought I was getting so many problems in my lower limbs. He suggested that I went to the local hospital with him for an epidural injection in my back to try to relieve the neural tension he thought I had in the base of my spine. The amazing thing was that after only a couple of days it worked. The pain in my calf had eased so much that I was able to start running again. Certainly I began to improve even more after I had started seeing Ali as well. I was finding new hope although I was still far from recovered. Most nights I cried myself to sleep in despair.

All the gym and pool work Margo got me to do paid dividends. I'd kept my fitness up and I slipped back into running again quite easily. I decided to make a comeback by competing in three races within eight days: a 1500 metres in London, which I won; an 800 metres in Berlin, where I came fourth, and a golden league race at Zurich, the last race before the World Championships, where I ran atrociously, coming in ninth. At that stage I was beginning to doubt my ability to compete in the World Championships but I found that being back running brought back my determination.

The last stop before the World Championships in Paris was a training camp in St Moritz with Maria and Jeff. Although we were training well, I still felt very low about myself, about my chances in athletics and about my life. After a massage one day, I asked to see the local doctor to see if she could help lift my spirits. I spoke to her and we established that anti-depressants weren't an option in case they came within the IAAF's list of banned drugs. Instead, she gave me some herbal capsules that tasted like chocolate and were to help increase the serotonin levels in my brain and to lift my spirits. She wanted to tell my coach but I insisted that our meeting should be entirely confidential. I didn't want to burden Margo, particularly as she had returned to the States by this time. Besides I didn't want to share my feelings with anyone else. Normally, I cope with things on my own and I didn't want to make this an exception.

I was nervous after my performance in Zurich and decided to speak to Zara about my concerns and to ask her if she would check with Max Jones, the performance director of UK Athletics, that it would be all right to put me in the 800 metres at this stage. He agreed on the understanding that I would see where my best chance lay when the Championships began. When we arrived in Paris, I had to make what seemed an impossible decision. The 1500 metres was the second of the two races on the programme. To race in that alone, I would have to pull out officially from the 800 metres for medical reasons. I went over and over the possibilities open to me. Finally, after much deliberation, and having spoken to Ali who gave me a lot of encouragement, I decided I would only enter the 1500 metres.

The morning after I made the decision, I went with Maria and Margo to the athletes' village, where Maria wanted to meet up with some of her friends on the Mozambican team. The three of us went over my options again: which big names were racing and who was the major opposition in each race. Then, someone told us that it looked as though Jolanda Ceplak was pulling out of the 800 metres. That changed everything. With Maria and Stephanie as the two favourites, without Jolanda the third place was now open. The race seemed more appealing now so we decided I should go for it. Margo had to rush over to the UK accommodation block to catch the medical team before they made their official withdrawal. They should have made it at 9 a.m. It was now 11 a.m. Would she be too late? She bumped into the team coming out of the block. When they had gone to see the official at 9 a.m., there had been no one there. They'd been asked to return at 11 a.m. She had caught them just in time to tell them not to pull me out. I was going to run in the 800 metres. My mind was made up.

For a couple of nights, I had stayed at the hotel with Margo, Maria, Jeff and Maria's masseur, just to get out of the village. Maria and I went over the start lists for the heats, with Margo advising us on the other runners and how we should play each of our races. I got through my heat. Maria got through hers. Then we received our semi-final draws. We were in the same semi-final. Margo briefed us as always, advising me that I would have to use my strength. 'If you make a break, make it from a long way out and just go for it without looking back,' she recommended. I decided that I would go at the 200-metre mark. I had to chance it if I was going to be one of the three who made it into the final. As far as Maria was concerned, she could have run it any way she wanted – from the back or the front, fast or slow. She was so much better than anyone else in the field. We both got through to the final.

Again, we knew each other's race plans but that didn't really help either of us because, of course, we had no idea how the other six runners would race and what tactics they'd use. Then we heard that the other favourite, Stephanie, was pulling out because a bottle had fallen on her foot. That changed the race further, opening it up for me. I knew Maria was going to take the lead but my plan was to sit back again, and then go round at about the 250- or 200-metre mark and hold on for dear life, no matter what. Sure enough, at the gun, Maria took the lead and slowed the race right down, almost playing with the rest of the field as she controlled the pace. I stayed somewhere in the middle because I thought it would be better for me to run a more even race. Maria picked up the pace and as we went down the back straight, most of the other runners were in front of me. Then I went wide (what I usually do to avoid being tripped) and legged it past them all to take the lead. The other runners should have followed me but they stayed behind Maria who was still controlling the race. As I led down the home straight, Maria came flying past, looking over her shoulder to check that no-one else was coming after her. As I saw her, I hit the gas. I was so used to running with her in training that I automatically notched up a gear and ran as fast as I could. Natalya Khrushchelyova from Russia was coming up to challenge me on the inside but didn't get past me. Not only did I win the silver medal, the press acclaimed it as the best performance by a British athlete. It was a fantastic end to a bad year – until the controversy began.

We were apparently accused by two of the other runners of fixing the race by running as a team. How ridiculous. Nobody had stopped those other runners from making a break when I did. We didn't put our arms out to prevent them from overtaking us. We were running a damn race. Yes, we did know what each other planned to do, but we had no control over what the others would do. If they thought there was a danger of us running as a team, why didn't someone try to upset our game by blocking me in at the back or passing Maria during the beginning of the race? Then we would have been forced to change our tactics. This was the last thing I needed after the year I'd had.

The next thing was that word went round that a journalist was spreading rumours that Maria and I were having a relationship. The rumours seemed to be based on the fact that we were single, very good friends and I was staying with her while training. Where else would I live in Johannesburg? Why would I want to buy a house there when there was a nine-bedroom house I could live in? Of course I was going to stay there. Both of us had been dedicated to reaching our peak performance at the World Championships, and were glad of each other's company when we weren't training. Simple as that. I could cope with the insinuations because there had been speculation about me before because of my closeness to certain people when I had been in the Army. I had kept true to the vow I'd made to myself then about keeping my private life private. There are always some people who think that they know more than they do, so I just let them think. However it was a different thing for Maria who was very upset by them. She is a big celebrity in Mozambique, having brought so much glory to the country through her athletic prowess. These insinuations could be terribly damaging to her reputation there. What enraged me even more was that the rumour-mongering did affect our friendship badly. As a result of the gossip, we both felt awkward talking to one another in public or hanging out together, in case it was misconstrued. It caused a lot of stress between us that was completely unnecessary and spoiled what had been a very good friendship.

It was during these Championships that the BALCO (Bay Area Laboratory Co-operative) scandal broke. Someone anonymously passed a syringe to the US Anti-Doping Agency. It contained a substance that was later identified as a designer steroid called THG that until then had gone undetected in the athletes using it. The discovery was to point the finger at some of America's biggest and best-known athletes. There had been speculation on the track about some of them for years. We were pleased that these issues were being investigated. I would be happy to go through any number of tests if it helped keep the sport clean.

As the season drew to a close, I decided I wanted to run the rest of the circuit. In Brussels, I came fourth, so I expected that people would again question how I had won a silver in Paris. As a result, I had something to prove at the grand prix final that was coming up in Monaco. As for Maria, she proved yet again what a fantastic athlete she is by winning the golden league – the only person to have ever won the jackpot on their own. To win all seven races at world-class level is an extraordinary achievement by any standards. To be the only person to have ever done it is amazing. The prize money of $1,000,000 is a nice bonus.

The grand prix final in Monaco was the last race of the season. The field included many of the same runners who had competed in the World Championships, Diane Cummins and Natalya Khrushchelyova among them. Maria went to the front of the race again, fighting off Jolanda and the others who were all challenging each other for position. However I had decided to stay at the back and watch everyone make their move until we reached the back straight. I knew it was a risk but I stuck to my plan. I watched every single person making their bid for victory and then, as I came round the top bend with about 110 metres to go, I went like a bat out of hell, my knees high like a sprinter's as I passed everyone in the home straight, although I left it a bit too late to catch Maria. Yes, we did know one another's race plan, but so what? I felt very pleased. I had run against almost identical opposition to the opposition I'd faced in the Paris final but I had run the race completely differently and still had beaten them. I felt it was a moment that justified my medal position in Paris. So, after all my troubles, the year ended with my winning two silvers.

Two thousand and four was looming. And with it came the Athens Olympics. I knew that, now I was in my thirties, it would be my last attempt to win the gold I had dreamed of since I was fourteen. I felt as if this was the year that would make or break my future. My spirits had recovered, but in the back of my mind there was one thing I wanted most of all – to be Olympic champion. Over the years, my dream had begun to seem unattainable, but whatever happened, I was going to try to realise it. Everything I did had to be focused on reaching my peak in Athens. But there were some difficulties that I would have to iron out first.

# 19. NOW OR NEVER

Olympic year: 2004. This would be the most important year in my athletics career. The Olympic Games represent the culmination of the previous four years of every international athlete's life. It was what every training session and every race we'd run was geared towards. I was only too aware that, at thirty-four years old, I might not get another chance at that Olympic gold. This was it. I couldn't afford to let anything go wrong. Margo and I agreed that my success would hinge on my being injury free. With such a terrible track record, I knew I couldn't afford to take any chances.

When it came to discussing the allocation of my funding from UK Athletics, I was very clear. To stay injury free, I needed access to as much medical support as I required. I made a conscious decision that if I had the slightest twinge in my leg, I would immediately see a physio, Ali, whenever possible, and have extra preventative massage. Zara was great and ensured that the cost of whatever treatment I needed, whether medical services or physiotherapy, would be covered. I was to do most of my training work on my own or with a training partner, with Margo faxing me weekly training schedules. The crucial thing we had to sort out was a plan for the year that would incorporate warm-weather training and four-day-long blocks of time when, regardless of my stage of training, I would see Ali and Bryan for treatment and check ups. Ali would give me one of her tough treatments and fix my body. It only seemed to hold up for about three weeks before I would get some sort of back problem, muscle spasm or sore hips – all the niggles that were part and parcel of my daily life as an athlete. Bryan would go through my blood test results, taken monthly in South Africa by a local doctor, Paul Dijkstra, to try to pre-empt problems such as low haemoglobin (the blood cells used for transporting oxygen to the muscles), low ferritin levels (iron stores needed for formation of blood cells) or low magnesium counts, allergy and minor asthma problems that had persisted since my twenties, or any infections that might be lurking. He also checked whether or not I needed more mesotherapy on my back or calves.

Towards the end of 2003, I had suddenly realised that my recurring stomach pains had stopped ever since Bryan had administered the epidural that had helped my injured calf. It seemed like a miracle. After so many years of being crippled by them during training and racing, we seemed to have hit on a solution at last. As a result, we decided that he would also give me what has since become a regular six-monthly update of the epidural. It has made all the difference to me. I have lost count of the amount of physio treatments, stomach injections, X-rays, blood tests, bone scans and MRI scans I have had over the years for my legs, back, Achilles tendons and feet, but without them I wouldn't have been able to keep on running.

With all that settled, I was able to continue my training in South Africa in earnest, looking forward to the World Indoor Championships in March. I had been back in South Africa since October. I only wanted a maximum of three weeks off so I could get straight back into my preparation. Maria was spending quite a lot of her time training away, so I was finding Johannesburg pretty lonely. I realised that if I was going to progress I needed to train with other people therefore I started travelling back down to Potchefstroom more and more for my longer, more demanding sessions. It made all the difference. Having other people supporting me and training with me kept me going. Especially helpful was a South African guy called Charlie, a slim black long-distance runner who was coached by Jean Verster. Being back there felt like a change for the good. Although I felt at home in Johannesburg, I found that being in Potch refreshed my head again. I enjoyed being in a team environment but I found I could also be my own person again.

My training went really well with no injury problems. I felt confident and strong. I won the 1500 metres in Glasgow, the 800 metres at the AAA Championships in Sheffield, now my fourteenth British title, and came second in a 1500 metres in Stockholm. The last race I was due to run before the World Championships was a one-kilometre race in Birmingham. I thought it would be good preparation for my running the championship 1500 metres in Budapest. Maria was running in the same race in Birmingham and had been talking about possibly trying to establish a new world record over the distance.

During training, I regularly called or emailed Margo with my times and repetitions so she could keep an eye on my progress. 'You're in great shape,' she said. 'I think you could run a fast time in Birmingham.' As the meet was on my home turf, I was definitely up for it. I knew Maria would go off with the pacemaker from the start so I had to make my own race plan. I decided to go off at my own pace and run as evenly as possible. Come the race, I started as planned, keeping in the middle of the field. Gradually I made my way past the other runners. Then, coming up to the bell, I went into overdrive as I went past Maria to take the lead. I don't know which one of us was more shocked. I took off and headed for home. Initially, I thought that Maria would charge past me again on the next straight. As I came up to the bend, all I could think about was the finishing line. The next thing I heard was 'Aaaaaah,' and I felt someone trip. Maria had fallen. I stuttered for a moment as I looked over my shoulder, then thought, God! I'd better keep running. The other athletes were getting dangerously close. I raced to the finish, crossing the line and breaking both the British and European records. It was fantastic. My next thought was for Maria so, as soon as I'd been interviewed trackside by Sally Gunnell, I went off to find her. My mum, dad, my brothers, my manager Jane, Zara and my other friends came down to the warm-down track where I had found Maria and Jeff. As we arrived, Maria stormed off. Then I heard that a couple of people were creating a problem over who had tripped whom up and I felt that Jeff wasn't helping matters.

It was a difficult situation, even though everyone else who had seen the race (including the TV commentators) said that Maria had run up very fast behind me, trying to go on the inside where there wasn't a gap. Then Margo called from America. Being a school teacher, she is unable to get much time off to come to support us on the track. She hates not being able to be with us when we're racing so always calls us straight after our races to see how we are doing. She is so good at listening to both versions of events and comes up with her own spin on them. This time, she said that not being there made it hard for her to comment but that we should try to let the situation settle down and not let it get to us, because we had a championship coming up.

I was concerned that Maria might have hurt herself so I thought the least I could do was ask Pedro, a masseur, if he could help. He called the meet doctor and together they examined her and booked the appropriate scans to be run on her injured hip. I'd rather solve the problem of her being hurt than deal with all the nonsense that was going on. I reckoned that, despite everything, we were still a team. The only person there who I could confide in was Zara. She supported me wholeheartedly and we talked a lot, trying to establish what had really happened.

Jeff and I had exchanged strong words because I was so disappointed by what had gone on. I suppose we still didn't know each other very well and both of us feel very passionately about racing. Being able to speak honestly with each other made our relationship stronger. Now we have got to know each other's personality better, we get on well; we're able to say what we want and take digs at each other without them becoming personal.

As a result of her fall, Maria decided not to return to train in Valencia where we had been training earlier in the season before Birmingham. She wasn't used to injury and wanted to nurse her bruised hip at home. Jeff flew off to the States, leaving me to go on my own to Spain. Fortunately, my great friends Andy Graffin and Ali were able to come with me and help me with some intensive training. Being away from everything I knew was ideal. I could focus 100 per cent. I made the conscious decision to be nothing but an athlete until after the Olympics and not to be side-tracked by anything. Margo and I spoke regularly about how I was doing so that she could help me grow the confidence I needed. She is one of the most motivational people I have met. She always gives me a quote on my training plan to keep me focused.

The first time I saw Margo after the problems at Birmingham was in Budapest at the World Indoor Championships. She never normally went to the Indoor Championships but since she was coaching me I had wanted her to be there for support. She was excited to be there and I was feeling good. With two silver medals under my belt the previous year and an injury-free winter, I was thinking everything was on the up. I got through the 1500-metre heats quite easily and was ready for the final. I decided to warm up outside where it was cooler and airier, away from the stuffy warm-up arena I had used before the heats. I went through my normal warm-up procedure of a fifteen-minute easy run and about forty minutes of drills and strides, in between doing my stretches. By the time I got to the track, I was ready, really ready, for the final.

At the gun, I felt fantastic, very bouncy. I knew my biggest rival was going to be Ethiopia's Kutre Dulecha. She had been running very well throughout this indoor season so, out of everyone, I kept her in my sights. For the first four laps I decided to run at the back. I wanted to conserve my energy as much as possible. With three laps to go, I saw Dulecha was up at the front. As I came round the top bend with 500 metres to go, I was watching to see if the leaders made a break. If they did, I would have to go with them. If they didn't, I would wait for another 150 metres before making my move. I can win this, I said to myself. I can win. At that moment, BANG. I fell, hitting the track hard on my left-hand side, ricocheting along the floor. I picked myself up, aware that my side was hurting quite a bit but, ignoring it, I ran on. The crowd were screaming, carrying me forwards as I caught and passed some of the field with another lap to go. Then suddenly with about 120 metres left, I hit that brick wall and I was running on empty. My legs turned to jelly and I could barely put one foot in front of the other. Everybody ran past me and I trailed in a sorry ninth.

My back was hurting badly and I'd been grazed all down my side. I was devastated, convinced that I was jinxed. That could be the only explanation. It was nobody's fault. I couldn't help asking myself why everything had gone wrong for me yet again. The 1500 metres on an indoor track is seven and a half laps, so it becomes very tactical. There's a lot more pushing and shoving for position. You have to be careful and watch out for yourself. Tripping, whether intentional or unintentional, is a regular hazard.

Maria was running in the 800 metres. We hadn't spoken much since Birmingham as I had been in Valencia. I decided to shut off what had happened and to support her. She flew round in her heat, proving that she was still the best in the world, and went on to win the world title. I was delighted at her success and that her leg wasn't causing her a problem. I couldn't help thinking about our different reactions to our separate falls. They made me reflect on myself as an athlete and on the mind-set that I would need for success. Having a fall in the championships was awful. It meant that I had to pick myself up immediately, both physically and emotionally, if I was going to approach the season in a positive frame of mind. If I didn't, I would be lost. I do believe that things happen for a reason. Fate, you might say. I just couldn't work out what the reason for my falling could be. This was the point when I decided to think only about myself. Nobody else. No-one was going to deflect me from my aim.

I had one week at home before I returned to Potch. All my family and friends knew how distraught I would be over Budapest so rallied round to cheer me up. Usually I would have a three or four week break before the summer season but I couldn't stay any longer than the week. I stayed with Mum who understood that I didn't want to hang around. The Olympics were approaching and I knew I wasn't going to get a second chance. I had to get away to refocus and motivate myself. I had to go back to South Africa and get back to training as soon as possible. Eban Verster has been my regular physio in Potch since 2000. He was a brilliant help, and worked every day on my injuries, releasing the effect of the whiplash injury I'd sustained when I fell, so that I could get back to training as soon as possible. My neck and my back were sore for ages. I also began having more regular consultations with Paul Dijkstra, who treats a lot of South African Olympic athletes, to discuss my anaemia, allergy and breathing problems again. It was a very beneficial time for me as I was able to sit down with both Eban and Paul to go through a plan of action for the treatment of my slight injury as well as checking my health status to ensure I was in the best possible shape in the lead up to the summer season. They liaised with Ali and Bryan in the UK. Together they ensured that I was given the best care possible. They gave me an enormous amount of time over the next few months, which was invaluable to me. Without their help and commitment, I would have had a much harder struggle to get over the problems. During the time I was getting treatment, I went to the gym and the pool, gradually getting back into running so that I never stopped training completely. As a result, I was able to go into the next phase building up from quite a high level of fitness. Now all I had in my sights were the

Olympics. My heart and head were both set on my winning gold in the 1500 metres.

My training was going well again, and Margo asked me and Maria to travel to her hometown of Eugene, Oregon so she could supervise our training more easily for a while. We thought the high pollen count in Eugene might affect both of our allergy problems so we stayed in a forest in the mountains where the air was much clearer. As usual my year had been very limited race-wise. I prefer to have good blocks of training to gain confidence. While we were there, I entered the Prefontaine Classic, my second track race of the season, where, after running a not very positive race, I came second in the 1500 metres. I was thinking far too much about how I should be performing, worrying that I should be fitter than I needed to be at that stage of the year. I was also putting too much pressure on myself because it was Olympic year. I ran erratically and was just not completely focused.

By the time I reached the Olympic trials in July, I was feeling strangely unsure of myself. I kept panicking that everything was going to go wrong again. I was nervous because I felt the Olympics were the be all and end all. Whatever happened there would mould the rest of my life. That was a scary thought. At the trials, people were asking me why I was entering the 1500 at the Olympics when I'd only won two races over that distance that year, unlike the 800 where I'd had so much more success. I didn't even really know the answer and worried that I was going to muck up my medal chances. But I just had a feeling that the 1500 metres, the race that I'd been training for, was going to be my race this year.

Margo, Jeff, Maria and I had agreed that in July we would go to a training camp in Madrid just before the Madrid Grand Prix but, because of a niggle in her hamstring, Maria opted to go to St Moritz for treatment. It was so close to the Games that I didn't want to unsettle myself by changing my plans for anyone. So I decided to go to Madrid on my own. The hotel was an hour's taxi ride from Madrid airport into the mountains en route to Segovia. My room was so tiny, I could virtually reach from wall to wall, and the bath was minute, just big enough to curl up in. I'd sit in that room watching DVDs, feeling so lonely, as if there was only me left in the world. I had to keep reminding myself that I was there to train for the Olympic Games, nothing else. I could hardly speak a word of Spanish so I had to resort to sign language and ate the same thing on the menu every day I was on my own. Fortunately I knew Brian Tracey, an Irish ex-runner who lives in Madrid, since I had rented my flat there with Wes in 1999. Most days he would drive up the mountain and take me down to Segovia for my track session's where he would time me and give me loads of encouragement. He of course spoke fluent Spanish, so every now and then he would choose a new meal for me until I got bored with it and had to ask him to choose another!

Inevitably I spent time reflecting on what a lonely life athletes lead. It's exactly the opposite of the life I led in the Army, when I was surrounded by people for most of the time. It's possible to go for days without talking to anyone when I am totally focused on my training. When I do make new friends or form new relationships with people, my athletics has always had to come first. So, unless they're in the athletics world themselves, it's hard to establish and keep contact with people. Having to travel a lot makes it difficult to fit in with anyone else's life and career. If I were to take someone with me, the press would inevitably start talking. I'd rather avoid the hassle, so I prefer to go on my own. I count myself lucky to know that I have my small group of close friends. They are just on the end of a telephone or an email. But when I'm in my training environment, I'm very focused on whichever championships are coming up and I don't let anything distract me. I have to stick rigorously to my schedule, making sure I get early nights and plenty of rest between training sessions.

While I was there I went down to a race meeting in Madrid to run in the 1500 metres. Madrid is slightly at altitude and the track is very hard. The previous year I had a problem there when I had to pull out of the race because of a calf injury so I was determined to put that straight. I was very confident that I would race well but, when it came to it, I just couldn't focus. I ran very negatively, hanging at the back but not making a move when I needed to. With 300 metres to go I put in a huge spurt and came second. As soon as I finished the race my calf started troubling me again and I had to limp off the track. I immediately telephoned Ali. I got the first plane out of Madrid the next morning and went straight up to Sheffield for treatment from her and Bryan. I had reached a point where all my experience of injuries, particularly in 2003, had taught me that the best way to deal with whatever came up was to act immediately.

Ali was astonished to see me. 'I can't believe you've actually done what you said you were going to do,' was her reaction. All through 2004, we had joked about how I was stalking her. Whenever I had the slightest twinge, I'd turn up on her doorstep in Sheffield or Leeds, wherever she was. All year I was having little niggles that might last a few days but were helped by homeopathic injections or physiotherapy. I couldn't have asked for more commitment from anyone. She would even change her appointment book around so that I could be fitted in. I spent so much time with her that I regard her as a friend as well. This particular time, my calf was really sore so one day we spent as many as eight hours in physiotherapy – now that's dedication for you. When she thought I was ready to go back on the track, she'd go with me to time me, watch how I was doing and then give me another session of physiotherapy. At about that time, I joked to Zara that neither she nor Ali could retire, leave the country or disappear from my life until I retired from athletics. I had found in them the best support team.

Even though Margo was now my coach, I still wanted to keep Dave in the picture, so throughout the season I texted him all my session times and recoveries. I was on my own a lot and I was anxious to keep everything perfectly on track for the Olympics. Just having that bit of input from him was fantastic because he knew what I was capable of and I knew he would give me an honest opinion of my form.

My last race of the season before the Games was the Zurich Golden League. I went down to the track for a couple of training sessions with Margo, who was now over for the summer with her husband Bobby. After I finished one session with a fast 200 metres, I started to question which event I should run in at the Olympics. I sensed that I could run a great 800 metres but, because the 1500 metres was second in the programme, I faced a dilemma. Margo also explained to me that if I decided to run in the 800 metres at the Olympics, she wouldn't be able to be on my team. Although she supported me, her first loyalty had to be to Maria in that race since they had a thirteen-year history together. I was a bit disappointed but understood her position. All the same, I couldn't tell her which of the races I wanted to compete in until I could assess my fitness nearer the time. I wasn't sure whether Margo wasn't keen for me to run in the 800 metres because she wanted to avoid any confrontations with Maria or whether, more likely, she thought I might jeopardise my chances in the 1500 metres. I kept going through the different scenarios with her and Bobby until they said they thought I should run the 1500 metres. Margo and I decided to get the Zurich Golden League out of the way before sitting down to go through a potential plan. I gained a lot of confidence from that race in Zurich, even though I came second. I ran it in a much more positive frame of mind, probably only losing because I went to the front with 400 metres to go – something that I hadn't done for a while. It meant I was an easy target for others to attack. When I walked off the track I felt upbeat about going to Athens, especially with the thought that I still had two and a half weeks of preparation left before my racing began. I knew that would benefit me immensely.

That night Margo and I sat down to speak about my preparation. Margo told me to go and write ten track sessions down that I thought would benefit me and she would do the same. When we got back together, we had both come up with about fifteen different sessions each and we combined them to make a plan that could be adapted, depending on how I felt and how the sessions went. This was my blueprint for training when I arrived at the Olympic holding camp in Cyprus the next day.

Most of the British team were staying down in Coral Bay but the endurance runners were put up in Aphrodite Hills, an exclusive resort development on a plateau with golf courses, not far from the beach. We were booked to stay in the hotel but luckily for us it hadn't been completed, so instead we were put up in the villas on the estate. Jo Pavey, whom I planned to share with, hadn't arrived so I was sharing a lovely, quite small apartment with Liz Yelling, a marathon runner. There were two pools, it was beautifully quiet and I was very happy to be there. Whatever happened in the next two weeks would mould whatever happened at the Olympics.

Training was extremely intensive. Ali was on hand for physio as part of the athletics medical team, and Bryan was there in case of emergencies. Ali and Zara pretty much forced me to climb in the dreaded wheelie bins filled with ice and cold water after sessions to help boost the recovery of my leg muscles and avoid injury. Zara had told me that I was able to take a training partner to help me with my sessions. Andy Graffin had been ill before I went to Cyprus but, although he was now back in training, I made the decision with Zara to ask Tony Whiteman, former British number one 1500-metre athlete, to step in. I felt bad about leaving Andy because he has always been such a fantastic friend but I couldn't risk him not being fit enough to cope when I was stepping up to the next gear. I had to think of myself. Sometimes an athlete has to be selfish and do what's best for them. This was the only chance I had to get everything right.

Tony took over as pacemaker for every single session I did. I gave Zara the schedule that Margo and I had devised and she would tell Tony what the time splits and pace had to be. I relied on him and followed his lead. Everything we did had been well thought out and was extremely demanding, with back-to-back sessions that would push me to the limits until I was left exhausted, crawling on my hands and knees on the track. The volunteers (British ex-pats living in Cyprus) rallied to help all the athletes with whatever they needed. They fetched me bags of ice so that I could cool my legs or neck down during my sessions. Ali was always there to give me a massage, and along with Zara would force me into the ice bin. Bryan was panicking that I was pushing it too hard and would cross that fine line between peak fitness and illness or injury. But I put all my faith and trust in the people around me and risked it. The only way I would have a chance at winning that elusive gold medal was by building up strength and confidence in these final sessions. I relied on Tony and he did a really good job. He, like Ali and Zara, was extremely motivating at a time when I most needed him to be.

Although Margo wasn't there I trusted her strategy implicitly, but I needed the input from an outsider, especially one who knew me and knew what I had achieved in the past. I didn't change anything in Margo's plan but I am eternally grateful to Dave, whom I was constantly texting with my times, for spurring me on and giving me confidence, telling me whether I was looking strong or where I was lacking in speed. He had kept my training diaries over all the years we'd been together so it was useful to be able to compare my achievements and fitness levels from previous years – something I was unable to do with Margo.

I was getting into the best shape of my life and was totally focused on what I had to do but nonetheless was able to relax and enjoy the company of everyone there. One night Ali and I were walking back from The Retreat (eventually to be transformed into a beautiful health club) where we'd been watching television and refuelling on the available snacks. I turned to her and said, 'I can't believe everything's going so well. Something is bound to go wrong.'

'Don't be so pessimistic. Why should it? Of course nothing's going to happen.' Ali was quite confident but experience made me uneasy.

'Something is bound to go wrong,' I insisted. 'I'll probably get bitten by one of those black snakes that we saw on the golf course yesterday.'

'Of course you won't. Everything is going to be fine,' she reassured me. 'You're in great shape.' She was determined to stop me from being at all negative so we ended up laughing about the idea of the snakes. Then we said goodnight and went to our respective apartments.

At 2 a.m. I was woken by the most excruciating pain just under the back of my left knee. As I grabbed my leg, it felt as if a bolt of lightning had ricocheted up my arm. I lay there, petrified, convinced I was having a heart attack as the pain shot up my arm and into my shoulder. For the third time in my life, I thought I was going to die. I reached across the bed to the telephone so that I could get hold of Ali or Zara. Their phones were off. Holding my shoulder, I got myself out of bed and managed to get to Zara's place, where I found the key left in the front door. Lucky for them I wasn't a burglar! I let myself in and tiptoed round, knocking quietly on the bedroom doors, whispering Zara's name as loudly as I dared. I had no idea which room was hers. Eventually she heard me. Together we went to wake up Bruce Hamilton, another of the UK Athletics doctors. As I described my symptoms, I could tell he thought I must be having a heart attack or a stroke. He checked every thing, then asked where I had felt the original pain. I showed him the point behind my knee. After looking at it carefully, he said he could see two little red marks where I'd been bitten by something. Terrified as to what it might be and yet not wanting to sleep until we knew, Zara and I went back to my room to see if we could find the culprit. She slowly removed the sheets from my bed, one by one, gently shaking them. As she took off the last one, a wriggling black something shot out of my bed. It was at least four inches long. We screamed. There was no way I was getting back into that bed while that was in the room, whatever it was.

When we called Bruce to tell him we'd found something, he came down and helped take the room apart until we found the creature hidden between the window and the shutter. Zara squirted an entire can of insect repellent on it before they picked it up and dropped it into a mug of water, ready to take to the hospital. Immediately, it began to shed its skin. I've never been so glad to say goodnight to someone as I was to Bruce when he walked out, taking the beast with him. For the rest of the night I wore my tracksuit and socks and slept with my light on.

The following day, the hospital told us that it was a large millipede known as 'forty legs' – more like forty million legs! – and recommended treatment with anti-histamines. Meanwhile Liz had appeared bleary-eyed from her room asking, 'Are you all right?'

'Didn't you hear what went on?' I couldn't believe she'd slept through it all.

'Well, I did hear something. Then I heard a bloke's voice so thought it must be someone you'd brought back to the apartment and ignored it. Then, when I heard screaming, I thought you must be being mugged so I didn't dare come out.'

'Thanks, Liz. Charming. I could be dead by now!' By this time I could see the funny side of the whole episode. The story went round the camp like wildfire. As I told everyone, they were then to be found anxiously checking their bedding every night. Meanwhile I breathed a huge sigh of relief, along with the rest of my team. We were all being so cautious to ensure that I didn't trip, twist my ankle or pull a muscle that none of us had thought of the Cypriot wildlife as a potential threat. Surely there couldn't be anything else that would jeopardise my chances when I was so close to my dream?

# 20. GOING FOR GOLD

Knowing what I know now, I look back at that fortnight in Cyprus and see the omens that presented themselves to me, although I didn't see them then. Some of them were trivial enough at the time but seem weighted with significance now. It's almost as if everything was meant to happen the way it did.

Throughout my life, my relationship with my hair has been erratic, fraught with difficulties one minute and going brilliantly the next. Over the years, I have experimented with what must be hundreds of different styles, starting with my Afro days and moving through short, straight, curly, long, layered, loose, tied back, up, down ... You name it, I've tried it. By 2004, my hair was braided. Superstitiously, I decided that I had to get it redone while I was in the Cyprus holding camp. I wanted my hair to be just right when it came to my first heat of the Games. I went on and on to everyone about how I had to find a hairdresser. I had arranged to go down to Coral Bay to see British sprinter Joyce Maduaka but because of a slight change in my programme that day, I had to cancel. I was getting very nervous until the sprinter Daniel Plummer – one of the those who had 'gate crashed' the endurance team's base along with Darren Campbell, Linford Christie and a few others – stepped up to the plate. 'I'll do it,' he volunteered.

'Are you sure?' I was hesitant about taking up his offer. A guy? An athlete?

'Oh yeah. I do my sister's. It's no problem.'

I was so relieved to have found someone who could help me so we fixed a time during the Sunday evening before he was due to fly to Athens. The same day after training, a bunch of us went to Aphrodite's Rock, a massive chunk of stone that rises from the crystal clear sea at the spot where the Greek goddess of love and beauty is said to have risen from the waves. The beach beside it is one of the most beautiful on the island. We were mucking around, skimming stones, when we were approached by a small knot of tourists who had recognised us. We stopped to have our photos taken with them and then they went off. As we played, I kept going on about my hair, telling everyone that this was the last go and nervously looking at my watch so that I wouldn't be late. After I won the aptly named title of Olympic skimming champion, one of the women from the group of tourists came back. She said, rather sheepishly, 'I never do this but my name's Patricia. Here's my card. I'm a hair braider back home near Wembley.' What a weird coincidence. I just said, 'I wish I had met you earlier. I needed a hair braider.' I stuck the card in my pocket, said goodbye and we all left to get back to the camp.

Daniel had gone off somewhere with Darren Campbell and I couldn't find them anywhere. I was beginning to panic about getting my hair done at all. At last he appeared at about 9.30 p.m. but took half an hour to do the first parting. He couldn't find a comb so was struggling to do my hair with a pen top. I began to worry as I sat there with my hair undone, with just one parting and the beginning of the first corn-row. Then he charged off to be with Darren who had sustained an injury problem. I was left sitting there with my hair all over the place. Without thinking, I put my hand in my pocket and found Patricia's card. I had completely forgotten about it. Zara, Tony and Amy Terriere, a member of the BOA support team who became my ice-bath buddy, encouraged me to telephone her. How could I? The poor woman was on holiday. She probably didn't have her English phone with her, but it was my last option. I dialled. The call wouldn't go through. Encouraged to try again, I dialled once more. This time Patricia answered.

'Hi. It's Kelly Holmes. We met on the beach this afternoon.'

'Yes, I remember.'

'I know you're on holiday but I need you to save my life. I need someone to do my hair before the Olympics and I'm leaving the day after tomorrow. I'm desperate,' I concluded.

'Sure, I'd love to,' she replied.

We arranged a time for her to come over the next day. She did a fabulous job and, just as importantly, we immediately hit it off. Patricia is one of those warm, calm people who, once they jump into your life, you want them there all the time. She did my hair that day, brought me luck, and has done my hair ever since.

The last day in the camp, I was still undecided as to whether I should compete in the 800 metres or the 1500 metres. I needed one session to tell me what to do but I had to make up my mind by the next day. Just as in Paris I would have to withdraw officially from the 800 metres in good time so that I would still be allowed to run in the 1500 metres. On the way to my last session, I was in the car with Tony and Zara, flicking through the radio stations. I was humming along and happened to say, 'I'm just in the mood to listen to Tina Turner's 'Simply the Best'. To our amazement, just as we drew up at the track, the song started playing. Zara just said, 'Oh my God.' The coincidence gave me goosebumps. We listened to the whole song before we got out of the car, with me fired up for my session, the last one before the Olympics. It had to go well. Just as we started, I became aware of that same strange feeling that I had experienced before I broke the British record in 1997 and before I won the Olympic bronze in Sydney. I was floating. My body was working perfectly. Nothing could touch me. The last session was two 400-metre repeats. I ran them in the best time of my life, in times that even the 400-metre girls would have been proud of. I went mad, running round the track, screaming at the top of my voice. 'I'm ready. I'm reeeaaadddy.' At last I knew was in great shape. I had my confidence. I now could believe I had a chance of winning a medal.

Seeing those times, Zara and Ali said I had to go for the 800 metres. I knew they were right but first I had to text Dave for his opinion. I trusted him to give me direct answers. He had been warning me not to overdo it but his reply came back, 'You have to go for it.' At last I was ready to enter both events. I phoned Margo to tell her. It must have been difficult for her, torn between two runners, but I appreciated her loyalty to Maria. Besides, I had my own fantastic support team who were seeing me through. All Margo could say was, 'Go with your heart. I can't be with you but I support you.' The one thing I didn't tell her was the times that I'd achieved that afternoon. I was on my own now and they were my ammunition. I didn't want a chink to be exposed in my armour. If I told her, it might give them an extra advantage over me, as I knew nothing about how Maria was doing in training. For nearly two years we had both known every one of each other's strengths and weaknesses but the time had come for me to keep my extra strength secret. We were in two camps now.

That night I wrote the press release announcing my decision to run both the 800 metres and the 1500 metres. I made a conscious decision not to do any pre-race interviews. When the BBC came to the camp, the others smuggled me out in a van to escape them. This time, my legs were going to do the talking.

When we got to Athens, I went to my room in the village and immediately rearranged it so that I felt comfortable, moving the two beds together and doing the same with the two wardrobes. I pinned the cards and letters wishing me luck and the motivational sayings I had received onto the wardrobe doors. My first heat was the next day. I opened the door to let in some air. I was sitting on my bed, listening to music, when a gust of cold air blew in round my face. I'm not religious but for that brief moment I felt as if there was something watching over me. It made me feel completely relaxed. I knew I was ready. I decided to adopt Alicia Keyes' 'If I Ain't Got You' as my song of the Games, while the Ben Sherman dog tag we had been given would be my lucky charm.

I agreed to do one interview with the BBC once I was in Athens to explain why I'd decided to run the 800 metres, although I still kept my form close to my chest. My reticence with the press helped keep the pressure off me, as well as the fact that all the British hopes were pinned on Paula Radcliffe. She had to cope with so much going into those Games. Everyone was expecting her to win a gold, while although people in the sporting world assumed I'd get a medal, nobody was expecting me to win a gold.

The atmosphere in the Olympic village was fabulous. I was sharing an apartment in one of the British blocks with Tracy Morris and Liz Yelling who were both running in the marathon, Kelly Southerton who was in the heptathalon and Jo Pavey who was in the 5000 metres and the 1500 metres. We arrived six days after the official opening of the Games and were expecting Goldie Sayers (javelin) and Kathy Butler (10,000 metres) to join us. Denise Lewis was downstairs and Paula was next door. Everybody was nervous about what lay ahead but there was a terrific sense of camaraderie and mutual support.

On the day of my first heat, I discussed with Bruce Hamilton my anxieties about not having enough time to recover between the 800-metres final and the start of the 1500-metres heats. We agreed that the best thing would be for me to make up a carbohydrate drink, a protein drink, a rehydration drink and a cheese and ham roll before the race and take them to the track with me so they would be instantly available when I'd finished racing. I spent the day before doing some drills and acceleration work at the track. It was very odd seeing Jeff, Margo and Maria there but not being able to talk to them, although Jeff did come over to say hi and how good he thought I looked. Focusing 100 per cent on myself and on what I wanted to achieve made me feel stronger. In the evening I forced myself to have an ice bath in the cellar of one of the blocks before going to the dinner hall. The hall was vast but a little disappointing after the excesses of Sydney where the choice of food had been so great. In Athens, the choice was more limited but I always managed to find something good. The most important thing was to get an early night, so I retreated to my room, where I laid out all my kit on the bed for the morning, and took a mild sleeping pill – something I had never done before but I wanted it to help me relax. I needed to be as chilled as possible. As I listened to my song, I dozed off.

The most important thing I wanted to do on the day of the first heat was suss out where everything was so that I knew how long the bus would take to the stadium, and what to expect of the warm-up area and the call room. My mind had switched into racing mode. I just wanted to get on with my heats. At last the time came for Zara to take me down to the track, establishing the pattern for the rest of the week. At the warm-up track I concentrated on warming up and doing a fifteen-minute jog while singing my theme tune out loud. Then I went back to where all the physios were, to do my drills and stretching, before Zara put my numbers on my vest, another ritual we were to repeat for every race. I went through the call room, having my kit checked, before going down the tunnel to the stadium. I noticed Agnes Samaria, who was in the heat before mine, and wished her luck. Then it was my turn. I entered the stadium, kissing my lucky charm, the silver dog tag engraved with the British flag, as always looking out for the British flag, then took up my position. We were off. I hung back off the pace as much as I could, trying not to expend too much energy by racing as efficiently as possible. With 250 metres to go, I made my move towards the front and won quite comfortably. Afterwards I went to the mixed zone and got my bag from Bryan English, and immediately began replacing my energy by taking the drinks I'd prepared. I put on some compression socks that I had been told would help with any inflammation, warmed down and went for a massage with Ali and an ice massage with Bruce.

The semi-finals were the next day. I knew I was facing Jearl Miles Clark, who always pushes the pace, and the Russian Tatyana Andrianova, who was a bit of an unknown quantity. I wanted to repeat exactly the routine I had established the first day, so I texted Sally Gunnell who was the first person I had seen when I came off the track. I asked her if she'd have some peanuts and a bottle of water for me. I wanted my recovery to begin as soon as possible after the race. Usually I tend to go into my shell at championships but this time I felt so relaxed that I was quite sociable, even having lunch with Agnes. At last I was at the track again, eying up my opponents for signs of tiredness. They all were looking good. I had decided to adopt the same tactics as I had used the day before. At the gun, Jearl went to the front but I was watching her while not letting the others get too far away from me. Once again I made my move on the back straight into third place. With 100 metres to go, Andrianova, Miles-Clark and I were fighting for the winning places but I got home first. Sally was waiting for me with my peanuts and water but I kept my interview with her very brief. I didn't want to destroy my focus.

That night, Kelly Southerton came home at about two in the morning having won a bronze in her first Olympics. Fantastic. I remembered what I'd felt like in Sydney and decided there was no way she could come back to a quiet apartment so I got up and we had a good chat. I refused to look at her medal though, just in case it jinxed my chances.

During my rest day, the atmosphere in the apartment was charged. Liz and Tracy were both running in the evening. I went to the physio room to watch the race on television. We were surprised to see that Paula didn't break away, wondering whether she had another tactic up her sleeve. Then she pulled up. It was heartbreaking to watch her cry. We all knew how much pressure she had been under and how much winning the marathon meant to her. I was so pleased however for Liz and Tracy when they eventually arrived back, delighted with their own performances.

The 800 metres final would be one of the toughest I'd faced. The contenders were very strong indeed. Dave texted me, giving me exactly the support and advice that I needed with his view of the other runners' strengths and weaknesses.

The final was in the evening, just as the heats had been, so I could stick to the same routine. Throughout the day, I kept myself to myself, watching a DVD of *Finding Nemo* to pass some of the time. When I got to the track, I spotted Margo. She had been on a run in the morning and had come to my room to wish me luck. I could tell that she felt awkward. As my coach, she wanted to be with me and to give me guidance. I understood why she couldn't. We didn't discuss the race or my form and she left me with the words, 'Be strong.' That was enough to tell me she was behind me. She confirmed it when, at the warm-up track, she made the effort to come over, wink, say good luck and pat me on the back. At last we were on the track itself. The time had come. As I did my strides, Maria ran past, touched me on the hand and said, 'Good luck.'

As the fastest qualifier, I had drawn lane three. Lanes three and four are normally given to the top seeded runners to allow them a good break. I focused, feeling good. At the gun, Jearl went out hard again with Tatyana following. They pushed up the pace but I stayed calmly at the back of the field. Maria and Jolanda were in front of me. Along the back straight, we were running together alongside Hasna Benhassi. At the bell, I tried to move around some of the athletes but I was bumped. I didn't let it affect me and I just carried on forward without losing my focus. As we approached the 300-metre mark, I determined not to go too early. The field closed together and I began to make my move again. Maria was on my inside. As I tried to pass her around the top bend, she overtook someone else. I was bumped again but dealt with it. I came wide off the top bend and was level with Maria as we overtook Tatyana and headed into the home straight. I didn't think about Maria or the way she was running as I sometimes had in the past. This time, I was going for the line. Ten metres from it, I told myself, 'Relax.' I dropped my shoulders as I had practised in training, using my arms even more strongly. Those ten metres seemed more like one hundred. I crossed the line first with Jolanda and Hasna right on my shoulder and Maria just a stride behind. I had won. I started to celebrate, my eyes popping out of my head, my mouth wide open, but then had a second of doubt. I lowered my arms a little as I realised that I couldn't possibly have won the gold. I looked up at the giant screen waiting for the replay. Then a British photographer yelled, 'Kelly. You've won.' I heard the words but they didn't register. He shouted again. At that moment, I could see for myself that it was true. My eyes almost popped out of my head again as I watched the winning moment. It was true. I didn't know whether to laugh, cry or scream. I desperately wanted someone to hug me or pinch me. I don't imagine I will ever recapture that extraordinary feeling. I was in a complete daze as I completed my lap of honour, before going to the mixed zone for interviews with the press who were as surprised as I was.

At the medal presentation, I was shaking like a leaf but Sebastian Coe – Lord Coe – came over to give me a hug to congratulate me. My hero. This couldn't be happening. During a delay before the medal ceremony, while there was an inquiry into whether Hasna or Jolanda had come second, Seb kept talking to me and then suggested I do my cool-down. Of course, I would be racing again the next day. 'Yes, I'd better,' I agreed. But he knelt down and helped me off with my spikes. Lord Coe helping me take off my spikes! This was getting more surreal by the second. I asked Jolanda if she wanted to join me so we cooled down together, so the muscles wouldn't stiffen up.

At last the inquiry announced that Hasna had won the silver and Jolanda the bronze. As we walked into the stadium, our national flags draped round us like sarongs, a massive cheer went up from the crowd, almost drowning out the trumpet fanfare. After the other two had received their medals and flowers, it was my turn. 'And Olympic Champion for 800 metres in Athens 2004 is ... Kelly Holmes.' The roar from the crowd was deafening as I stood there, wanting the moment to last forever. Seb presented me with my medal – another unforgettable experience – before we turned to the flags for the national anthem. As the Union Jack rose above the Moroccan and Slovenian flags, 'God Save the Queen' boomed out across the stadium. I tried to sing but could only look at our British flag and take in the stadium, packed with people singing at the top of their voices. This was the best moment of my life.

After the obligatory press conference, I was whisked off to doping control, where it was compulsory for the first four athletes in every final to be given a blood and urine test. I have no complaints about having to go through this routine but irritatingly it always seems to take me about two hours before I can produce a sample when, all the time, I was dying to go and celebrate. I didn't get back to the village until late, but I only wanted to be with the two people who had helped me so much, Zara and Ali. Jo was in the dining room too, having come fifth in the 5000 that evening. Another brilliant result. Like me, she was going to be running in the heats of the 1500 metres the next day so it was good to know I wasn't the only one thinking, 'Do I have to?' Zara reminded me that I should have an ice bath before going to bed. What a way to end the day but I knew she was right.

At last I was alone in my bedroom, sitting on my bed. I looked at my medal and tears came to my eyes as the realisation hit me, for the first time, that I really had achieved my lifetime's dream. I put the medal on the pillow beside me as I went to sleep.

The first heat of the 1500 metres was in the evening of the next day. Winning the 800 metres was a complete bonus. The 1500 metres was the race I had come to Athens for. In the morning I enjoyed congratulations from everyone I bumped into before going for a BBC interview, where I even got to talk on air to Ann Packer, the 800-metre champion in the 1964 Tokyo Olympics – another great moment. At 11 a.m., I went with Bryan to the doping control centre in the village for my post-race blood test. After making myself eat some lunch, I had one of Ali's more agonising treatments. Every muscle in my body was stiff, crying out in protest as she concentrated on my legs, ankles and back. To relieve the tension in my back, she used some acupuncture needles – a blessed relief from her elbows. I went for a much-needed rest before leaving for the track with Zara about two and a half hours before the race.

I warmed up using exactly the same routine that I had used in the 800-metre races. This time Margo was at the track, able to join my team because of course Maria was not racing. She was sensitive to the fact that Zara and I wanted to keep to our routine so stood back to let us follow it, just letting me know that she was rooting for me all the way. The race itself went by in a blur. I had decided to adopt the same tactics as I had in the previous races and stuck to the back, coming up to qualify by finishing second to Natalya Yevdokimova of Russia. This time Sally welcomed me with cashew nuts, which I munched through the interview. Keeping the interviews to a minimum, I made my way to Bryan and my routine recovery programme. All I wanted to do was sleep, so I returned to the village for something to eat, the obligatory ice bath and bed.

I had two priorities during the rest day: getting checked over by Ali, and getting my hair done. The other thing I wanted more than anything was breathing space, so I escaped with Kate Howey and Lorraine 'Cleo' Shaw to the British Lodge where we lay by the pool with friends and family who had come from the UK to support us. It was what I needed to make me relax and unwind, countering the nervousness I was feeling about the next race. Just as with the 800 metres, I had a tough semi-final draw with Olga Yegorova as my biggest threat. I spent the day of the race quietly, playing my Alicia Keyes' song and other music, and seeing Ali for a little more work on my back.

When I reached the warm-up track with Zara, Margo was there to offer advice. 'Run as you normally do. You're looking great. Hang back for the first two laps.' It was great for me that she was there but Zara, having been with me since Cyprus, was the one who was really keeping me going, intent on maintaining our routine and my focus. Once I was on the track, I could hear the British fans calling my name but I shut them out as I prepared myself to race. I knew I had it in me to reach the final and I was not going to mess up. As I stood on the start line I heard them announce, 'Kelly Holmes, the 800-metre Olympic champion.' It felt so weird to realise they were talking about me. But there was no time to think about that. I was ready to run. Remembering Margo's words, I stayed at the back for the first 800 metres, keeping an even pace. I gradually made my way up the field, making sure that I stuck close to the runner in fifth place. I had to be in the first five to qualify so, if the worst came to the worst, I'd only have one person to sprint past. The day off had benefited me, as had those back-to-back training sessions I had done in Cyprus. I was doing well, feeling good. As I went down the home straight, we were fighting for position. I glanced to the left to see how many people were there. Zara and Margo had said, 'Hang back. Don't show everything you have.' I ran past four of them, then did as they had suggested, hanging back to finish second. I was in the final.

On the rest day before the final, I was forced into playing mind-games with myself. I hid my medal in my room and tried to convince myself that the 1500-metres final was the first of my races at these Olympics. Zara kept reminding me there was only one race to go and it was the race I had come here to win. The 800-metres medal was a bonus. Ali worked on my back again and then it was at last time for my hair. Zara had found out that Aleen Bailey, the 100-metres runner on the Jamaican team could and would do it for me. While she was neatly plaiting the corn-rows, in walked Merlene Ottey, the amazing sprint heroine. At 44, she is a great ambassador for our sport and is still competing. Talking with her took my mind off the race. Aleen did a great job on my hair, especially since she was competing herself that evening in the 4 x 100-metres relay. She had told Zara that she welcomed the distraction of doing my hair. While she worked, she suddenly said, 'I can't believe I'm doing the hair of an Olympic champion. Maybe if I touch it, it'll give us good luck for tonight and we can come back with gold.' Later that evening, as I watched her and her team-mates take their lap of honour, having done just that, I wondered again about the role Fate was playing at those Games.

I woke up early on the day of the race. Margo and Zara had gone to watch the footage of the semi-finals so Margo could come over to chat about the final. I hadn't wanted to discuss tactics on my rest day because I wanted to empty my mind as much as possible. She appeared in the late morning to go through my game plan. Assuming the pace would be fast, we decided that I should stay at the back for the first 800 metres, making sure I didn't become detached from the field. I would only start moving a couple of places up to fifth or sixth just before the bell, then moving up a little further so that I would be in contention with about 200 metres to go. Then I would be in a position to kick for home whenever I wanted. We talked about the other runners, all of them fantastic athletes. It was not going to be an easy race. Afterwards we went for lunch to be joined by Agnes and by Ali and Zara later. On the way back to my apartment to rest, I bumped into Max Jones, UK Athletics' performance director, who said that what I had done had made me one of the greatest athletes, but if I were to win tonight, I would become a legend. I hadn't even thought about what it would mean if I won again. All I wanted to do was run the best I could and finish.

That evening, many of my precious routines were upset. Ali and another couple of people were on the same bus as Zara and I. Would it be significant? I tried to block it out of my mind. When we got to the warm-up track, I was to find the UK physios had moved from their normal spot. I wanted to go back to where they had been before, at the bottom of the track, but another team had already got there first. I kept telling myself it was only a place on a track. How much could it matter? Ali worked on my ankles and Pedro, the team masseur, gave me a massage while I watched the men's 4 x 100 relay team warming up. I remembered Sydney when my mind had been a million miles from winning the 1500 metres once I'd won my bronze. This time it was different. I was an Olympic champion. I had to stay totally focused. My lucky song was going round and round my head. I prepared myself by doing my stretching and drills, my strides and some sprints. I was feeling good. The relay guys were jogging around, looking good too.

It was time to go. Margo told me how strong I looked, how I must believe in myself and stick to my plan, then Zara took over as we went together to the call room. The atmosphere was very intense. Few people were speaking as I took in the whole field for the first time, weighing up who they were. I put on my spikes, kissed my lucky charm and went to do my strides on the track. In the background, the sound of the crowd was like a distant buzz. My mind was on the race. At the sound of the gun, I headed for the back of the pack, keeping exactly to our plan. The only runner I was aware of was Benhassi. I must not forget she was behind me because I was only too aware of her strong finish. I had no idea who was in front or even who I was behind. I began to move up the field exactly to plan. At one point someone caught me but I stuck out my arm to push them back and carried on running. Along the back straight, I began to pick up the pace, making sure that I was going to be in contention for the last 150 metres. Coming round the top bend, I looked behind me to check for Benhassi. I couldn't see her. I had to be sure because once I changed pace that would be it. With ninety metres to go, I made my move, then at fifty metres I kicked for home. Something took me to that line. As I crossed it in first place, the feeling was indescribable. I had achieved my lifetime's dream twice over.

It had taken years of dedication, commitment, focus, emotional, struggle and pain but now I had done it. I was double Olympic champion, with a new British record of 3:57.90. And yes, it was worth all the wait.

I dropped to my knees exhausted and overcome by emotion. As I got up, I had tears in my eyes. The crowd was ecstatic; the photographers in front of me were going crazy. Someone threw me a British flag so I could take the lap of honour. Although my legs could hardly carry me, I made my way round shadowed by a television crew on a buggy. I raised my arms but I hadn't the energy to keep them up for long. I felt as if I was in a dream that I never wanted to wake from. Sally was waiting for me with nuts again. I scoffed them as we talked even though I didn't really need them now that my Olympic journey was over. As I was interviewed by various television channels, I became aware of that tearing pain gripping my stomach again. Fortunately, Bryan was there to take me under the stands to give me a painkilling injection. It was a horrible moment but I was beyond caring. After it had taken effect, I crawled out, smiling.

BBC Radio 5 had my mother on the line. She didn't know that I was there when Sonia McLaughlin, their interviewer, asked her what she would say to me when we could talk. 'Well, what can you say to someone who has achieved her dream?' was her reply. As soon as she heard my voice, she didn't say a word. She screamed her head off. I could hear my family in the background, all screaming with her.

By then I was feeling very tired and light-headed but fortunately the presentation ceremony was announced quickly. This time, I had two Union Jacks around me and I could see plenty more waving in the crowd. What a brilliant feeling. Maria Cioncan happily stepped up to take the bronze; then it was Tatyana Tomashova's turn for the silver. As I stepped up for the gold, I still couldn't take in the enormity of what I had done. I kept shaking my head in disbelief. As the National Anthem played, the British fans sang along loudly but I couldn't get the words out. Tears were in my eyes but I was determined not to let them get the better of me. Meanwhile Cioncan was completely overcome and sobbed through the whole thing. It was an incredible moment.

During the press conference, I heard someone shout, 'Did you see that?' Our 4 x 100-metre guys had won gold too. What an amazing night. After the drugs test, which took an age while I filled myself with water and fizzy drinks in an attempt to provide a big enough sample, I found Margo and Zara. They were both over the moon for me and I gave Margo my victory flowers. I would never forget how instrumental they and the rest of my team had been in my success. The media interviews seemed endless so that by the time I arrived back at the village, everyone, including Ali, had already gone out. I linked up with Matt Elias (400 metres) and Catherine Murphy (400 metres) who came over to my apartment. We had tried to join the others but it was 2 a.m. and there weren't any taxis. An hour later we met up with the Australian Tamsyn Lewis, and decided to give up and resort to the dining hall – not the greatest place to celebrate. At 5 a.m., I called Mum. Back in Tonbridge they were still up and celebrating too. At that time, I had no idea of the impact that my double win had made in Britain. I don't think I'd have believed it if I had.

The next day was the closing day of the Olympics where I was given the honour of carrying the British flag. I couldn't have asked for these astonishing ten days to end in a better way. The flight home had a real buzz. All thirty medallists got to sit in business class but, because all our team-mates were at the back, I went back to spend most of the flight in half of Jo Pavey's seat. After we landed at Heathrow, there were posed photos taken of all the medallists on the steps of the plane, before we disembarked and went straight into a press conference. I was about to discover the media frenzy that had hit Britain.

## 21. WHAT NEXT?

Crossing that line changed my life forever. Only seven days earlier, I had been someone with a dream. Only four minutes earlier I had been an Olympic champion going for an unprecedented second title. Now I was the first British woman ever to become a double Olympic champion, the second Briton since Albert Hill to achieve the feat in 84 years, and only the third woman in the world ever to achieve the middle-distance double. I had run into the sporting history record books.

At Gatwick, I led the team out of the arrivals area into the terminal where our friends and family were waiting for us. It was bedlam with people crying, cheering and asking for autographs. The officials tried to rush us through but I felt that if people had made the effort to come and see us, the least we could do was spend some time with them. So there was a change of plan. We walked through the crowd, chatting to people and signing autographs. I spotted Dad, Kevin and his wife Clare, Stuart and his fiancée Emma, Penny, Lisa and Danny. They were all waiting for me but I couldn't see my mum. She had been told to hide so that she could surprise me. It was a great welcome. We all drove back to Hildenborough in a limousine so large that it couldn't get down my mum's street. Mum said we had to go to Hilden Manor where everyone had parked their cars. In fact, when we arrived, I was taken inside and the place was decked in flags and banners with all my family, friends and people from the village who had known me for years waiting for me. As I walked in to this brilliant surprise party, the DJ played my tune, Alicia Keyes' 'If I Ain't Got You.'

Two days later, the Town Council had organised for me to go on an open-topped bus through Tonbridge town centre. I still didn't understand how caught up everyone had been in my success and was very nervous, worrying for the organisers that nobody would turn up. The house was filled with flowers sent by hundreds of well-wishers. Mum had told me about the BBC and Sky trucks parked round the corner from her house during the Games, but I only half believed her. When the morning of the parade dawned, I peered out of the curtains to see the road jammed with TV crews and people wielding cameras. I was thrilled and stunned that everyone was being so supportive. Mum was laughing. 'Kelly,' she said. 'You haven't got a clue.' She was right.

Two bodyguards had to escort me to the bus that was parked by the 'Rec' at the end of our road. Everyone was screaming as if I was a pop star. I couldn't stop laughing as we climbed aboard with all my family and friends in tow. Without them, it wouldn't have been the same.

Hildenborough was packed with people lining the streets, waiting. I couldn't believe it. The houses were decorated with red, white and blue bunting, Union Jacks and banners that read Special K; Kelly, Simply the Best. The atmosphere was fantastic as everyone waved and shouted as we went by. People tooted their car horns. Some were sitting out in the sun, others were having barbecues in their front gardens. I could see some people had brought their babies and young children. It was just the same all the way down the main road to Tonbridge. Outside the old people's home, men and women were out sitting in their wheelchairs, waving flags. As we headed into Tonbridge, the crowd was getting larger and larger. It was so cool. Then as we got to the NatWest bank at the top of the High Street, I couldn't believe my eyes. I had never seen anything like it. The jaws of everyone on the bus dropped. My brothers had tears in their eyes. 'My God. They've all come out because of you.'

All the way down the high street was jam-packed with people. They were hanging off lampposts, leaning out of windows, standing on roofs with drinks and bottles of champagne. Everyone was cheering and giving me the thumbs up. In the crowd, I spotted Tess Theobald (née Porter), one of my circle of friends since we'd played together as kids. I yelled at her to get on board. I wanted to share the moment with everyone I'd been close to over the years. Union Jacks were everywhere. My grin could have split my face. Instead of the anticipated 15,000, over 80,000 people had turned up. The bus crawled through after another thirty police and the Tonbridge Lions Club were called in to help and even then it took hours. A Sky TV helicopter circled overhead. We eventually reached the Castle where there was a civic reception in the midst of two thousand people who had squashed themselves into the grounds. After the Sydney Olympics I'd been admitted as an Honorary Freeman of the Borough of Tonbridge and Malling, so I was welcomed by the Mayor, the councillors and other Freemen. I tried to follow their speeches with a few words of my own, but every time I opened my mouth I was drowned out by the screaming. It was as if I was a movie star. I was completely overwhelmed and humbled at the same time. Out of all the things I've done since returning from the Olympics, this is the one thing I will never, ever forget.

Even so, I still thought that this was local attention for a local girl. I had no idea how Olympic fever had gripped the nation and how many people had been rooting for me. It was only when I started being asked to do things outside the area that I began to get a glimmer of the real scale of the support there had been for me – whether I was getting a standing ovation by the crowd at Charlton Athletic FC or when I came down the steps to applause on the Michael Parkinson show. I was even taken into the world of fashion when I was invited to London Fashion Week. I wore a grey dress by Roland Mouret and joined various celebrities in the front row of the Fashion Fringe Competition that took place in Selfridges. I was surrounded by the legends of the fashion world and was happy knowing that my manager, Jane, was sitting right behind me. As the show began, I must have been staring with my mouth open. It was like landing on another planet. The models had legs up to their armpits and I was baffled by them appearing wearing only a top with their knickers and nothing on their legs except shoes. They pranced like horses, balanced on the highest heels I'd ever seen. Music blared out of the speakers and fireworks blazed by the side of the runway as we 'ooohed' and 'aaahed'. It was a bizarre experience but an amazing glimpse into another world.

The London Olympic Parade was held in the middle of October and, although it was a fantastic event, for me it didn't come close to the one that had been held in my home town. It was particularly good to have the Paralympians with us though. Taking place so long after the Games, it slightly missed the moment but the people who turned out for it were great, especially the school kids who were chanting our names and cheering.

Of course, the racing season wasn't quite over. I had three more meetings to attend. It was hard for me to remain motivated but I was extremely lucky to have my good friend Andy Graffin around. He gave me his time and encouraged me to remain focused for the rest of the season by training with me no matter what the weather or time of day. But all the same at the golden league in Berlin, I didn't fight for the line and was just pipped by Tomashova in the 1500 metres. Four days later, I was racing again in Monaco where the world rankings were to be decided. Of course the press were whipping up the competition between Tomashova and me. I was only too aware that I had to beat her if I was to be ranked number one in the world. On went my championship head, only this time I adopted different tactics. Tomashova was the only danger. I had to beat her, so I made sure I did by racing further up the pack, never giving her a chance to escape. I charged down the final sixty metres as if I was a championship sprinter, crossing the line, screaming like a mad woman. 'Yeeeeah.' I had done it.

The final race of the year was the Newcastle Road Mile, held traditionally the day before the Great North Run. I had won it twice before but had lost to Sureyya Ayhan from Turkey in 2003 when I'd run a dreadful race, running like an 800-metre runner and using the wrong tactics altogether. I'd kicked myself for ages afterwards and swore I'd never run like that again. This time I completely changed my approach. Everyone was probably expecting me to run from the back but I took the race on, running at the front from start to finish. In the last 300 metres I felt a sharp tearing sensation in my calf. I gritted my teeth. 'This is the last race of the season,' I told myself. 'There's no way I'm stopping now.' The atmosphere was great, the crowd was cheering me on as I broke the course record in 4:28.7 minutes. Fortunately the injury was a minor pull that soon recovered during my rest period.

To round off my sporting year I was thrilled to be voted BBC Sports Personality of the Year by the British public. I'd always watched other people receiving it in the past and thought what a brilliant feeling it must be to win. The fashion designer Scott Henshall made me a dress especially for the night. A couple of days earlier when the toile (a mock-up of the real thing but made in calico) turned up, I was horrified. Was the real thing going to look like this? I didn't realise that it would be made of a completely different material. I've never been a particularly dressy person before but now I love planning what I'm going to wear. I was persuaded to wait to see the finished dress. I was so relieved when it arrived, a fabulous black knee-length dress cut away at the shoulders and midriff, although I felt nervous about exposing so much flesh. I usually cover up more but, slightly to my surprise, I felt very comfortable in it and was made more confident by the number of compliments I received.

Patricia came up to my hotel to do my hair. She had been astonished when I returned from Athens I had called her to ask her to continue doing my hair. She had thought that now I was double Olympic champion I would never contact her again. What she didn't know was that if I meet a genuine person and we become friends, they become friends for life. My room was bombarded by people: Scott was there with his PR team, my manager Jane, James from Boodles the jewellers arrived with diamonds for me to wear, along with a make-up artist and a photographer. They all took over, handing out advice as to how I should look and what I should do. I was sitting there, overcome, thinking, 'Oh, my God!'

I think I was more nervous that evening than I was for the 1500 metres final at the Olympics. Whether I was voted for or not was out of my control. Being told I had a good chance of winning made me even worse. I was shaking like a leaf all night. I was sitting with Steve Cram and Natasha Kaplinsky, the BBC news reader. Mum, Mick, Dave, Wes, Kevin and Stuart were in the audience supporting me. The award for the Sports Team of the Year was given to Great Britain's rowing coxless four before attention turned to the individual award for Sports Personality of the Year. Each of the nominees was introduced by a short film. Mine featured previous British female Olympic gold medallists including Ann Packer (800 metres), Dame Mary Peters (heptathlon), Tessa Sanderson (javelin), Sally Gunnell (400 metre hurdles) and Denise Lewis (heptathlon). I felt extremely flattered by their tributes. When they finally announced that I had won, I was so choked that I could barely speak. It was a huge honour.

Since then, I have been fortunate enough to receive so many awards for my achievements, an amazing twenty-seven at the time of writing, among them European Athletics Association Sportswoman of the Year, International Sports Journalists' Sportswoman of the

Year, Athletics' Writers' Sportswoman of the Year, TV Golden Moments and Transworld Sportswoman of the Year. But the two greatest accolades of all have to be first the Sports Personality of the Year Award because it is the highest form of recognition given to a sports person that is voted by the public, and then, of course, my Damehood, the highest recognition bestowed by the State.

Although the season was over, my diary was crammed. I was being invited to things that I would never have imagined I'd be involved with. I have been invited onto more TV programmes than I can count, including guest appearances in the *EastEnders* Christmas special, *At Home with the Kumars*, *Des and Mel*, *Richard and Judy*, *BBC Breakfast* and *GMTV*. The list goes on and on.

Top of my invitations has to be being invited by Tom Cruise to the premiere of *Collateral* after we'd both appeared on *The Parkinson Show*. I had just got home when he called and asked my mother to pass on the invitation for that evening. I was exhausted, and besides, the only suitable clothes I had were those I had been kitted out in for the show. No way was I going to turn up in the same thing. I had to say I couldn't go. Imagine turning down Tom Cruise!

I was the chief guest of the Football Association at the England-Wales International at Old Trafford. David Beckham introduced me to the English team and the Gary Speed introduced me to the Welsh squad before I stood on the sidelines as the packed stadium reverberated to the sound of the National Anthem. Tears came to my eyes as it brought back that moment on the rostrum at Athens.

I appeared on the *Royal Variety Show,* where I had a bit of trouble squinting at the autocue without my glasses as I introduced Girls Aloud. Before the show, I had been chosen with Liza Minnelli, Jill Halfpenny and her dance partner from *Strictly Come Dancing* to be presented to Prince Charles. I had to pinch myself to make sure it was really happening. I met all the celebrities who had been on the show, getting lots of cuddles from Barbara Windsor and being kissed and hugged by Elton John who said he had been rooting for me to win Sports Person of the Year. All I could think was, 'Oh my God. It's Elton John.'

My life turned upside down as the invitations increased in the run up to Christmas. I went on *The Ant and Dec Show* with Robbie Williams and Nadia from *Big Brother*. While Robbie was rehearsing, he kept breaking off to ask me questions about athletics and fitness training. How surreal that felt. My part in the show involved flying across the studio in a harness to whack at boxes with a stick so that they opened and the contents fell on the audience. It all went well in rehearsal but in the live final, I was whirling round over their heads as I tried to stab at the boxes that weren't co-operating. As I spun around all over the place, feeling sicker and sicker, I thought time up would never be called. When the clip ended, all that could be heard was my voice saying, 'Get me down. Get me down.'

Princess Anne hosted a dinner for some of the British Olympic sponsors and that year's successful athletes, including Matthew Pinsent, Shirley Robertson and myself. We were in the Chinese Room at Buckingham Palace, seated at a beautifully dressed, long table. That was a really good evening although I struggled a bit with the protocol. There were so many knives and forks that I couldn't work out which ones to use when. I had a laugh with the guy sitting beside me as we watched what everyone else was using so that we didn't embarrass ourselves. At the end of the meal, we were offered fruit. Tons and tons of it. The waiter leaned over us discreetly asking us what we would like. I'd never tasted anything like the honey ice cream that came with it. I kept asking for more and my neighbour kept encouraging me. We had a real scream, giggling about everything that was going on.

The athletics season may have ended in September but I had one thing on my agenda that I had set up way back at the beginning of the year. 'On Camp with Kelly' is an initiative that I had developed that is sponsored by Norwich Union. I had selected eight British junior athletes to take to South Africa so that they could learn what it takes to be a full-time athlete. I wanted to share my experiences, both good and bad, as a PTI and as an athlete, to help them find a smoother pathway through their careers and to give something back to the sport. What I was looking for were eight girls who showed passion and determination. I wasn't interested in anyone who thought athletics was going to put them on a path to becoming rich and famous. I had also talked to Jean Verster about the possibility of introducing some junior South African athletes half way through the four-week course. Sharing their different perspectives would be useful for both groups since South African athletics has little or no funding for young athletes.

I was very familiar with Potch as I had been going there since 1997 and had bought a house there so this seemed the perfect place for the camp. It has become my second home and I'm lucky to have found a sweet Mozambican guy, Fesbem, who does all the odd jobs round the house and garden as well as looking after the place when I'm away. When the girls arrived in South Africa, I gave them a serious talk. 'This is NOT a holiday. This is an education training camp. For those of you who don't remember, I was in the Army for nine years so to some of you it might seem more like a boot camp.' I watched their faces fall. Of course I was joking ... or was I?

My army training meant that I knew exactly how to organise everything and I loved doing it. I thought it was most important to be honest with the girls, emphasising that athletics is not an easy sport. To succeed in any walk of life, you must have passion, desire and the will to overcome any obstacle in your path. Sometimes in your life you have to make sacrifices. There is no easy road to success or achievement but with total dedication and realistic targets you can make them happen. I hope the girls on the camp learned a lot from the experience. The media coverage was fantastic in the UK and South Africa so it was nice to know that all the press guys who have followed my career over the years were totally supportive of my first initiative.

Since winning, I have had opportunities to do so many different things that are a far cry from the athletics world. The invitations have kept on coming and I've grabbed every chance I've been given, sometimes because I am curious and sometimes because I think, 'Why not?'

I travelled to Beijing to receive the Top Ten Sports Person Award voted by the Chinese public. As an ambassador for the London Olympic bid, I felt that being in the city hosting the 2008 Games, was also a good moment to voice my support for Britain becoming the host in 2012. It was a fleeting but worthwhile visit during which I was also given a new translation for the tattoos on my shoulder. When they were originally done, I was told that one meant Will to Win Against Adversity and the other meant Strength, Power and Success. But Liu Guang, our interpreter, explained how Chinese characters are open to different interpretations and that he would translate them together as Exceptional Victory. I loved the idea of them being so appropriate to different stages in my life.

Making a Sainsbury's ad for an Active Kids campaign comes high on my list of rewarding new experiences. It was two days of filming with my old PE teacher, Debbie Page, and what seemed like hundreds of screaming kids from my old school, Hugh Christie and Longmead Primary School in Tonbridge. I loved every minute of it. Then, in April 2005, I was very privileged to be invited to become godmother to the

P & O cruise ship, Arcadia, the biggest ever British superliner built for British passengers, and to officially name her in Southampton. Normally they are named by royalty so how amazing was that!

However, life was put back into perspective when I returned home from Athens. My good friend from the Army, Jackie Gilchrist, had been diagnosed with breast cancer. She hadn't wanted to tell me before because she knew it would ruin my focus so I only found out when I saw the letter she had written to my mum that was waiting for me when I got back. Jackie was worried what I would say when I saw her because she had lost her long red hair during chemotherapy – she should know me by now! I am so pleased to say that after nearly a year she is making a full recovery.

Something else that made me realise that my struggles were insignificant was meeting Nathalie Richards, a fifteen-year-old girl who has a brain tumour, through the charity Starlight Foundation. Nathalie's wish was to meet me and so she did, when she came to watch me race in Glasgow in January and afterwards when I took her and her family for a meal. The highlight of my thirty-fifth birthday was going to visit her in hospital as she waited for her fourth operation in three weeks. I had the day off so I went to surprise her and the look on her face said it all. Love is the biggest healer. Sharing my chocolate cake with her was one of the most rewarding things I have done.

Now that I've achieved my dreams, I'm looking to my future, wondering what it has in store. My life so far has been a full one and I hope to be able to put my experiences to good use. I have a lot of imagination when it comes to things that I enjoy doing. I loved setting up and participating in the camp in Potch, using my knowledge to make the learning experience fun and informative for young athletes. I want to stimulate activity in the sports arena for as many people as I can. I also hope to run similar camps in the UK. Another project I would like to start would be to bring more sport and opportunities to the townships around Potchefstroom.

On 23 April 2005, I announced that this will be my last season on British soil which is a very sad thought. I had already won indoor races in both Glasgow and Birmingham, although I was forced to pull out of the Madrid Indoor European Championships because of a pulled hamstring. I loved racing in front of a home crowd who never fail to boost my performance. I may go to the 2006 Commonwealth Games but won't make a decision until much nearer the time. My body isn't coping well with the demands I put on it but I will remain focused for as long as I still choose to race. My motivation for running now is the unbeatable experience of standing on the track, being announced as 'Double Olympic champion, Dame Kelly Holmes and hearing the enthusiasm of the crowd.

I've always had a goal to fight for and it is very strange for me not to have a major one now. I began as a child with two dreams – to be an Army PTI and to be an Olympic champion. The road I've taken to achieve them both has been a long and often difficult one. Obstacles have presented themselves time and time again but I have always kept my sights fixed on what I wanted to accomplish and have let nothing deflect me. Anyone with similar dreams should never give up on their ambitions. I believe that if a person wants something badly enough, it is within their power to achieve it. I am living proof that dreams can come true. I'm not for a moment saying that it will be easy, but determination and single-mindedness will get you there in the end. As I have said so many times: never put less than 100 per cent into what you want to do. At least then, like me, you will never live with regrets. There have been times when, in my darkest days, I have wondered how I could keep going or whether my dreams would ever come true. In my athletics career, my injuries have caused frequent and frustrating setbacks and tears but I have always picked myself up thanks to the help and support of the fantastic people I have been lucky enough to have round me. I owe them all a great deal.

When I won the 2004 Olympic gold in the 1500 metres, I remember going to the press conference afterwards, feeling as if a weight had been lifted off my shoulders. I was filled with a sense of peace. At that moment I was certain that I would not let what had happened to me change me. I realised that I don't have to prove anything to myself or to anyone else any more. I may have achieved my own long-standing goals in life but it does not make me a better person than anyone else.

The strange thing is that I still often cry when I am on my own but now it is with the realisation that I have achieved all my long-term dreams. I sometimes still can't believe that it was me who became the double gold medallist. People seem to expect me to be different as a result but I'm not. Just as my sponsors Reebok say in a poster campaign in which I feature, 'I AM WHAT I AM'. Of course I like to wear the designer clothes and the diamonds. What woman wouldn't? But now I have reached a point in my life when I can be who I want to be no matter what people think. I can just be me. I can just be Kelly.

# KELLY HOLMES – CAREER HIGHLIGHTS

**KEY**
i = Indoor

**Personal Bests**

| Event | Mark | Venue | Date | |
|---|---|---|---|---|
| 200 metres | 24.8 | Portsmouth | 2 Jul 96 | |
| 400 metres | 53.8 | Portsmouth | 2 Jul 96 | |
| 600 metres | 1:25.41 | Naimette-Xhovémont | 2 Sep 03 | British Best |
| 800 metres | 1:56.21 | Monaco | 9 Sep 95 | British Record |
| 1000 metres | 2:32.55 | Leeds | 15 Jun 97 | British Record |
| 1500 metres | 3:57.90 | Athens | 28 Aug 04 | British Record |
| One Mile | 4:28.04 | Glasgow | 30 Aug 98 | |
| 3000 metres | 9:01.91 | Gateshead | 13 July 03 | |
| **Road** | | | | |
| One Mile | 4:23.5 | New York | 26 Sep 98 | |
| **Indoors** | | | | |
| 800 metres | 1:59.21 | Ghent | 9 Feb 03 | British Indoor Record |
| 1000 metres | 2:32.96 | Birmingham | 20 Feb 04 | European Indoor Record |
| 1500 metres | 4:02.66 | Birmingham | 16 Mar 03 | British Indoor Record |

## Major Championship Placings

**Gold**
1994 Commonwealth Games 1500 metres
2002 Commonwealth Games 1500 metres
2004 Olympic Games 800 metres
2004 Olympic Games 1500 metres

**Silver**
1994 European Championships 1500 metres
1995 World Championships 1500 metres
1998 Commonwealth Games 1500 metres
2001 Goodwill Games 800 metres
2003 World Indoor Championships 1500 metres
2003 World Championships 800 metres

**Bronze**
1995 World Championships 800 metres
2000 Olympic Games 800 metres
2002 European Championships 800 metres

**4th**
1996 Olympic Games 800 metres

**Finalist**
1996 Olympic Games 1500 metres
2000 Olympic Games 1500 metres
2001 World Championships 800 metres
2004 World Indoor Championships 1500 metres

**Semi-Finalist**
1993 World Championships 800 metres
1999 World Championships 800 metres

**First Round**
1997 World Championships 1500 metres
2002 European Championships 1500 metres

**Other Achievements**

AAA Champion at 800 metres in 1993, 1995, 1996, 1999, 2000, 2001 & 2004 and indoors in 2001 & 2004

AAA Champion at 1500 metres in 1994, 1996 & 2002. Unbeaten in AAA finals as a senior

UK Champion at 800 metres in 1993 & 1997

European Cup Winner at 1500 metres in 1995 & 1997; second at 1500 metres in 1994 & 800 metres in 1996; fourth at 800 metres in 2002

World Cup Third at 1500 metres in 1994

Grand Prix Final Second at 800 metres in 1995; second at 800 metres in 2001

World Athletics Final Second at 800 metres in 2003; first at 1500 metres in 2004

Army Championships Winner at 200 metres, 400 metres and 800 metres in 1991; at 400 metres and 800 metres in 1992; at 400 metres and 1500 metres in 1993; at 1500 metres in 1994.

Inter-Services Championships Winner at 1500 metres in 1989; at 400 metres in 1990; at 1500 metres in 1993; at 200 metres, 400 metres and 4x400 metres in 1994; at 800 metres and 3000 metres in 1995; at 400 metres and 1500 metres in 1996; second in 800 metres in 1989

English Schools Champion at 1500 metres in 1983 & 1987

The first athlete to contest both the 800m and 1500m finals at three successive Olympic Games

## Annual Progression as of April 2005

| Year | Age | 400 metres | 800 metres | 1500 metres | 3000 metres | British Caps | Sub-2 min at 800 metres |
|---|---|---|---|---|---|---|---|
| 1983 | 12/13 | | 2:22.9 | 4:37.8 | | | |
| 1984 | 13/14 | | 2:15.1 | 4:35.2 | | | |
| 1985 | 14/15 | | 2:13.1 | 4:41.4 | | | |
| 1986 | 15/16 | | 2:11.0 | 4:26.9 | | | |
| 1987 | 16/17 | | 2:09.45 | 4:26.1 | | 2 Junior | |
| 1988 | 17/18 | | | | | | |
| 1989 | 18/19 | | 2:12.1 | 4:38.7 | | | |
| 1990 | 19/20 | 59.7 | 2:14.7 | | | | |
| 1991 | 20/21 | 57.6 | 2:11.8 | | | | |
| 1992 | 21/22 | 58.6 | 2:03.94 | 4:27.7 | | 1 Under-23 | |
| 1993 | 22/23 | 55.3 | 1:58.64 | 4:17.3 | | 1 | 3 |
| 1994 | 23/24 | 54.7 | 1:59.43 | 4:01.41 | | 3 + 1 England | 2 |
| 1995 | 24/25 | 54.51 | 1:56.21 | 4:03.04 | 9:08.7 | 2 | 5 |
| 1996 | 25/26 | 53.8 | 1:57.84 | 4:01.13 | | 2 | 8 |
| 1997 | 26/27 | | 1:57.14 | 3:58.07 | | 2 | 3 |
| 1998 | 27/28 | | | 4:06.10 | 9:10.23 | 1 + 1 England | 0 |
| 1999 | 28/29 | | 1:58.24 | 4:04.58 | | 2 | 7 |
| 2000 | 29/30 | | 1:56.80 | 4:05.35 | | 1 | 2 |
| 2001 | 30/31 | | 1:57.88 | 4:31.68 | | 1 | 8 |
| 2002 | 31/32 | | 1:59.83 | 4:01.91 | | 3 + 1 England | 1 |
| 2003 | 32/33 | | 1:58.69 | 4:01.96 | 9:01.91 | 3 | 5 |
| 2004 | 33/34 | | 1:56.69 | 3:57.90 | | 4 | 4 |
| 2005 | 34/35 | | 2:05.8i | 4:14.74i | | 1 | 0 |
| | | | | | | 26 + 3 England | 48 |

**Records set at 600 metres**

| | | | |
|---|---|---|---|
| 1:25.41 | Naimette-Xhovémont | 2 Sep 03 | British |

**Records set at 800 metres**

| | | | |
|---|---|---|---|
| 1:56.95 | Gothenburg | 13 Aug 95 | British & Commonwealth |
| 1:56.21 | Monaco | 9 Sep 95 | British & Commonwealth |
| 1:59.21i | Ghent | 9 Feb 03 | British Indoor |

**Records set at 1000 metres**

| | | | |
|---|---|---|---|
| 2:32.82 | Sheffield | 23 Jul 95 | British & Commonwealth |
| 2:32.55 | Leeds | 15 Jun 97 | British |
| 2:32.96i | Birmingham | 20 Feb 04 | British & European Indoor |

**Records set at 1500 metres**

| | | | |
|---|---|---|---|
| 3:58.07 | Sheffield | 29 Jun 97 | British & Commonwealth |
| 4:02.66i | Birmingham | 16 Mar 03 | British Indoor |
| 3:57.90 | Athens | 28 Aug 04 | British |

With thanks to Mark Butler

## AWARDS SINCE THE 2004 OLYMPIC GAMES

Dame Commander of the British Empire

BBC Sports Personality of the Year

International Athlete of the Year – Voted by International Sports Journalist

European Female Athlete of the Year

International Amateur Athletic Federation – Female Performance of the Year

Sport Writers Association Sports Woman of the Year

British Athletic Writers Association Female Athlete of the Year

London Sports Personality of the Year

BBC Radio London Sports Personality of the Year

BBC Radio London Athlete of the Year

BBC South East Sports Personality of the Year

BBC South East Courier Award

Celebrity Sports Star of the Year

Transworld Sports Women of the Year

Sunday Times Sports Woman of the Year

Norwich Union Award for Best Performance in a British Vest 2004

Kent Invicta Award for Outstanding Achievement

T4 Honours Award

Great Britons Award – Sport

Diva Best Female

TV Moments Awards – Best Sport Moment of the Year

TV Moments Awards – Golden Moment of the Year

World Top Ten Athletes Award – Voted by the Chinese Public

Glamour Magazine Sports Woman of the Year

Women of the Year Outstanding Achievement Award

Walpole Award for British Sporting Excellence

Glasgow – Lord Provost Award

Laureus World Sportswoman of the Year

# INDEX


AAA Championships 93, 95–96, 103, 110, 124, 149, 156, 168, 173
AAA Indoor Championships 166, 201
ABSA series 133
Active Kids campaign 235
Adkins, Julie 32
Afanasyeva, Yelena 128
Akabusi, Kriss 57, 58
alcohol 79, 87–89
Andrianova, Tatyana 218, 219, 220
Anne, Princess 233
*Ant and Dec Show* 233
apartheid 133–134
*Arcadia* P & O ship 235
Army 3, 4, 119
  ambition to join 26–27, 30–31, 34, 40
  basic training 43–49
  drill 45
  driving training 51–55
  Physical Training Corps 102, 109
  PTI training 56–60, 61–68, 109–110, 115–116
  recruitment 120–121
  retirement 132–133, 135–136
  tournaments 101
  work as PTI 71–72, 83–86
Army Championships 58, 94, 103
Army School of Education, Beaconsfield 81
Army Track Athlete of the Year 121
Army Youth Team 116, 119–121
Arnold, Carol 100
Arnold, Dave 19–22, 31–32, 33, 75, 99–101, 103, 104, 109, 110, 112–113, 121–123, 129, 136–137, 148–149, 153, 158, 160–161, 163, 166–167, 181, 186, 207, 209, 219
Arnold, Malcolm 127
Asgill, Julie 139
Asics 100, 179
asthma 36, 200
athletics 51
  army 58–59, 77, 81, 94, 121, 135–136
  lifestyle 206
  school 24

Atlanta, Georgia 126
Augee, Myrtle 106
awards 121, 230–232, 234
Ayhan, Sureyya 179, 230

Backley, Steve 163
Bailey, Aleen 223
Bay Area Laboratory Co-operative (BALCO) 197
Barber, Eunice 150
Barrett, Sue 138
Basham, Jane 150, 155
Basham, Peter 150
Baulch, Jamie 127
BBC Sports Personality of the Year 230–231
Beckham, David 232
Benhassi, Hasna 156, 219, 220, 224
Bennett, Liz 59
Bidert, Roland 139
Bislett Games 124, 135
Bosnia 129–130
Boulmerka, Hassiba 110–112
Bray, Johnny 35–36
Brazier, Debbie 23, 24
Brighton University 123
British Championships 135
Brown, Malcolm 125, 127–128
Brussels League 170
Buckingham Palace 1–4, 147–148
Budd, Zola 131, 134
Budget, Dr Richard 166
Budokan martial art 15
Butler, Kathy 170, 216

Campbell, Darren 127, 163, 175, 213, 214
canoeing 117–119
CBE award 1–4, 232
Ceplak, Jolanda 170, 171, 177–180, 195, 197, 219, 220
Charles, Prince of Wales 148, 232
Christie, Linford 97, 213
chronic fatigue syndrome 166
Cioncan, Maria 225
Clark, Jearl Miles 218, 219
Coe, Sebastian 25, 220
Commonwealth Games
  1994 106–108
  1998 145, 146–147
  2002 173, 174–176
  2006 235
Connor, Nan 34, 35
Cowmeadow, Jane 178, 179, 201, 229, 231
Craft, Lara 23, 27–28, 50
Cram, Steve 25, 231
cross-country running 59, 77–78, 154
Cruise, Tom 232
Cummins, Diane 169, 170, 197
Curbishley, Alison 159, 162
Cyprus 208–211

D N Galan race, Stockholm 95
Davies, Gareth 179
Davies, Sam 159
De Klerk, Evette 134
Deaves, Susan 107
Decker, Mary 134
Devenish, Marlon 175
DeWitt (van Zijl), Benita 123
Diana, Princess of Wales 140
Dijkstra, Paul 200, 204
Dixon, Karen 122
Djate, Patricia 114, 115
dogs 11, 137, 144–145, 188
Dooley, Michael 122, 173
drugs and drug-testing 107–108, 168–169, 176–177, 197, 221
Duchess of Kent Barracks, Aldershot 57, 61, 100, 101
Duke of Edinburgh's Award Scheme 27–28
Duknove, Natalya 96
Dulecha, Kutre 151, 203
Dulforce, Jason 87
Dunbar, Joe 149
Duncan, Anne 77, 80
Duncan, Wesley 69–70, 76–81, 93, 94–95, 100, 147, 149
Dupuy, Jason 155
Durban, Captain 62–64, 66
Dynamic Energy 142, 144

East, Mike 175
Edwards, Jonathan 162, 176
Edwards, Paul 107
Elias, Matt 226

Elizabeth II, Queen 1–4
English, Bryan 181, 193, 200, 204, 206, 208, 209, 218, 222, 225
English Schools Championships 8, 20–22, 31, 32
Europa Cup Championships 94
European Championships 33, 103–106, 110, 124, 135, 174, 176–177
European Indoor Cup 3

Fenn, Jo 176
Fern, Tony 58
Football Association 232
Formanova, Ludmila 151
Foster, Brendan 168
Fourie, Johan 134
Fraser, Donna 162
Freeman, Cathy 161, 162
Fryer, Paula 93
Fuchsova, Helena 161
Fund, Jeff 180–181, 189, 194, 195, 201, 202, 205, 217

*Generation Game* 7
Gibson, Sharon 106
Gilchrist, Jackie 59, 73–74, 136
Goodwill Games, Brisbane 170
Graf, Stephanie 160, 161, 169, 170, 171, 183, 189, 195
Graffin, Allen 137–138, 157
Graffin, Andy 137–138, 157, 178, 180, 202, 208, 230
Graham, Yvonne 111
grand prix races 95, 110, 114–115, 123–124, 131–132, 156, 168, 170, 197, 205–206
Great North Mile 170–171
Griffith, Michelle 32, 106
Griffiths, Gwen 108
Guildford Barracks 41–42
Guang, Liu 234
Gunnell, Sally 97, 127, 159, 177, 201, 218, 222, 225, 231
Gurina, Lyubov 96

Halfpenny, Jill 232
Hamilton, Bruce 210–211, 217
Hamilton, Suzy 131
Hanson, Ashia 106–107
Harrop, Marcus 135
Hartmann, Gerard 145–146, 155–156
Hattingh, Burt 154
Havens, Kerrie 23, 27–28, 30, 38, 50, 155
Henry, Connie 32, 107
Henshall, Scott 231
Hildenborough, Kent 5, 8, 9
  reception 227–228
Hildenborough Primary School 13, 14–15, 16
Hill, Albert 227
Holmes, Derrick 5, 37–40
Holmes, Kelly
  allergies 205
  asthma 36, 200
  boyfriends 13
  childhood 5–16
  chronic fatigue syndrome 166
  early jobs 33
  earnings 148, 171
  endurance 24, 185
  family 5–13, 143, 175, 201, 204, 227, 231
  hair 1, 29–30, 94, 213–215, 222
  injuries 3, 122–123, 125–130, 137–139, 141, 145–146, 154, 155, 190–194, 206, 230
  first races 17–22, 31–33
  mentality 20, 21–22, 59, 112
  relationships 55, 87
  stomach pains 91, 97, 121–122, 125, 146, 173–174, 183, 200, 225
  style 19
  tactics 104, 160–161, 189, 201, 223
Holmes, May 39
Howey, Kate 157, 163, 222
Hugh Christie Secondary School, Tonbridge 17, 18, 22–24, 30, 235

Imphal Barracks, York 67, 70
Inter-Counties Championships 94, 154
Inter-Services Championships 58–59, 77, 81, 110, 124

Jackson, Colin 97, 127, 159, 171
Jackson, Captain Tanya Collier 73
Jacobs, Regina 129, 139, 151, 189

Jarrett, Tony 122
Jennings, Bobby 191, 192, 207
Jennings, Margo 180, 184–188, 191, 192, 195, 199, 201, 202, 205, 207, 208, 209, 215, 217, 219
Johannesburg 180, 181, 183–188, 200
John, Elton 232
Johnson, Michael 133
Jones, Marion 150
Jones, Max 194, 223–224
judo 75–76

Kaplinsky, Natasha 231
Kelly Holmes School Challenge 142–144
Kent Schools Championships 20
Kenteris, Costas 163
Keough, Linda 93
Khrushchelyova, Natalya 196, 197
Kovacs, Ella 96
Kremlyova, Lyubov 105

Leconfield Barracks 50, 51–55
Lewis, Danny 37
Lewis, Denise 32, 106, 127, 150, 163, 216, 231
Lewis, Emily 178
Lewis, Linda 37–39
Lewis, Lisa 37–38, 39, 155
Lewis, Tamsyn 226
Lidlow, Kevin 138, 139, 141, 145
London Fashion Week 229
London Olympic Parade 230
Longhorn, Jackie 86
Lough, Gary 158
Lyons, Major 136

Madrid Grand Prix 205–206
Maduaka, Joyce 213
Maranga, Jackline 147
Marchwood, Southampton 55–56
martial arts 15, 75–76
Martinez, Mayte 177, 178, 189
Masterkova, Svetlana 124, 128, 129, 133, 151
Maughan, Professor Ron 123
May, Fiona 150
MBE award 147–148
McBride, Michelle 59
McCord, Lieutenant Colonel 115–116, 132–133, 136, 147
McKenzie, David 106
McLaughlin, Sonia 225
Merah-Benida, Nouria 163
Merry, Katherine 162
Middlesex County Championships 94, 103
Middlesex Ladies' Athletics Club 69, 76–77, 80, 81
Minnelli, Lisa 232
Minnesota University 33
Mitchell, Jeina 155
Modahl, Diane 94, 97–98, 106–108, 147, 156
Modahl, Vicente 107, 108
Monaco grand prix 197–198
Montalvo, Niurka 150
Morgan, Deirdre 34, 36
Morris, Tracy 216, 218
Mugo, Naomi 147
Murphy, Catherine 226
Murray, Yvonne 103
Mutola, Maria 95, 97, 113, 114–115, 123–124, 128, 140, 147, 151, 161, 169, 170, 180–181, 183–198, 200–203, 205, 207, 215–216, 219

Nevill, Barry 124, 143, 167, 178
Newcastle Road Mile 230
Nike 124, 126, 135–136, 144, 167–168
Nikolayeva, Yelena 131
Nolan, Geraldine 105
Norman, Andy 94–95, 106, 123, 124, 131, 133, 167–168, 171, 172
Norman, Elsie 8, 9
Norman, Pam 1–4, 5-13, 15–16, 29, 32, 34, 67, 106, 114, 137, 138, 143, 147, 150, 204, 225, 227, 228
relationship with 36–40, 50, 58, 64–65, 104
Norman, Percy 7, 8–9, 143
Norris, Aud 8, 12, 28
Norris, Geoff 8, 11, 12, 28
Norris, Kevin 9–10, 14, 15, 38, 50, 64, 114

Norris, Mick 1–4, 7–10, 14, 38, 40, 49–50, 64, 147, 154
Norris, Pam *see* Norman, Pam
Norris, Sheila 7–8, 10, 34
Norris, Stuart 10–11, 15, 38, 50, 64, 65, 114, 120
Norwich Union 233
Grand Prix 189
Notting Hill Carnival, London 80–81

*Olympic Diaries* TV documentary 122
Olympic Games 99
  Athens 2004 3, 25, 199, 213–226
  Atlanta 1996 114, 121, 126–130, 132–133
  Barcelona 1992 79, 95, 134
  Los Angeles 1984 25, 134
  Moscow 1980 25
  Munich 1972 176
  Seoul 1988 95
  Sydney 2000 149, 153, 158–163, 229
'On Camp with Kelly' 233–234
Oslo Grand Prix 95
O'Sullivan, Sonia 124, 131
Ottey, Merlene 223
Ovett, Steve 25

Packer, Ann 221, 231
Page, Debbie 17, 18, 235
*Parkinson Show* 229, 232
Patricia (hairdresser) 1, 214–215, 231
Patricios, Dr John 190
Pattinson, Helen 156, 159, 171, 175, 177
Paulino, Tina 96, 147
Pavey, Gav 157, 158
Pavey, Jo 157–158, 159–160, 170, 174, 175, 176–176, 208, 216, 226
Peters, Mary 231
Peters, Zara Hyde 153, 193, 194, 199, 201, 208, 209, 210, 215, 217, 221–226
Pinsent, Matthew 122, 233
Plummer, Daniel 213–214
Podkopayeva, Yekaterina 104, 105
Porter, Julie 13
Porter, Steve 13
Porter (Theobold), Tess 13, 229
Potchefstroom, South Africa 133–135, 154, 165, 180, 200, 204, 234, 235
Prefontaine Classic 205
Princess Christian Hospital, Hildenborough 34–36

Quirot, Ana 113–114, 115, 128, 135, 140

race and racism 10, 29, 107, 133–134
Radcliffe, Paula 145, 155, 159, 175, 176, 216, 218
Radisson Resort, Australia 156–157
Rainey, Meredith 114, 115
Rawlinson, Chris 175–176
Redgrave, Steve 122, 163
Reebok 179, 236
Reeder, Annika 122
Roach, Bridie 97
Robertson, Shirley 122, 233
Rogachova, Lyudmila 105
Rose, Alison 193, 194, 199–200, 202, 204, 206–207, 208, 209, 215, 221–226
*Royal Variety Show* 232
Rozenberg, Yekaterina 189
Ruck, Kim 23, 27
Russell, Ian 13, 14

Sacramento, Carla 139–140
Sainsbury's Active Kids Campaign 235
Salisbury, Barry 181
Samaria, Agnes 186, 188, 192–193, 217, 218, 223
Sanderson, Tessa 25–26, 127, 231
Sayers, Goldie 216
Schnurr, Paula 108
Schubert, Renate 190
Scott, Dave 167
Sevenoaks, Kent 120
Sharp, Sue 59
Shaw, Lorraine 157, 159, 175, 222
Sheffield Grand Prix 131–132
Sheringham, Teddy 124
Signal Regiment 71, 101
Skelton, Matt 149
skiing 76
Smith, Alan 155
Smith, Captain Lester 119

Southampton Athletics Club 58
Southern Championships 81
Southern Women's League 146
Southerton, Kelly 216, 218
Speed, Gary 232
sponsorship 100, 124, 126, 135–136, 167–168, 179
St George's Children's Home, Tonbridge 6, 7, 15
Stellenbosch, South Africa 122, 166
Stewart, Glen 135
Sutton, Marian 159
swimming 46–47, 61–62
Szabo, Gabriela 124, 129, 179

Tallahassee 121, 125
television shows 232–233
Temane, Matthew 134
Thomson, Gary 38, 50, 58, 67
Thomson, Pam *see* Norman, Pam
Thomson, Penny 67
Tomashova, Tatyana 179, 225, 230
Tonbridge 228–229
Tonbridge and Sevenoaks County Championships 18
Tonbridge Athletics Club 18–20, 32
Top Ten Sports Person Award, China 234
Tracey, Brian 205–206
training 20, 31, 59, 80, 100–101, 129, 135, 137–138, 149, 154, 180–181, 183–189, 205, 208–209
  heat and humidity 121, 123
Tsyganova, Natalia 150
Tullett, Hayley 156, 159, 162, 163, 175
Tulloh, Katherine and Jojo 31–32

UK Athletics 193, 199
UK Championships 93, 94

Verster, Eban 204
Verster, Jean and Alta 133–134, 155, 200, 233
View From clothing 168, 169, 179
Vriesde, Letitia 114, 156, 169, 170

Wagner, Robert 171–172, 177, 178, 179, 180, 189
Washington, Stacey 17, 19, 32
Watkins, Captain 66
Whitbread, Fatima 133
Whitcombe, Andrea 159
Whiteman, Tony 135, 208–209
Whitlock, Janine 159
Whitlock, Sarah and Sandra 150, 155, 174, 175
Wickson, Roy and Marg 28
Wickson, Simon 13, 28
Williams, Robbie 233
Windsor, Barbara 232
Wolfhart, Dr Hans Muller 138
Women's Royal Army Corps (WRAC) 70–71, 101
Woodward, Lisa 23
World Anti Doping Agency (WADA) 176
World Championships
  Athens 1997 130, 136, 138–140
  Edmonton 2001 165, 168–169
  Gothenburg 1995 109–114
  Paris 2003 195–197
  Seville 1999 149–151
  Stuttgart 81, 91, 96–98
Wang, Yuan 96
World Indoor Championships 188, 189, 200, 202–204

Yegorova, Olga 168, 222
Yelling, Hayley 168, 177
Yelling, Liz 208, 216, 218
Yevdokimova, Natalya 222
York, Lisa 79–80, 99
Youth Olympics 32

Zurich golden league 140, 169, 194, 197, 207–208